Shelter burden

CONFLICTS IN URBAN
AND REGIONAL DEVELOPMENT
a series edited by John R. Logan
and Todd Swanstrom

Edward G. Goetz

SHELTER BURDEN

Local
Politics
and
Progressive
Housing
Policy

TEMPLE UNIVERSITY PRESS | PHILADELPHIA

Temple University Press, Philadelphia 19122
Copyright © 1993 by Temple University. All rights reserved.
Published 1993
Printed in the United States of America

∞ The paper used in this publication meets the minimum
requirements of American National Standard for Information
Sciences—Permanence of Paper for Printed Library Materials,
ANSI Z39.48-1984

Library of Congress Cataloging-in-Publication Data
Goetz, Edward G. (Edward Glenn), 1957–
  Shelter burden : local politics and progressive housing policy /
Edward G. Goetz.
    p.   cm.—(Conflicts in urban and regional development)
  Includes index.
  ISBN 1-56639-055-9 (cloth : alk. paper)
  1. Housing policy—United States. 2. Housing development—
Government policy—United States. 3. Public housing—United
States. I. Title. II. Series.
HD7293.G582   1993
363.5′8′0973—dc20   92-2463

For Susan and Hanne

Contents

Tables and Figures		ix
Preface		xi
Abbreviations		xiii
1	INTRODUCTION	1
2	DEVOLUTION THROUGH RETRENCHMENT: THE END OF THE FEDERAL ERA IN HOUSING	19
3	THE LOCAL HOUSING MOVEMENT	45
4	HOUSING POLICY INNOVATION IN U.S. CITIES AND STATES	77
5	THE ROLE OF NONPROFIT HOUSING DEVELOPERS	114
6	THE POLITICS OF HOUSING IN LOS ANGELES	139
7	EXPLAINING THE SPREAD OF PROGRESSIVE HOUSING POLICY	168
8	SOCIAL ACTION, ECONOMIC RESTRUCTURING, AND PROGRESSIVE HOUSING POLICY	187
Notes		201
Subject Index		239
Author Index		245

Tables and Figures

TABLES

1.1	Comparison of responding cities with all cities having populations greater than 100,000	18
3.1	Local housing advocacy groups by time of formation	54
3.2	Types of low-income housing advocacy coalitions in U.S. cities	57
4.1	Use of regulatory housing programs by cities and states	91
4.2	Use of community lending regulations by state governments	100
4.3	Use of policies to preserve and create low-cost downtown housing by cities and states	107
5.1	Number of nonprofit housing developers and number of housing units produced by nonprofits in responding cities, 1989	117
5.2	Support for nonprofit housing developers provided by responding cities and states	122
5.3	Sources of funding for support to nonprofit housing developers	123
5.4	Technical assistance provided to CDCs by state and local governments	124
7.1	Use of progressive housing policies by cities	175
7.2	Cities scoring highest on progressive housing scale	176
7.3	Use of progressive housing policies by responding states	182

FIGURES

3.1	States with low-income housing coalitions, 1991	53
3.2	Number of states and larger cities with housing coalitions, 1970–90	55

3.3	Percentage of states and larger cities with housing coalitions, 1970–90	55
3.4	States with homeless coalitions, 1991	60
3.5	States with nonprofit housing development coalitions, 1991	61
4.1	Spending for housing and community development in the fifty states	78
4.2	States with housing trust funds, 1990	103
7.1	Distribution of PHOUSING variable among cities	175
7.2	Distribution of PHOUSING variable among states	183

Preface

HOUSING PROFESSIONALS and academics who study housing policy issues use the term "shelter burden" to describe situations in which low- to moderate-income families spend too much of their monthly income on housing costs. The current guideline follows federal legislation and establishes 30 percent of income as the threshold. Low- to moderate-income families spending more than 30 percent of their income on housing are said to be suffering a shelter burden. This book is about public policies aimed at alleviating such burdens, and so in that respect the title is appropriate.

But there is another sense in which "shelter burden" describes the contents of this book. From 1933 until 1980 the federal government took the responsibility for meeting the housing needs of low-income families in the United States. We can argue about the effectiveness or efficiency of the federal effort, but the fact remains that it was the federal, not state or local, government that took the lead in affordable housing policy. In 1980, however, and throughout the remainder of that decade the federal government withdrew from the housing policy scene, cutting budget authorizations by over 80 percent. As a result, the burden of making and implementing housing policy in the United States fell squarely on the shoulders of state and local governments. This book is about what happened at state and local levels between 1980 and 1990, and how local governments have dealt with *their* shelter burden.

SOME OF THE findings reported in this book have been presented elsewhere. Much of the material on nonprofit housing in Chapter 5 appeared in *Urban Affairs Quarterly* 27, no. 3 (1992). In addition, an analysis of some of the regulatory policies discussed in Chapter 4 appears in the *Journal of Urban Affairs* 13, no. 3 (1991). I presented a very preliminary analysis of the city-level data (reported in Chapters 4 and 5 of this book) at the 1990 Urban Affairs

Association conference in Charlotte, North Carolina, and a version of the Chapter 7 statistical analysis at the Southwest Political Science Association meeting in San Antonio, Texas, March 1991.

I want to acknowledge the support of a University of Minnesota Graduate School Grant-in-Aid, which allowed me to conduct the surveys that form the basis for the original data collection reported here. Many people assisted in collecting information from the wide variety of publications and newsletters that reported innovations occurring simultaneously across the nation. Patty Beech contributed significantly to the collection of both the primary and secondary data used in this study, as did Norah Davies, Phil Dommer, Tracy Bach, Leslie Simon, and Jonathan Silverstein. Miriam Goldfein and Lori Gilbertson assisted with maps and graphs. Char Klarquist spent more hours on this manuscript than either of us anticipated, and for that I thank her profusely. Andrea Akita arranged a meeting in Seattle with leaders of the housing coalition in that city. Michael Bodaken and Joel Reynolds took time not only to answer my questions but also to read a draft of the Los Angeles chapter. Both politely tried to correct my mistakes and omissions. If I haven't got it right yet, it is despite their efforts. Thanks also to the others in Los Angeles who took the time to answer questions.

My "real life" experiences have contributed much to this work, and Barbara Smith and Bill Witte at the Mayor's Office of Housing in San Francisco, Andy Raubeson at SRO Housing Corporation in Los Angeles, and Alan Arthur of the Central Community Housing Trust in Minneapolis each provided me with opportunities to learn firsthand about local housing policy.

Todd Swanstrom provided constructive criticism and suggestions that improved the manuscript significantly, and probably more important and continuing support for this project than he knows. Mike Rich supplied data on cities that would have taken me months to collect (I know that, because it took *him* months). Better yet, he supplied them in a form that my computer could read.

To Gilda Haas, Calvin Welch, Chip Halbach, Burt Berlowe, and countless others working for housing rights in the United States, I offer my admiration for the commitment and dedication reflected in their hard work.

To my mother, thanks for all the child care—last year and thirty years ago. Finally, to my greatest inspirations, Susan and Hanne, I dedicate this book.

Abbreviations

ACORN	Association of Community Organizations for Reform Now
ALHFA	Association of Local Housing Finance Agencies
CBD	Central business district
CDBG	Community Development Block Grant
CDC	Community development corporation
CES	Coalition for Economic Survival
CHAS	Comprehensive Housing Affordability Strategy
COSCAA	Council of State Community Affairs Agencies
CRA	Community Reinvestment Act of 1977
CRALA	Community Redevelopment Agency of Los Angeles
FHA	Federal Housing Administration
FNMA	Federal National Mortgage Administration (Fannie Mae)
HAC	Housing Assistance Council
HACLA	Housing Authority of the City of Los Angeles
HFA	Housing Finance Agency
HMDA	Home Mortgage Disclosure Act
HOLC	Home Owner's Loan Corporation
HPPD	Housing Preservation and Production Department (Los Angeles)
HTF	Housing trust fund
HUD	U.S. Department of Housing and Urban Development
LIHAC	Low-income housing advocacy coalition
LIHTC	Low-Income Housing Tax Credit
LISC	Local Initiatives Support Corporation
MBE	Minority-owned business enterprise
MRB	Mortgage revenue bond
NAHB	National Association of Home Builders
NAHRO	National Association of Housing and Redevelopment Officials
NAR	National Association of Realtors

NAREB	National Association of Real Estate Boards
NCCED	National Congress of Community Economic Development
NCH	National Coalition for the Homeless
NLIHC	National Low Income Housing Coalition
S&L	Savings and loan
SCANPH	Southern California Association of Non-Profit Housing
SRO	Single room occupancy (residential hotel)
TIF	Tax-increment financing
UDAG	Urban Development Action Grant
WBE	Women-owned business enterprise

1
Introduction

THE PRINCIPAL argument of this book is that a combination of (1) dramatic budget cuts in federal housing programs, (2) the increasing economic polarization resulting from the economic restructuring of urban areas, and (3) the subsequent mobilization of a community-based housing movement has resulted in a dramatically new era of postfederal housing innovation. Local governments across the country have responded to federal cutbacks in housing assistance to the poor in ways that were unanticipated in current theory on federalism and the policy constraints of local governments. Further, they have done so in ways that have transformed housing policy and introduced a new housing policy paradigm.

That the federal government during the 1980s abdicated its leading role in housing policymaking has been amply noted.[1] Federal budget authorization for low-income housing assistance programs fell by more than 80 percent between 1979 and 1988 when adjusted for inflation. What new initiatives were developed at the federal level in these years represented a reduction in the commitment to the production of low-income housing, a shallower subsidy in most forms of assistance, and a more limited support for affordable housing.[2] Housing assistance programs were cut more dramatically than any other kind of domestic program.

President Ronald Reagan and his aides counted on the historical reluctance of local governments in providing housing assistance to the poor to effect a drastic reduction in governmental housing assistance. Indeed, the expectation among most observers, liberal and conservative alike, was that governments at both state and municipal levels would not respond with their own housing assistance programs. But, in fact, they did respond. Local governments across the United States answered the federal cutbacks with an array of innovative programs designed to marshal new resources for housing, involve new groups in housing development and management, and create new mechanisms for the delivery of housing assistance. Nathan has called this type of unexpected response, which he documents for a range of programs beyond housing, the "paradox of devolution."[3] A community-based housing movement has emerged as a strong political influence at state and local levels. Nonprofit housing groups have also emerged as the backbone of local service delivery systems. Local governments are spending more of their own money than formerly, improvising ways to attract greater levels of private investment, and using their regulatory powers to a greater extent in the effort to support affordable housing. This book is an effort to make sense of the vast local response to the housing crisis of the 1980s and to put it in the context of recent theoretical developments about the nature and scope of urban and local policy.

LOCAL HOUSING POLICY IN THE 1980s

The 1980s were a decade of extraordinary local policy innovation in housing. Government officials at both the state and the local level, prodded by a newly constituted community-based housing movement, worked to create alternatives to federal programs aimed at assisting low-income households. The degree of local housing policy activity is remarkable for two reasons: First, as Nathan and his colleagues argue, housing, perhaps more than any other urban program, has been very strongly identified in the minds of advocates and policymakers with the federal government.[4] This perception, fifty years in the making, was effectively altered in less than ten years. Second, much of housing policy, both local and federal, has traditionally targeted middle-income households. The clear challenge of the 1980s, taken on by advocates and officials, was to develop a local housing delivery system that would serve the needs of low-income people.

The devolution of policy responsibility in housing has been matched, predictably, by a devolution of politics on housing issues. Advocacy groups have formed at both the state and local level to pursue redistributive housing policy. Coalitions between previously disparate community-based groups have strengthened the voice of local housing advocates. Advocates of low-income housing are now overwhelmingly community based, oriented toward nonprofit housing development, and aggressive in their insistence that policy meet the needs of low-income households. These new advocacy groups have enjoyed success in both direct and indirect ways. They have successfully defended their positions in front of legislative bodies; they have been involved in the policy formulation process (indeed they are frequently the source of new legislative initiatives); and they have been successful in prodding local governments into research and needs-assessment efforts as a way of initiating a local housing response. More indirectly, these groups have been successful in electing candidates and, in some cities, governing coalitions that then pursue their progressive housing agenda.

Manifestations of the increased local housing response have been many. City and state governments across the country engaged in studies to assess housing needs and created special task forces, all in the hope of creating a foundation for a localized response to housing conditions. The policy response is notably characterized by the fact that cities and states are spending an unprecedented amount of their own money for low-income housing. New York City alone spent $740 million in 1989, Los Angeles around $50 million, Memphis $26 million, and Seattle almost $25 million.[5] Even midsized cities such as Omaha, Sacramento, Charlotte, and Minneapolis are spending from $1.6 to almost $10 million per year on affordable housing. States have transformed their housing efforts by moving from conservative housing finance agencies providing financial assistance to middle-income home buyers to dynamic state agencies creating new forms of assistance to low-income households.[6] A 1988 study, for example, counts more than 230 new programs enacted in thirty-nine states between 1980 and 1987.[7]

Though the response of local governments has been extraordinary, two caveats must be considered. First, to herald a dramatic increase in local housing activity is not to say that innovation in local housing policy is universal, or always embraced by local officials. In many areas officials remain reluctant to provide housing assistance for low-income households. One of the tasks of this book is to examine this variation in local policy response and explain why some localities have become very active in the housing arena while others have not.

Second, the aggregate budgetary response of state and local governments does not nearly match the severity of federal budget cuts. Between 1980 and 1987, budget authorization for HUD (Department of Housing and Urban Development) fell by $19.2 billion. The increase in state expenditures for housing in the combined fifty states between 1980 and 1990 was $2.2 billion—a more than 350 percent increase but a far cry from matching the federal withdrawal. Factoring in increased expenditures by local governments (estimated at $3.1 billion between 1982 and 1987) still leaves a sizable gap. The significance of the local response to housing, however, is not in expenditure levels. Though threefold expenditure increases should not be ignored, the innovations at the state and city level have been more substantive than financial.

The housing movement has effectively advocated a set of approaches that together form an alternative policy paradigm. This new paradigm is characterized by a redefinition of public and private responsibilities and obligations related to low-income housing. Whereas housing policy during the federal era centered on the public subsidy of private production, the new approach more carefully regulates private development while fostering through community development corporations (CDCs) the growth of a nonprofit sector for the development and ownership of low-cost housing. The progressive housing paradigm includes the following objectives or techniques:

1. *Reliance on nonmarket relationships for the production, management, and ownership of land and housing.* Specifically, a lead role is given to the nonprofit sector in the delivery of housing assistance. More generally, the expansion of the "social sector," both public and nonprofit ownership in housing, is emphasized. According to some estimates, CDCs were producing some 30,000 to 45,000 units per year in the late 1980s, roughly matching the output of HUD.

2. *Greater regulation of the private sector in ways that promote the production and preservation of low-income housing.* The progressive paradigm emphasizes the importance of local land-use regulatory powers and their role in supporting and preserving low-income housing. Techniques such as moratoria on the demolition or conversion of affordable units, linkage programs and one-for-one replacement requirements, and rent

control are each looked to as means of constraining market behavior detrimental to affordable housing.
3. *Taxing the private development process to provide financial resources for low-income housing.* State and city governments have imposed real estate transfer fees, escrow fees, and similar means of taxing the land development process to provide funds for housing production. Generally, these fees have been channeled into "housing trust funds" dedicated to the production of affordable housing.
4. *A reversal or mitigation of the impacts of downtown development and the subsequent re-use of inner-city land for low-income housing.* The new housing paradigm seeks to preserve low-cost housing opportunities in downtown areas, notably in SRO (residential) hotels.
5. *Community-based planning on housing issues.* Community-based planning has been advocated as a means of building consensus on housing issues as well as mobilizing official response to neighborhood housing concerns.

CONVENTIONAL WISDOM AND THE LIMITED LOCAL STATE

The increased globalization of the economy, the greater mobility of business and investment, and the perceived dependence of local economies on decisions made by economic actors and political actors beyond the control of local authorities has given rise to an interpretation of urban policy in the 1980s that can be characterized as the *Economic Constraints Model*. This analysis questions whether or not local officials can make meaningful policy choices in the face of the overwhelming influence of non-local (usually economic) factors. Studies with such titles as *City Limits, The Dependent City,* "Semi-Sovereign Cities," and *The Decline of Urban Politics* analyze the diminished ability of local officials to engage in meaningful decision-making that is not strongly shaped by economic and political factors outside of their control.[8]

Paul Peterson's *City Limits* set the stage for more than a decade of debate among urban scholars as to the nature and extent of the institutional, economic, and political constraints that restrict the autonomy of local policymakers. Peterson's argument holds that cities have a unitary interest in creating economic activity that employs residents, generates tax revenues, and creates an attractive locational choice for both capital and households.[9] He emphasizes the mobility of both people and capital and the need for cities to pursue policies that will enhance local wealth. Relying on a public-choice model of urban development, Peterson claims that businesses and residents will be attracted to places with the most favorable ratio of taxes paid to services received.[10] Further, according to this approach, "developmental" policies serve to enhance that ratio, and it is thus "in the interest of the city" to enact them. These developmental policies, according to the argument, benefit all of the residents of a city and are therefore pursued with a good deal of consensus. Although there are problems with the specifics of Peterson's argument—namely, that developmental politics are consensual[11] and that they benefit all residents[12]—the basic premise that local governments have a strong incentive to pursue economic growth is really not arguable. This logic has resulted in the political hegemony of "growth machines" made up of local landowners, property interests, business and public officials, and the subsequent pursuit of "privatistic" policies that bestow incentives and subsidies upon private actors in order to induce growth.[13]

The underlying premise of this model is that the mobility of capital forces local officials to cater to business interests in order to attract the investment necessary to maintain the local economy. City officials give primary consideration to the need to make the city attractive to investors, and create a good business climate by providing abatements, incentives, subsidies, and other perks to business interests. The economic imperative is all the more compelling because officials know they are in competition with their counterparts in other locations.[14] As a result, the 1980s saw a proliferation of giveaway mechanisms, some masquerading as public-private partnerships designed to induce private-sector market activity.[15] The assumptions of the economic constraints model began to take on the characteristics of conventional wisdom; that is, they were widely accepted and infrequently evaluated. Public concession simply represented the way of doing business with business during this era.

Introduction   7

The logic of the economic-constraints model leads to the additional conclusion that redistributive policies are not in a city's interest, given the burden such policies place on the "productive" members of a locality for the benefit of "unproductive" members.[16] According to the argument, redistributive policies do not serve the local economy well for at least three reasons. To the extent that finite local resources are spent on redistributive purposes, these resources are then not available for use in any of a number of other ways to enhance or maintain the economic vitality of the city. That is, there is an opportunity cost associated with redistributive programs. According to the limited-city model, public resources at the local level are better spent on developmental policies that will create or maintain economic growth. Another implication of pursuing redistributive policy is the potential for making the city a welfare magnet that attracts poor people. The welfare-magnet hypothesis holds that because of variation in the redistributive policy from one municipality to the next, the poor are attracted to areas with relatively generous redistributive programs or, at the very least, are discouraged from moving away from those areas.[17] An increased dependent population only puts further strains on local resources. A third way in which redistributive policies are seen as counterproductive to a growth agenda is the extent to which they discourage private capital investment. Given the high degree of mobility that private capital enjoys, investment decisions are likely to favor those areas most attentive to the needs of the business sector, including lower taxes and greater municipal encouragement of trade and economic activity.[18] Further, a large dependent population may discourage locational decisions of firms that wish to avoid the prospect of future taxation or the potential for social disruption.

Economic Constraints and Urban Restructuring

It is not by coincidence that this analysis of urban policy emerges during an era of global economic restructuring characterized by the reorganization of capital, the internationalization of markets, and the restructuring of labor markets. Indeed, changing economic trends are an explicit part of the argument in some cases.[19] That is, these trends are seen as imparting an imperative of growth and urban restructuring away from centers of industrial production toward service centers of finance, real property investment, and corporate management. Urban officials either lead their cities down the path of regeneration, or they fail to do so and allow the city to lag behind as an outdated, overindustrialized anachronism. Typically, of course, the way to urban regeneration is through the developmental policies described earlier. For example, urban regeneration has meant dramatically changed land uses, especially in the downtown core. The wide-scale demolition and clearance of low-income housing, light industry, and warehousing has generally been either facilitated by or directly achieved through public effort. In the place of these outdated land uses are upscale housing, commercial and retail developments, and cultural centers to serve the increasing white-collar, downtown workforce. These too are frequently subsidized or underwritten by the public sector.[20]

Economic Constraints and Federalism

Kantor and David argue that the economic imperative to local policy is stronger at the municipal level than at the state level.[21] Indeed, it is the size and diversity of the local economy and the permeability of borders that define the strength of the economic imperative: "The general economic structure of federalism provides an economic context that favors developmental policy objectives at the local level and favors greater public choice on questions of policy at the national level."[22] This argument essentially echoes Peterson, who asserts: "Limits on local government . . . require that local governments concentrate on developmental as against redistributive objectives. By comparison, central governments are concerned with more than simply developmental objectives."[23]

Indeed, this understanding has focused the debate on national urban policy for the past thirty years. Democratic urban policy has attempted to maintain centralized control and oversight through categorical aid programs and "attached strings." This is done out of mistrust of local politicians and perceptions of how they would implement redistributive policy if given a chance. In fights over local discretion in public housing programs, public housing advocates and democratic policymakers favor national standards.[24] The major housing programs of the 1960s were federally administered under centralized authority.[25] Liberal Democrats thought the best way to achieve their objectives and reach their constituency was to reduce local discretion.²⁶ Republican urban policy, on the other hand, has aimed at devolving policy responsibility and discretion to local levels. Conservatives have in essence valued local control more than the redistributive intent of aid programs. Thus, conservative urban policy loosens federal oversight and guidelines and allows local officials greater flexibility in determining the use of federal grants. General revenue sharing and block grants were designed to maintain federal support for local activities while providing the greatest possible latitude for policy decisions at the local level. Behind these policies is the assumption that local discretion will result in less redistribution and greater attention to the local business interests that have traditionally constituted the Republican constituency within cities.

It is against this background of experience and expectation that Reagan attempted the most far-reaching reforms of federalism in recent times. Reagan's federalism proposals went beyond the reform attempts of Richard Nixon and Gerald Ford in the number of programs affected and the sweep of budget cuts simultaneously proposed. According to Nathan et al. there were three primary objectives in Reagan's domestic agenda; the retrenchment of social programs specifically and public spending generally, the devolution of responsibility to local (primarily state) governments, and the restriction of eligibility for social programs to the "truly needy."²⁷ These objectives, of course, were linked. Restricting eligibility would help to reduce spending levels by eliminating "nondeserving" recipients of federal funds. More important to this discussion, however, is the implicit link between the devolution of policy responsibility to local governments and the retrenchment of social programs. The conventional wisdom of the economic-constraints argument described above led Reagan and almost everyone else to expect that devolution would lead to retrenchment. In fact, that did not happen. Indeed, to a great extent it was the other way around: spending cuts at the federal level led to local government assumption of previously federal responsibilities.

Reagan's most sweeping federalism reform, the so-called "swap-and-turn-back" proposal, never reached Congress. Intense reaction by local government officials who were afraid of being stuck with greater responsibilities and fewer funds effectively killed the measure before it was heard. Massive budget cuts in many areas, however, especially in federal housing programs, allowed Reagan to achieve a de facto devolution. That is, faced with severe reductions in federal housing assistance and the elimination of several programs, and experiencing ever more acute housing crises, local governments were forced to replace federal programs with new local initiatives.

As many federalism scholars argue, federalism is a political accommodation more than a rigid legal construct. The history of housing policy in the 1980s is affirmation of that. Where legislative reform failed, dramatic budget cuts prevailed. As one observer of federalism noted in 1985, "The most important thing about federalism is the federal government has no money."[28] Whether the federal government had the money or not, it was certainly not spending much on domestic social programs. Budget cuts at the federal level put the onus of service provision on local governments. The arena of housing policy very clearly illustrates the dynamics of de facto devolution. Federal budget cuts in the 1980s were larger in housing programs than in any other domestic capital program.[29] The response of local governments to housing budget cuts has been equally dramatic.

HOUSING AND ECONOMIC CONSTRAINTS

The experience of states and cities with housing policy in the 1980s provides a strong counterargument to the economic-constraints thesis. A worsening housing crisis, increased income disparities, and the growth of poverty and homelessness amid affluence, combined with the activism of a local housing movement, have led to a new postfederal era of housing politics. The housing policy arena, which used to be dominated by federal action, large producer groups such as the National Association of Home Builders (NAHB) and National Association of Realtors (NAR), and national trade groups such as the National Association of Housing and Rehabilitation Officials (NAHRO) and Association of Local Housing Finance Agencies (ALHFA), is now increasingly dominated by local officials, nonprofit organizations, and community-based housing advocates, who wield influence at the state and national level through their coalition organizations. The National Low Income Housing Coalition (NLIHC) has statewide and citywide counterparts all over the country which serve as lobbying agents for community-based housing advocates. The adoption of policy innovations and orientations that go beyond previous federal initiatives in their emphasis on nonmarket (nonprofit) mechanisms and market controls (exactions and growth/conversion controls) was unanticipated by the economic constraints model. At most, Peterson argues, only cities with sufficiently growing economies could afford to engage in redistributive policy.[30] The housing policies described in this book have been widely instituted, however, conforming in their pattern of adoption less to patterns of economic growth than to the existence of credible political advocacy.

There is therefore a need for a better understanding of what is possible at the local level and what factors activate that potential. Indeed, such an understanding is becoming well developed in the literature, though perhaps not well integrated. This line of argument suggests that the economic-constraints model restricts appreciation of the political influence of disparate local groups on public policy. The economic-constraints model is also deterministic and overemphasizes the role of the economic imperative in determining local policy outputs.[31] It thus underestimates the range of policy responses available and empirically misjudges the breadth and nature of urban policy as expressed in the 1980s and beyond.

Indeed, the economic-constraints model suffers from only a partial application of the lessons of urban restructuring. That is, the model acknowledges the influence of changing economic relationships and the mobility of capital, the often international sources of investment decisions, and the attempts of local policymakers to harness that process to their benefit.[32] That much of the argument must be admitted. City officials do face a strong incentive to guide their city through restructuring in a way that facilitates a revitalized local economy. Faced with the prospect of becoming economically obsolete, local officials will do what they can to make their city an "intentional city";[33] that is, they will try to create the conditions for a postindustrial economy.

Yet urban restructuring is a more complex process than is suggested by the simple economic-constraints argument. The shift of economic resources away from production and into real estate development, abetted by the tax reforms of 1981, resulted in major shifts in land use across the urban landscape and especially in the physical reconstitution of downtown areas.[34] Redevelopment of urban areas involved the demolition of millions of low-cost housing units and their replacement with luxury housing and commercial and cultural developments aimed at upper-income markets. This attention to downtown development by local officials and private developers was matched by an equally dramatic neglect of neighborhoods. In cities across the United States, neighborhood conditions deteriorated while downtowns thrived. The spatial inequality of urban restructuring was reinforced by changes in labor markets and distribution of income. Economic restructuring bifurcated the wage distribution by creating high-paying, technologically based jobs on one end and low-wage, menial and irregular employment on the other end.[35] Declining wages hurt the poor the most as unprecedented numbers became submerged in a poverty that either cost them their homes or thrust them into the growing category of poor households spending exorbitant portions of their income on housing. The development of these objective conditions and their political implications were as important in producing a local policy response as were the economic constraints of global competition for private investment. In fact, far from neutering local politics, economic change activated politics through the creation of deep economic and social divisions.

The experience of housing in the 1980s definitively indicates that there is greater policy latitude available to local officials than the constraints model suggests. In fact, greater latitude is evident even in the economic development field, where various cities have pursued developmental policies that contradict the expectations of the economic-constraints model.[36] A better understanding of local policymaking therefore requires recognition of the importance of local conditions and political action. Regime analysis, for example, is an attempt to describe the properties of governing coalitions and to put policymaking into a political as well as an economic context.[37] An examination of governing coalitions and their actions and interests avoids the deterministic pitfalls of the constraints model. Another method of investigating the politics of urban policy is to focus on the impact of local social movements. By describing the conditions that nurture the formation and expansion of social movements, and by examining the strategies and policy impacts of such movements, we can construct a fuller and richer explanation of local policy. This book relies primarily upon the latter form of analysis by using national data to assess the impact of a community-based housing movement in the United States. Local officials act on the basis of a number of cues, only one of which is the economic imperative identified by the constraints model. Other motivators include ideology, electoral concerns, and institutional incentives.[38] Identification of the elements of governing coalitions and the ways in which those coalitions interact with local political institutions can also provide meaning for policy outcomes.[39] The access of oppositional movements, made more or less viable under certain institutional arrangements and under certain economic conditions, can constrain a blindly privatistic development policy agenda. In the housing arena such groups have been influential in defining alternatives, providing solutions, and working toward the enactment of new policy approaches. The interests expressed by the housing movement are not often congruent with the pro-growth agendas of many urban regimes, yet they have been adopted in a wide range of localities.

A comprehensive model of local policy should also account for the ways in which needs are expressed. The low-income housing crisis forced local policymakers to respond in the 1980s. Yet this was not, of course, an automatic relationship; one must examine the mediating structures that gave expression to the needs created by the housing crisis. The organization of community-based groups and their strategies for influencing officials are especially important here. For example, the housing movement has benefited from and effectively used media attention to housing issues and homelessness as a means of mobilizing community consensus and policy responses.

We must revise our expectations regarding the impact of growth on public policy. Heretofore we have regarded economic growth as a liberating influence on public policy. That is, according to the economic-constraints model, only those localities that enjoy the greatest level of economic prosperity can afford to engage in more progressive or redistributive policy.[40] Similarly, comparative case studies show growing cities to be more energetic in low-income issues than cities with stagnating economies.[41] This book will show that the particular kind of growth experienced by municipalities during the 1970s and 1980s has been liberating in that it creates the financial capacity for policy autonomy, but is also burdening in that it creates social and economic conditions requiring a more autonomous, redistributive policy response. Cities with greater levels of both wealth and poverty are the cities most aggressively utilizing the new local housing policy paradigm.

CDCs AND THE HOUSING MOVEMENT

My focus on the impact of the local housing movement introduces another thematic issue that is related to the political strategy of social movements. There is a body of analysis on neighborhood-based and community political movements that locates conservatizing influences in government funding. According to Frances Piven and Richard Cloward, political movements lose momentum and bog down in organizational imperatives if they institutionalize themselves.[42] A study of citizen participation by Marilyn Gittell found a shift from more politically oriented advocacy strategies to more apolitical service provision over time as community groups incorporated and became coproducers of government services.[43] This position maintains that (1) organizational maintenance takes an increasingly large proportion of time and effort, thus reducing the time and effort devoted to community-based organizing and political mobilization, and (2) the receipt of government funds necessarily compromises a group and makes it less willing to speak out against government policies—a matter of not wishing to bite the hand that feeds.

This argument is especially relevant to the local housing movement of the 1980s and 1990s. Community development corporations play a large role in the movement as advocates for greater governmental support of low-income housing. At the same time, CDCs are heavily reliant on government funding for their housing production activities. In addition, more recent arguments suggest that CDCs may be incapable of maintaining a democratic structure and preserving a truly "alternative" political orientation.[44] One might therefore expect CDCs to conservatize, modify, or even abandon their political advocacy goals because of both their highly institutionalized structure (as legally incorporated agencies with paid staff and a board of directors) and their heavy dependence on government funding. In fact, the data presented in Chapter 5 suggest the opposite. Despite heavy government support, individual CDCs tend to channel their political advocacy through other coalition bodies of housing advocates, and because of their technical expertise and neighborhood-based constituency they provide local officials with both technical and political resources. As a result, CDCs have become an integral part of the housing service delivery system in many major U.S. cities.

OUTLINE OF THE BOOK AND DATA SOURCES

The book first establishes the political context for the postfederal era in housing, then describes the new progressive policy paradigm, and finally analyzes the postfederal era in the context of current models of state and local policymaking. Chapter 2 more fully describes the federal era in housing policy in order to provide a relief against which the new policy paradigm can be compared. The inherently conservative and regressive nature of most federal housing assistance is detailed, along with the institutional and political underdevelopment characterizing the local housing policy arena during the federal era. The chapter then turns to the documentation of the declining federal commitment to housing during the 1980s in both fiscal and political terms. The complementary increase in local funding for housing activity and in innovative thinking and problem solving at local levels are also introduced. The argument that we are indeed in a "postfederal era" in housing is predicated on three premises: (1) there has been a fundamental shift in leadership on housing issues from national policymakers to local officials; (2) there has been a shift in policy innovation and design from national-level interest groups to local groups; and (3) there has been a replacement of national debate on housing with hundreds of local political contests in state capitols and city halls across the country. The first of these premises is established in Chapter 2, the latter two in following chapters.

The political context for the postfederal housing era is further described in Chapter 3 where data and analysis of the local housing movement in the United States are presented. Emerging as an important force in the mid-1980s, this movement was the vehicle through which the new housing policy paradigm was created and introduced to local policymakers. The chapter describes the evolution of the movement and documents its community-based orientation. The growth of the movement, its policy prescriptions and its growing influence throughout the past decade are described.

Chapter 4 outlines the contours of the new local housing policy paradigm. It presents the progressive housing paradigm in full and analyzes the diffusion of this paradigm throughout larger U.S. cities and the fifty states. The most prominent element of the new paradigm is reliance on and the expansion of a nonprofit or "social" sector in housing development and management.[45] Chapter 5 recounts the emergence of this sector, the means by which local governments have come to integrate the nonprofit sector in housing policy implementation, and the methods by which local governments support nonprofit housing production.

Chapter 6 presents a case study of the city of Los Angeles. The case study is meant to illuminate and illustrate the processes described in the earlier chapters; that is, given the explanation previously provided for increased local activism and innovation in housing across the nation, this chapter shows how those processes were played out in one locality. Between 1980 and 1990 Los Angeles underwent a transformation from a city without any meaningful debate on housing policy, or any locally initiated housing programs, to one of the more active and progressive municipalities in the country. The progressive housing agenda is well established in Los Angeles as the result of years of advocacy for the housing needs of low-income households and the coalescence of a loose but extensive network of advocates that constitute the local housing movement. Objective conditions of homelessness, poverty, and poor housing conditions combined with the electoral vulnerability of the mayor and the opportunism of the movement to create a flurry of policy and policymaking changes in the city. As a result, Los Angeles represents a paradigmatic example of the politics of housing in the postfederal era.

In describing the housing movement and the nature of the progressive policy response in U.S. cities and state, the book presents a good deal of evidence and data to develop its central argument. Chapter 7 presents a statistical analysis of that argument by examining the determinants of innovative housing programs. The analysis is a multivariate study of the factors that determine which state and local governments adopt elements of the progressive policy paradigm. The analyses indicate that progressive policies at the local level are explained by a combination of contradictory economic conditions and the impact of community-based advocacy. The findings challenge the assumptions and predictions of the economic-constraints model of local policy that autonomous policymaking takes place only in wealthier jurisdictions. Instead, the empirical analysis supports an understanding of policy autonomy that acknowledges not only the role of political action but also the impact of economic polarization in creating both the need and the capacity to provide redistributive local policy.

Chapter 8 reiterates the main findings of the book and discusses the implications of the findings. Further, the chapter puts the new policy paradigm in a larger context and evaluates its significance. The optimism that accompanies the observation of a new and vigorous local housing approach is tempered by an analysis of the continued lack of resources of local and state governments. The book closes with prescriptions for a more integrated approach to housing assistance in a federalist system.

The information used in this book comes from a variety of sources. First, national and local publications on housing issues have carried a steady stream of information about the placement of progressive housing items on local political agendas and their more-than-occasional passage. These reports provided examples and illustrations for many of the political and policy developments described here. In addition, secondary sources—scholarly studies and public documents related to local housing programs and the issues faced by housing movements across the country—have been supplemented by government data on expenditures and socioeconomic conditions.

But the book's primary foundation is the original data collection from three separate national surveys and a series of interviews in the case study location (Los Angeles). First, surveys were sent in 1990 to 173 U.S. cities with populations over 100,000 (using 1980 census counts). Completed questionnaires were received from 133 municipalities (a 73.9 percent response rate). As Table 1.1 shows, the respondents reflect the full population of large U.S. cities on each of the dimensions listed. These survey responses

TABLE 1.1
Comparison of responding cities with all cities having populations greater than 100,000

	All Cities		Respondents	
	N	%	N	%
Region				
Northeast	22	12.7	18	13.5
Midwest	40	23.1	28	21.1
South	64	37.0	49	36.8
West	47	27.2	38	28.6
Population				
100,000–250,000	114	65.9	87	65.4
250,000–500,000	35	20.2	26	19.5
500,000 +	24	13.9	20	15.0
Type				
Central City	145	83.8	111	83.5
Suburb	28	16.2	22	16.5
Total:	173		133	

form the basis for the analysis in Chapters 4, 5, and 7. Second, questionnaires were mailed to housing officials in each of the fifty states; follow-up phone interviews were completed with those not returning the initial survey in order to contact the forty-eight states that have a separate agency for housing functions (that is, all but Arizona and Oklahoma). These data form the basis for the analysis in Chapters 4 and 7. Finally, telephone interviews with officials in thirty-four statewide housing advocacy groups were conducted throughout 1990 and 1991.[46] These data are presented in Chapter 3.

2

Devolution through Retrenchment: The End of the Federal Era in Housing

THE FIRST fifty years of housing policy in the United States were a story of federal government initiative and leadership. From the depression-induced policy response of the 1930s and beyond President Nixon's moratorium in 1973, the federal government was the locus of political battles over the nature and scope of public policy related to housing. That era effectively came to a close during the Reagan administration when massive budget cuts signaled an end to federal leadership. State and municipal governments, though financially incapable of completely filling the void, now play much larger roles in determining the nature of the country's housing effort. As policy responsibility devolved to local governments, so too did the politics of housing, to the point that state legislatures and city halls have become the source of most of the new ideas and innovative initiatives characterizing housing policy in the 1980s and 1990s.

THE FEDERAL ERA IN HOUSING

Heavy public-sector intervention in housing and housing markets began with a series of New Deal initiatives aimed at responding to crises created by the Great Depression.[1] The nature of industrial and financial failure in the 1930s shaped the policy response of the federal government and contributed to the lasting character of housing policy for most of the federal era. In essence, federal housing policy in the United States during these years was characterized by three approaches: efforts to increase the efficiency of the private market, a brief and halfhearted attempt at public production of housing, and subsidies to the private sector to stimulate production of affordable housing.

Impact of the Depression

The Great Depression was the event that triggered large-scale federal intervention in housing in the U.S. The depression revealed serious flaws in the housing and real estate industries as they had evolved to that point, flaws that resulted in staggering market failure during the 1930s. Before and during the depression typical home mortgages were two- to five-year loans with balloon payments at the end. The typical mortgage covered only 50 to 60 percent of the full cost of the home. Second and third mortgages were common, as was the practice of refinancing the mortgage at the end of its short term.[2] The impact of the depression on such a system of home financing was devastating. With unemployment rising and incomes declining, many people could no longer afford mortgage payments on their homes. Those borrowers who could still make monthly payments generally had no way of meeting the final obligation of the balloon payment, and lenders became reluctant to refinance mortgages because of the declining earnings of borrowers. Real estate dropped in value, and second and third mortgages became worthless. As mortgage values declined precipitously, lending institutions began to fail. At the height of the depression fully one-half of all home mortgages in the United States were in default, and 1,000 foreclosures a day were occurring throughout the country.[3]

The federal government's first response was to head off this financial disaster. The 1932 Federal Home Loan Bank Act provided both a short- and long-term response to the crisis in the financial industry. The Home Owner's Loan Corporation (HOLC) was created to refinance troubled mortgages. Though in business only four years, HOLC revolutionized the industry by introducing a new form of credit instrument: the long-term, fully amortized mortgage. By stretching payment over time and reducing immediate liability, HOLC eased the credit crunch experienced by most borrowers during the depression. The more longer-term approach in this legislation was the creation of a system of home mortgage financing. The Federal Home Loan Bank and the system of Federal Reserve Banks were created to provide guidance and supervision to the savings and loan (S&L) industry, institutions that were to be devoted to providing home financing.[4] This regulatory structure remained intact until legislation in 1979 and 1982 altered the system of incentives and oversight for S&Ls.

In 1934 the federal government addressed another pressing problem in the home financing system, the lack of mortgage insurance. With the creation of the Federal Housing Administration (FHA) the federal government announced that it would insure mortgages provided by private lending institutions. Prior to this intervention the only protection lenders had against default was the property itself, and the depression had shown that this was unreliable protection at best. The ability to shift the risk to the public sector made lenders more eager to make loans and helped to resuscitate the mortgage market.

The creation of the Federal National Mortgage Association (FNMA) in 1938 was another attempt to create a more efficient credit system for home financing. The FNMA was created to provide a secondary market for home mortgages by purchasing FHA and conventional mortgages and selling them to investors, thereby brokering the secondary market and providing more funds for home lending.[5]

These initial policy responses were primarily intended to address specific deficiencies in the residential finance industry and, by extension, the larger financial industry. Additionally, their impact in spurring employment was used as justification for their adoption. That is, these policies were fundamentally antirecessionary in intent. They were not attempts to broaden the social contract significantly, that is, to provide better housing for "disadvantaged" people. The FHA's emphasis on single-family homes and suburban locations guaranteed a quite conservative impact in social terms. The underwriting criteria and program guidelines adopted by FHA ensured that the programs targeted the white, middle-class, and suburban markets.[6] FHA objectives, in fact, meshed quite well with national economic and transportation policy in the postwar era, which encouraged the development of suburban areas at the expense of inner cities.[7] This federally subsidized migration had direct and negative effects on the low-income and increasingly nonwhite population left in the inner cities. Thus, far from being designed to assist low-income households, the program targeted other populations and indirectly had a detrimental impact on low-income, inner-city households.

At the same time, housing reformers were pushing the concept of public production and ownership of housing for low-income households. The public housing advocates were at least partially motivated by a desire to increase the standard of living for poor people.[8] Meehan argues, however, that public housing, on its face a more radical policy in that it involved direct public production of housing, was also a "multipurpose" policy similar to the credit market interventions of FHA, FNMA, and HOLC: "In both the 1937 and 1949 housing acts [authorizing public housing], the major articulated concerns were unemployment and slum clearance; the provision of housing for persons of low income was a peripheral rather than a central goal. And with respect to housing, primary emphasis was placed on development and construction and not on the provision of housing services."[9]

The ways in which the public housing program was designed and implemented guaranteed that public production did not compete with private-sector housing development.[10] Strong conservative and industry-based opposition to public housing limited the scope of the program. Tenant amenities, construction materials, and maintenance requirements were neglected in the design, construction, and management of the "projects" (as public housing complexes came to be called). The program limped along from the onset, chronically underfunded. As a result, it never evolved into the meaningful and important housing alternative in the United States that it did in other industrialized countries.[11] Indeed, because of underfunding and critical administrative mistakes,[12] combined with the deteriorating economic standing of inner-city minorities, U.S. public housing has become the holding pen for the most impoverished, and the projects themselves are ridden with crime, substance abuse, and other behaviors associated with near total economic, social, and political marginality.[13]

Postwar Housing Initiative

The urban renewal program was even more naked in its nonhousing objectives. The concept of publicly funded "slum removal" originated with a coalition of banks, merchants, realtors, and large corporations representing land-based interests in and around the downtowns of U.S. cities.[14] During its formative years the urban renewal coalition had little in common with public housing advocates. Most early urban renewal advocates were opposed to restricting the re-use of cleared slum areas to housing, and they attempted to limit provisions for public housing in urban renewal legislation. It was only later that public housing and urban renewal made a politically expedient marriage to enable passage of the Housing Act of 1949.[15] Under the urban renewal program, public agencies cleared blighted areas in the inner city and prepared the land for re-use, a certain percentage of which had to be public housing.[16] Nevertheless, the implementation of the program was such that it maximized clearance, removal, and commercial development and minimized the development of affordable and public housing; urban renewal eliminated more affordable housing for low-income people than it ever produced.[17] The history of urban renewal, moreover, has been an extremely volatile one, clouded with controversies about the destruction of working-class neighborhoods and the displacement of poor people and people of color without the provision of adequate replacement housing or relocation assistance.[18] The program was first and foremost an economic development tool for urban real estate interests and was used as such to facilitate the revitalization of downtown land.[19]

After nearly a decade of little federal innovation under the Eisenhower administration, President John F. Kennedy redirected federal involvement in housing. The housing programs of the 1960s embraced the idea of offering private-sector owners/developers loan subsidies and incentives to produce affordable housing. Programs such as Section 236 and Section 221(d)(3) provided private-sector developers with inexpensive financing through loans at below-market interest rates and interest rate buydowns. The private owners made the housing units available at regulated rent levels for as long as their federal mortgages required, rent levels affordable to low- and moderate-income households. In the 1960s, an era of rapidly expanding federal urban and antipoverty policy, housing policy was directed toward low-income, inner-city families more than before. The Kennedy and Johnson administrations were able to channel FHA assistance and other housing programs such as Section 235 and 236 into inner cities.[20] Yet even in these, there were substantial benefits to industry. The 235 and 236 programs were "oriented toward housing production—units, starts, and property—with people being a secondary consideration."[21] That is, the subsidy programs of the 1960s were fundamentally builder programs. Drafted with major input from the National Association of Home Builders (NAHB), they provided much-needed sources of housing finance to the building industry, especially during the credit crunch of 1969–70.[22] The contradiction of housing policy in the 1960s is that even as it more directly targeted lower-income, inner-city neighborhoods, it also became more dependent on private-sector implementation. Indeed, the federal government was simply more activist and more direct in providing inducements to the private sector than it had been before.

In an attempt to simplify and reduce the federal housing effort, Nixon collapsed a number of categorical housing assistance programs into the Community Development Block Grant (CDBG) and introduced a program that provided a rental subsidy to the household itself. The Section 8 programs (for newly constructed housing, rehabilitated units, or existing units) closely reflected Nixon's conservative ideology by providing an income supplement and allowing the consumer to use the added purchasing power in the marketplace,[23] an idea that was taken further by Reagan in 1983 with the housing voucher program. The CDBG program also reflected a more conservative policy prescription in that it devolved program control from federal officials in HUD to local governments. The block grant contained more general guidelines about the use of funds than did the categorical housing programs, giving local officials more discretion in how these federal funds were to be spent.[24]

In addition to these direct-expenditure housing programs, the federal government provided tax deductions for the interest paid on home mortgages and reductions in tax liability for those investing in low-income rental housing. The mortgage interest deduction was put in place to provide an incentive for homeownership. The other so-called tax expenditures were meant to induce greater private-sector participation in low-income rental housing. During the general inflation of the 1970s and the hyperinflation in housing costs of the 1980s, these tax expenditures came to dwarf the rest of the federal government's housing assistance system.[25] By far the largest portion of these tax incentives are the homeowner deductions that disproportionately benefit middle- and upper-income homeowners. Thus, the largest single program of assistance in the federal housing package is also the most regressive.[26]

By the beginning of the 1980s, despite Nixon's attempts to simplify the federal approach to housing, policy was being implemented through a combination of ever expanding efforts to control and channel credit to housing production,[27] an almost moribund public housing program, and a set of tax and financial subsidies to the private sector to produce affordable housing. As public policy, these approaches shared certain characteristics. First, the wide range and great mix of federal policies were argued by some to indicate an inability to agree upon the primary objectives of housing policy.[28] In most programs, especially the earlier ones, the affordable housing implications were subordinated to the true policy objectives. The real objectives were generally economic in nature and related to reviving failing financial or construction industries, revitalizing downtowns, or providing employment in times of widespread job loss. In other words, housing policy was being used primarily as a means of achieving nonhousing objectives. This was perhaps most evident during the depression, when the economic impact of housing policy was openly used as justification for government action, but even into the 1960s, housing policy was serving to support suburbanization and other nonredistributive goals. The scattered objectives of federal housing account for the wide variety of income levels assisted and populations targeted, the variety of subsidy techniques used, and the particular program and eligibility guidelines established.[29]

Second, federal housing policy has historically emphasized homeownership.[30] Beginning with the FHA reforms in mortgage credit, the establishment of secondary markets for residential mortgages, and the homeowner tax deduction, the system has been biased toward increasing homeownership rates. Furthermore, middle-class and suburban homeownership have been the true beneficiaries of government subsidy. For the first twenty years, FHA explicitly targeted nonminority and non-inner-city housing for assistance. The impacts on housing in inner-city neighborhoods have largely been a legacy of the unfulfilled promises of public housing and the documented malignancy of urban renewal.

Third, federal housing policy has been ultimately conservative.³¹ By the 1980 presidential election, it had become characterized by a conservative reliance on private-sector production, rent subsidies, local administration of block grant housing funds, and regressive tax incentives for homeownership. The public housing program was chronically underfunded, and the quality of housing and the quality of living it offered residents were showing signs of unarrested decline. Housing policy implicitly and explicitly supported the primary role of the private sector in producing affordable housing. Direct subsidy programs such as Section 221(d)(3), the finance and credit programs of FNMA and FHA, and the tax incentives were all aimed at boosting private-sector housing development. The reliance on the trickle-down of benefits through the "filtering" of housing units to the poor was another manifestation of the reliance on private-sector production to solve the country's housing problems.³² The orientation of federal housing policy toward support of the private sector was due to the measure of influence wielded by such groups as the National Association of Home Builders (NAHB) and the National Association of Real Estate Boards (NAREB). Indeed, these groups benefited from a very close relationship with federal agencies through frequent interaction between NAHB lobbyists and HUD and FHA officials. Personnel shifted easily between these public and private agencies, as frequent job switching between the lobbying organization and the federal agencies occurred.³³

State and Local Housing Policy during the Federal Era

The number and scope of federal housing programs grew through the years, as public policy objectives were redefined.³⁴ Each administration tended to put its own mark on housing policy, Democrats gently expanding its scope and Republicans restricting it or devolving influence to lower levels of government.³⁵ Despite these changes, the underlying premise that housing is a federal responsibility remained intact from the first legislative act in 1932 until the Reagan administration. Each Congress since 1932 has acted on that premise and adopted its own housing legislation.³⁶ Even the most radical tinkering with the housing system, Richard Nixon's restructuring of the assistance delivery system through the consolidation of categorical programs and introduction of rental subsidies (as significant as they were), did not alter the basic fact of federal leadership in housing assistance.

The programs enacted during the federal era, with the exception of the Nixonian reforms, tended to bypass local governments altogether. Local governments were not relevant to the finance and insurance reforms of FHA and the Federal Home Loan Bank Board legislation. At the local level, public housing and urban renewal required only the establishment of separate quasi-public bodies for the implementation of what were federally designed and federally funded programs. Even some of the private-sector subsidy programs bypassed local governments, transferring funds directly from the federal government to the subsidy recipients. Only with the block grant consolidation of the 1970s was local government given a direct role in the implementation of federal housing policy.

This heavy federal bent stunted the growth of local housing initiatives. Public officials assumed that affordable housing was a national responsibility and were thus reluctant to provide assistance locally. For their part, advocates for housing programs believed that the chances for enactment of low-income housing assistance were better in Washington than in local legislative chambers.[37]

The role of local and state housing agencies has thus been quite limited historically. In fact, state-level housing finance agencies (HFAs) are very recent phenomena. It was not until 1960 that the state of New York created the first HFA. There were eleven such agencies by the late 1960s, 30 by the mid-1970s, and forty-four by 1981.[38] They were formed in order to take advantage of the federal subsidies and tax incentives for housing production introduced in the 1960s. In the 1970s, HFAs were heavily reliant on federal programs, especially the Section 236 program, creating the majority of their units through this subsidy program.[39]

In 1974 the Virginia HFA was the first to issue tax-exempt bonds for the production of housing.[40] Thereafter, the issuance of tax-exempt mortgage revenue bonds (MRBs) became the primary function of state HFAs. By 1978, 62 percent of all housing funds raised by HFAs was acquired through mortgage revenue bonds.[41] The popularity of MRBs steadily increased to the point that Congress in 1980 limited the bonding authority of states and imposed restrictions on sales price and income eligibility. Still,

MRBs were extremely popular with state and local agencies, especially in the early 1980s when they represented nearly the only large source of housing capital. Between 1976 and 1986, state and local agencies issued close to $76 billion in MRBs.[42]

State housing finance agencies have generally been conservative in their lending practices and have not been innovators in housing assistance.[43] The heavy reliance on bond financing has given most state HFAs a conservative, bankerlike outlook on housing development. In order to sell the bonds and create program proceeds with which to retire the bonds, they have generally targeted moderate- to middle-income households for the housing assistance they provide. Even prior to their great dependence on mortgage revenue bonds, HFAs exhibited a conservative lending philosophy. The heavy reliance on Section 236 funds in the late 1960s and early 1970s meant that a large proportion of their beneficiaries were moderate-income households. Nationwide, in fact, only 13.6 percent of HFA-assisted households through the year 1973 were in the low-income bracket.[44] A study of HFAs in the early 1970s found that most of the units they offered were suburban, most were new, and almost all were for middle- and moderate-income households.[45] Conservative underwriting practices in the bond programs of the 1970s merely continued that trend.

In many cases the conservatism of HFAs lasted well into the 1980s. In Minnesota, for example, the HFA was given credit for being one of the more innovative state housing agencies.[46] Nevertheless, a 1988 study by the state's legislative auditor concluded that the agency had neglected low-income renters and needed to increase the priority given to the homeless, low-income renters, and nonprofit providers.[47] In other states, such as California, the HFA has been eclipsed by the state's Department of Housing and Community Development (DHCD). The HFA still performs its function as a lender and issuer of mortgage revenue bonds, but it is the DHCD that implements the state's innovative programs for SRO housing rehabilitation, nonprofit housing assistance, and low-income rental rehabilitation. This is the pattern in a growing number of states in which separate agencies implement state-funded housing programs, while the HFA exclusively finances homeownership through the issuance of mortgage revenue bonds.[48]

City agencies in the past have been little more than conduits for federal program money. Immediately before the Reagan years the typical local housing assistance agency was located in a line department of Community Development or a mayor's special office. These departments generally were responsible for the allocation of CDBG money, and they often implemented other federal housing programs.

Typically, several city agencies were involved in housing matters. The local planning department guided and enforced land-use decisions, and in many cases, depending upon the size of the city, a separate office handled housing inspections and the enforcement of building codes. But planning departments did not often regard themselves as housing agencies, and building inspections were rarely a matter of policy. Thus, local housing policy tended to be indirect at best, developed and enforced through zoning, building codes, property tax rates, and the implementation of federal programs. City governments rarely expended their own resources in support of affordable housing. Indeed, they did not have to; the federal government had always picked up that tab.

The emptiness of big-city housing policy debate is reflected most in the fact that before the 1980s it was suburban zoning techniques that attracted most of the attention of analysts looking at local housing policy. That is, the most compelling local housing policy issue was the exclusionary zoning practice of suburban jurisdictions that limited the availability of affordable (usually rental) housing.[49]

THE DEVOLUTION OF HOUSING RESPONSIBILITY

The Reagan administration cutbacks in housing assistance for low income households were part of a larger domestic strategy of social program retrenchment and federalism reform. There is some disagreement as to whether the changes that occurred during the Reagan years constituted a "revolution" or whether they were blown out of proportion by public response. Analysts have variously attributed this alleged overreaction to (a) the media, (b) Reagan supporters wanting to trumpet the triumph of Reaganomics, or (c) opponents attempting to generate a public reaction to cuts they considered too extreme.[50] Regardless of public reaction, however, it is clear that significant changes did occur in the country's social policy arena. Public assistance cuts and program eligibility guidelines altered the social contract. The antigovernment, probusiness, and voluntaristic tenets of Reagan domestic policy were, according to the Reagan line, an attempt to reduce government intrusion into the private market, to revitalize the economy, to reassert the incentives of the market, and, by implication, to allow the market to address social problems. Trickle-down theory was a reaffirmation of the market's presumed ability to solve social ills and a negation of the proposition that the state could effectively sustain the provision of the social benefits that had been incrementally assigned to it during the previous eight presidential administrations.

As significant as the new direction in domestic policy represented by the Reagan agenda proved to be, there is evidence of an even earlier trend toward devolution and social retrenchment.[51] Specifically, federal aid to state and local governments had begun to decline immediately before the 1980 election. According to Liner, "Some devolution of responsibilities from the federal level to the state occurred in every administration since President Richard Nixon's first term in the early 1970s. However, the pace quickened with the beginning of the Reagan administration."[52] Federal aid as a percentage of state and local expenditures had peaked in 1978.[53] Municipal governments in the United States had responded to the fiscal crisis of the mid-1970s by cutting back on their spending; according to Nathan and his associates, this retrenchment "percolated up" through the federal system.[54]

A gradual reduction in federal aid to states and municipalities took place in the housing arena as well. Nixon's moratorium on housing assistance in 1973 signaled the end of the expansionary era of federal housing programs.[55] His introduction of the Section 8 rental subsidy programs represents the last major increment in federal housing assistance and is offset, with respect to the scope of federal leadership, by the devolutionary impacts of his CDBG reform. The emergence and rapid growth in the number of state housing finance agencies reflected a growing state-level concern for housing assistance well prior to the Reagan changes. In addition, by 1980 local governments had had five years of experience in implementing housing programs through the CDBG program. As studies of that program show, cities were steadily increasing the amount of CDBG resources devoted to housing programs.[56] The conservative and limited nature of these nascent local housing activities should be emphasized, however. As described earlier, state HFAs were almost exclusively providing housing assistance to moderate- and middle-income homebuyers. Block grant housing programs were heavily tilted toward rehabilitation of single-family homes for moderate-income households.[57] The limited capacities that were formed at both the state and municipal levels through the 1970s served as scant preparation for the period of dramatic federal budget cuts in the 1980s.

Reagan's Devolutionary Reforms

Although devolution had already begun to occur in a limited and gradual manner, Reagan was the first president to couple a wide-ranging plan for devolution with dramatic cuts in domestic social spending. Even without the serious retrenchment of social programs, Reagan's reform initiatives went beyond the scale of previous attempts to reshape intergovernmental relations. Nixon's federalism reforms were attempts to streamline procedures and eliminate federal oversight of programs, but they retained the basic premise of federal government funding of state and local activities.[58] That is, Block Grant consolidation and even general revenue sharing were seen as ways of improving the flow of funds from the federal to the local level, without questioning the underlying premise of that flow. The Reagan federalism reforms, however, were aimed at the elimination of federal support for a range of domestic programs. The Reagan administration attempted to turn back to state governments a number of policy responsibilities that had previously and traditionally been the responsibility of the federal government.

For example, Reagan's most sweeping reform proposition, the so-called swap-and-turn-back proposal, offered to give back to the states $47 billion worth of federal programs in exchange for federal assumption of the Medicaid program. Throughout the first half of 1982, Reagan administration officials negotiated with local officials over the details of the plan. At one time the administration prepared a list of forty-four programs that might be handed over to the states, encompassing 125 different grants.[59] State and local officials reacted strongly to the proposals, fearing that responsibility for domestic social problems was to be unfairly dumped in their laps. The Reaganites were never able to persuade them otherwise, and the proposal never picked up the momentum it needed. Ultimately, the plan was shelved before being introduced in Congress.

Many argue that Reagan's federalism reforms were ideologically based in a more traditional and conservative conception of the original intent of constitutional federalism.[60] Under this argument the states are the primary focus of governmental activity, and federal intervention in domestic affairs is inefficient, counterproductive, and damaging to economic growth. The federal government should especially avoid, according to this argument, the temptation to reduce geographic inequalities.[61] Others argue that Reagan's preference for public policy at the state level was political more than ideological. That is, Reagan was not so much seeking to shift domestic policy responsibility from the federal to the local level as seeking to abolish that responsibility.[62] According to this understanding, Reagan counted on the state legislatures to resist taking on the social policy obligations that the federal government thrust upon them. Devolution of policy responsibility was tied to a perception of state and local politics that emphasized the conservatism of local legislatures. Indeed, Reagan explicitly formulated this opinion of local politics: "It is far easier for people to come to Washington to get their social programs. It would be a hell of a lot tougher if we diffuse them and send them to the states. All their friends and connections are in Washington."[63]

The expectation among Reagan and his policy advisers was that devolution would lead to retrenchment. This expectation was shared by Reagan's opponents as well.[64] The linkage between devolution and budget cuts at the state and local level enjoyed a consensus among many observers: "Some supporters of devolution saw it as a way to cut both government services and involvement at all levels because they assumed that states and localities would have little interest in picking up the slack left by federal reductions and cuts."[65]

Given so strong a connection, it is hard to avoid the conclusion that social policy retrenchment was the underlying motivation for devolution. This conclusion is strengthened by the fact that the

Reagan preference for less government was not universal. The unprecedented peacetime military buildup of the 1980s suggests that Reagan preferred governmental spending of a certain type.[66] Thus the reforms in intergovernmental relationships that he proposed reflected not so much stricter interpretation of constitutional federalism as a political initiative aimed at reducing social programs and redirecting federal spending from domestic to military purposes. The federalism reforms that were mainly efforts at devolving policy responsibility to state and local levels were thus a (weakly) camouflaged strategy of reducing the "social wage." That is, devolution was part of the larger administration effort to support corporate strategies for economic restructuring, including deregulation, privatization, and social policy retrenchment.[67]

In summary, then, Reagan had little success in formally altering the basis of federalism in the United States. The centerpiece of his reform proposals, the swap-and-turn-back plan, failed even to be introduced in Congress. If devolution failed as an indirect attempt at social program retrenchment, however, the Reagan administration was much more successful in directly retrenching federal social programs through budgetary cuts.

Reagan's Budget Cuts

The Omnibus Reconciliation Act of 1981 represents the Reagan presidency's most far-reaching impact on domestic social policy. The budget called for absolute decreases in federal grants to state and local governments for the first time in twenty-five years.[68] The impact of the cuts was such that the ethos of government expansion was questioned. Nathan et al. argue that the Reagan budget approach established retrenchment as the norm for public agencies; program expansion became in effect unfashionable.[69] As mentioned earlier, there had been a modest trend toward budgetary retrenchment in the late 1970s, at both local and federal levels. The Reagan budget cuts, however, significantly accelerated the retrenchment introduced by the Carter administration. Attempting to cut the budget as a percentage of the gross national product (GNP) while expanding military expenditures, Reagan dramatically slashed domestic social spending, restricted program eligibility guidelines, and reduced benefit levels.[70] Though he was never again able to impose such large cuts as in 1981, his full eight years in office saw a concerted effort to reduce spending levels in a range of social programs.

Of all areas of domestic spending, housing received the most severe cuts: HUD's share of federal budget authority fell from a little over 7 percent of the total budget in 1978 to less than 1 percent in 1988; between 1978 and 1987 new budget authority for housing assistance fell $24 billion dollars, or more than 80 percent when adjusted for inflation.[71] In addition to budgetary reductions, the 1986 tax reform further reduced or eliminated a number of tax incentives for the production of low-income, multifamily housing, replacing them with the Low-Income Housing Tax Credit (LIHTC). Though the tax credit has become widely used, the lengthy learning curve endured by low-income housing developers produced a significant interruption in the production of affordable units. In addition, the LIHTC subsidy is not deep enough to produce low-income housing without additional subsidies. Thus, the tax credits represented further federal withdrawal from housing assistance.[72] Experience with the program through its first two years supports the notion that the LIHTC has often been used in conjunction with additional public subsidies. Three out of every four LIHTC projects in 1987 and 1988 had one or more additional public subsidies.[73] The Reagan administration's public housing policy was to encourage the *sale* of units to tenants—yet another attempt to reduce the federal government's role in housing assistance to the poor. The administration's "new" housing initiative, the voucher program introduced in 1983, was not a new idea at all but rather a variation (again based on a reduced government role) of the Section 8 rental subsidy.[74]

The entire thrust of federal housing policy in the 1980s, then, both financially and programmatically, was toward the reduction of the federal government's role in the production, management, and ownership of affordable housing for low-income households. Hence, housing provides the paradigmatic expression of the Reagan achievements in reforming federalism. Nathan argues that Reagan had "considerable success" in reforming federalism but only indirectly and incrementally, in the form of federal budget cuts, tax reductions, and changes in federal programs that devolved more implementation responsibility to states.[75]

De Facto Devolution

State and local governments responded to federal budget cuts by expanding their involvement in a range of previously federal policy areas, unexpectedly increasing their spending in areas cut by the federal government. Nathan et al. call their response the "paradox of devolution."[76] This significant reordering of policy responsibilities has in fact altered the face of American federalism; it has created a "budget-driven federalism" determined largely by what the federal government is willing to do in the area of domestic policy.[77] In few places is the local government assumption of policy initiative more prevalent than in housing.

According to Nathan et al., state and local governments responded to federal budget cuts in one or more of seven ways: by *replacing federal funds* with local revenues, *increasing fees* in an effort to increase revenues, *shifting other federal funds* into more highly prioritized spending categories, *increasing program efficiency* in an attempt to reduce the impact of budget cuts, *spending carryover federal funds* from previous years, ratifying federal cuts by *passing them through* to other governments or to program beneficiaries, or *compounding them* with additional local budget retrenchment.[78] The paradox of devolution refers to the widespread practice of local governments to engage in the first four of these responses. State and local governments shifted funds, replaced federal funds with local money, initiated fees and exactions, and attempted to create more efficient and streamlined programs in an attempt to maintain program benefits as pre-Reagan levels. This local policy response, furthermore, was not restricted to the larger or more "progressive" states.[79]

Where sweeping legislative initiatives to reform federalism failed to earn even a Congressional hearing, budget cuts and programmatic changes did succeed in creating a shift in program responsibility from federal to local levels. In fact, the Reagan formula was reversed: having attempted to reform federalism (by devolving policy responsibility from the federal to lower levels of government) in order to effect budgetary retrenchment in social policy, the Reagan administration ultimately found that budgetary retrenchment at the federal level created in its wake a devolutionary change in federalism. Devolution did not lead to retrenchment; rather retrenchment produced devolution.

The Devolution of Politics

The Reagan budget of 1981 made it clear to social policy advocates that the federal government was no longer interested in funding "their" programs. The congressional response to the Reagan budget proposals made it equally clear that there was insufficient support in the House and Senate to counter the president's intentions. Thus, the 1980s also saw a dramatic restructuring of the social policy advocacy community from a few national groups to a myriad of active locally based groups, and a reorientation of lobbying toward state and municipal government.

Within two years of the Reagan budget cuts in 1981, interest groups for low-income people had been formed in all but eight states.[80] Many credited the Reagan budget cuts with constituting the exclusive impetus for the formation of these groups; indeed, some, such as the Illinois Coalition against Reagan Economics (ICARE), did so in the organization's name. The initial response on the part of low-income advocates was to reorient themselves to local advocacy and focus their attention on state capitols and city halls.[81] In addition, however, the depth and breadth of the Reagan budget cuts forced a realignment of social policy advocates and created new political bedfellows: "Reagan's assault on federal social spending forced minorities, labor unions, church groups and liberals . . . to form new coalitions or expand old ones to oppose the cuts and the establishment of social service block grants that gave the state much broader latitude."[82]

Local governments were sometimes instrumental in mobilizing program constituencies to lobby Congress against additional budget cuts. In San Francisco, for example, the local office of community development helped organize a coalition of CDBG recipient agencies for the very purpose of combining with similar agencies statewide for a lobbying effort aimed at avoiding further cuts in the CDBG program. These new coalitions, however, focused primarily on state and local policymakers and were successful in demanding that local governments respond to federal cutbacks. As Nathan et al. argue, these groups formed and began to lobby locally just as many states were benefiting from the increased tax revenues from a round of tax hikes and the coincident end of the recession. Thirty-eight states increased taxes in 1983, and when the recession eased that same year, state governments experienced unexpected surpluses. Social policy advocates were organized by that time to take advantage of the positive revenue situation.[83]

The devolution of politics was especially prominent in the housing field. Before 1980 only seven states had statewide low-income housing advocacy coalitions (LIHACs). By 1989 over thirty states had such groups, half of which had been formed after 1984. At the municipal level, LIHACs are similarly a recent phenomenon. In two-thirds of a sample of larger cities with low-income housing coalitions, those coalitions were formed after 1979. Such groups have been extremely active at both state and local levels in prodding officials to provide locally financed housing programs for low-income households. Their efforts are, in fact, what has driven the post-federal era in housing policy. Their new policy approach rejects many of the federal-era strategies in favor of new ways to provide housing for low-income households.

THE POSTFEDERAL ERA IN HOUSING POLICY

We find ourselves now in a postfederal era in housing policy. Some argue correctly that despite budget cutbacks, the federal government still provides more housing assistance than do local governments.[84] Nevertheless, the trend at the federal level since the Nixon administration has been toward retrenchment and restriction of government's role in the provision of affordable housing. The last significant innovation in federal housing policy was the Nixon Section 8 rental subsidy program introduced in 1974. Since then, federal initiatives have been oriented toward reducing federal assistance and shifting greater responsibility to local governments. This dwindling federal presence has been met with a great deal of expansion at the state and local levels. These governments are increasingly spending their own revenues and innovatively creating new financing mechanisms and new housing assistance delivery systems. Indeed, the local housing policy arena is the primary source for new and innovative ideas for solving the nation's housing problems. Community-based advocacy, aimed at influencing the decisions of local officials, has infused the housing policy debate with a number of new and alternative means of providing low-income households with affordable and quality housing.

The postfederal reaction was not immediate. In their study of local government reaction to Reagan budget cuts, Nathan and his associates noticed little local activity in the area of housing. They suggest that this was the result of the historically prominent role of the federal government in housing assistance.[85] In addition, they maintain that because of the nature of housing assistance (in which the final production of housing occurs years after the initial budgetary allocation of funds), there was in all likelihood a lag period of three to four years before federal budget cuts were felt most dramatically. Indeed, this seems to have been the case: the analysis of state spending on housing in Chapter 4 shows a dramatic increase after 1982. Similarly, most of the innovation at the municipal level has also occurred since 1984.

In the face of draconian federal budget cuts, local governments struggled to develop new programs and find new sources of funding in order to continue to deliver low-income housing. Very little systematic research has been done, however, on the response of local governments to federal budget cuts in housing. What research has been done has often taken the form of cataloguing "innovative" local programs.[86] The extant literature offers at best a sketchy outline of the overall pattern of local government response. The following chapters attempt to rectify this by providing a fuller accounting of housing policy at state and local levels.

More and more states and cities have come to see the provision of affordable housing as a legitimate local concern. Furthermore, the level of local government response to federal budget cuts appears impressive. Despite the more than 80 percent decline in federal funding, the number of households assisted has dropped by only about 6 percent.[87] Assistance levels have been kept up, to some extent, by the replacement of federal funds with other (local) funds, a strategy employed by local governments in a number of policy areas.[88] Cities have used their taxing powers to raise revenue and have increased local expenditures on affordable housing. Most are financing these expenditures through the sale of bonds, and a majority are using funds from current operating revenues.[89] Local governments have also used new tax sources or increases in old taxes to provide housing capital.[90]

In addition to own-source spending, the funding gap has been filled by shifts in the way remaining federal funds have been used. Cities have increasingly used their Community Development Block Grant dollars from the federal government for low-income housing efforts.[91] This was true even as CDBG allocations themselves were being cut from $3.7 billion in 1981 to $1.9 billion in 1988. On the other hand, state governments, given new discretion over the small-cities portion of the CDBG program in 1982, have with few exceptions reduced the amount spent on housing and replaced it with economic development and public works projects.[92]

Beyond looking for new sources of financing, state and local governments have attempted to spread scarce resources by relying more and more on multiple sources for project funding. In this postfederal era of housing policy, many different groups have become significant actors: churches, labor unions, private foundations, and private corporations have begun to finance affordable housing production, and nonprofit corporations and community-based organizations have become active in financing, developing, and managing affordable housing units.[93] The reliance on multiple sources of support has been necessary "largely because no single resource is adequate to finance an entire project."[94] In 1987 twenty-nine percent of all rehabilitated units received funds from multiple sources, compared with only a negligible percentage in 1980.[95] This leveraging of multiple sources of financing has often taken a programmatic form; that is, many programs require multiple sources and matching funds as a condition of eligibility.

The use of nonprofit community development corporations (CDCs) as the providers of low-income housing has increased dramatically in the past decade.[96] Pickman and his colleagues argue that in certain markets CDCs are the only actors involved in low-income housing.[97] Two factors are important in the rise to prominence of CDCs. First, the crisis of expiring use restrictions has threatened the ongoing affordability of one to three million publicly subsidized, privately owned projects.[98] As the subsidy terms expire on older units, the potential looms for conversion to market rate. That threat to maintaining the existing stock of affordable housing was such in 1987 that it forced Congress into an emergency solution for the retention of subsidized units. The new legislation restricted the ability of private owners to convert their units to market rate and required notification of the intent to convert in order to allow for the assertion of first right of refusal by local public agencies and nonprofits. In the 1980s there was a growing sense among housing advocates that this type of costly, last-minute rescue operation could be avoided by relying on nonprofit organizations. Nonprofit ownership offers a better long-term solution to the problem of affordable housing than does the private sector, because the eventual or potential conversion of subsidized units to market rate is avoided.[99]

Second, CDCs have gained importance as a direct result of the devolution of policy initiative and innovation to local governments. Community development corporations have stronger ties to neighborhoods, better understand community needs and preferences, and often provide a more responsive form of housing management than most private developers.[100] Furthermore, through their neighborhood-based ties, CDCs represent important political constituencies to local officials.[101] Channeling housing programs through CDCs thus produces benefits that are both technical and political. The political and programmatic issues surrounding CDCs are explored in Chapter 5.

Cities have also turned to off-budget strategies to encourage the development of low-income housing. Off-budget items involve primarily the innovative use of local governments' powers of land-use regulation. As Chapter 4 shows, land-use regulations such as office-housing linkage, one-for-one replacement of housing, and various housing preservation initiatives are being used by almost one city in five in the United States. These programs are attractive, in part, because they involve little or no budgetary expense for local governments, relying instead upon housing-related obligations imposed on private developers.

The shift in housing assistance from new construction to rehabilitation between 1980 and 1987 was another example of the increasing use of shallow subsidies. To the extent that rehabilitation is less costly, it has become the predominant strategy of local governments. Although the number of households assisted has, as noted above, dropped by only 6.5 percent, the type of assistance has changed dramatically. Rehabilitation as a share of total assistance provided by cities has increased by 22 percent.[102]

City efforts to provide low-income housing assistance, then, have been characterized by

a. an increased use of local (nonfederal) dollars for housing,
b. an increased use of CDBG dollars for housing,
c. greater leveraging of private capital,
d. an increased reliance on nonprofit housing developers,
e. the use of off-budget and regulatory strategies,
f. a shift from new construction to rehabilitation.

Most of these characteristics derive from the agenda of housing advocates who mobilized themselves to lobby for increased housing activity at the local and state level. Their agenda has extended beyond merely demanding that local resources be devoted to housing assistance. The local housing movement has provided alternative forms of financing and ownership models; it has advocated an alternative to private-sector domination of low-cost housing; and it has suggested regulatory initiatives to support low-income housing.

The postfederal era in housing is thus not only (or even primarily) reflected in budgetary terms; the federal government is simply no longer the source of new ideas for housing, no longer the source of leadership on the issue. As urban journalist Neal Peirce argues, one part of the Reagan legacy is that "any sense of federal leadership on tough social issues . . . has been shattered."[103] The 1980s, the early years of the postfederal era in housing, saw state and municipal governments emerge as the source of new and innovative solutions to dealing with housing problems. Often these ideas began at the community level, initiated by local governments that were persuaded by the political and technical arguments of community-based advocates.[104]

SUMMARY

The policy strategies of liberals and conservatives alike were long shaped by the premise that state and local governments are inherently more conservative than the central government. This thesis was supported by an analytical framework that described economic constraints on local officials which bias policy in favor of economic development and growth, and against redistributive social policies. It was further supported by empirical evidence that local governments spend less money on redistributive programs,[105] or recast intergovernmental programs to serve non-redistributive needs.[106] It followed that if the federal government were able to devolve responsibility for social programs to state and local governments, the level of government activity in these programs would in all likelihood diminish. I have argued that this thesis provided the implicit motivation for Reagan's federalism reform proposals in the early years of his administration.

This thesis also served to motivate the opposition of social policy advocates to the Reagan proposals. The formal Reagan federalism reforms, opposed by both policy advocates and local governments that were worried about having additional policy obligations thrust upon them without the commensurate means to provide such benefits, ultimately went nowhere. Reagan was able to accomplish a limited amount of devolution through the consolidation of federal programs into block grants, the relaxation of program implementation guidelines, and the reduction of federal oversight of existing block grants. These policy changes allowed local governments more discretion in implementing federal programs. Limited as these reforms appeared next to the grandiose swap-and-turn-back proposal, they represented the extent of Reagan's formal devolution of policy responsibility.

On the other hand, the Reagan administration was very successful in directly retrenching social programs through massive federal budget cuts. This federal government retrenchment combined with moderate devolution in federal programs should have led to significant changes in domestic policy implementation. Yet in housing, at least, the expectations of the economic-constraints argument have not held. Housing policy during the 1980s faced a crisis situation in the form of federal budget cuts of 80 percent. During the decade, however, housing advocates reoriented their advocacy to local levels of government and were able to create a revitalized housing policy field. How did this occur? Most of the answer to that question is provided in the chapters to come, but some factors are already apparent.

First, federal housing programs were themselves limited and conservative in nature. Often the impetus for housing policy came from other needs such as employment generation, downtown urban development, or financial industry reform and rescue. Those needs led to policy design in which the interests of industry prevailed over the interests of low-income households. As a result, urban renewal was allowed to destroy more housing than it produced; the FHA was allowed to consciously discriminate against nonwhite and inner-city mortgage applicants for close to thirty years; public housing was allowed to wallow in its own physical decline without management subsidies sufficient to deal with festering social problems or capital subsidies sufficient to maintain livable conditions. Even the more targeted federal programs such as Section 235 and 236 were written largely by the homebuilding lobby in the interests of the homebuilding industry. Finally, the largest single element of federal housing policy, the enormously regressive income tax deduction, annually bestowed many times more benefits on the wealthy than on lower-income households. Given this characterization of the federal era in housing policy, it becomes less surprising that when state and local governments assumed the initiative in housing, the results were more progressive.

Yet the legacy of local housing policy during the federal era was also a conservative one. State programs were little more than subsidy programs aimed at providing homeownership opportunities to middle-class families in the suburbs. Municipal programs were equally conservative; suburbs were distinguished for their creative use of building code and zoning regulations in the service of excluding lower-income and rental households. Inner-city housing issues also revolved around land-use issues (primarily the siting of public housing), the enforcement of building codes, and single-family rehabilitation programs. When the federal era in housing policy ended with the Reagan budget cuts in 1981 and subsequent years, there seemed little reason to hope that the local policy response would be notable. Yet it has been.

A new policy paradigm has emerged in the postfederal era in a variety of locations across the country. This new paradigm emphasizes the role of nonmarket actors such as nonprofit development corporations and community-based organizations. It utilizes market restrictions and exactions that impose obligations upon private-sector actors to produce or maintain affordable housing units. It makes use of local resources and often attempts to reverse market trends in urban development. This paradigm is to be explicitly contrasted with that of the federal era, which relied nearly entirely on the private sector as the means by which affordable housing was produced. The federal era approach also relied increasingly upon demand-based income assistance to support housing, and used housing frequently to serve other more pressing domestic issues such as job generation, growth, and financial industry reform. The next chapters explain how and why the new paradigm emerged.

3

The Local Housing Movement

THE NEW HOUSING paradigm has been carried to state legislatures and city halls by a community-based movement of housing advocates, service providers, and neighborhood organizations. The concepts that constitute the new housing policy derive from the analysis of urban and housing problems developed by these groups. The movement's origins were many, including the antipoverty and civil rights activism of the 1960s, the tenant movement, the organizing of urban neighborhoods against urban renewal and displacement in the 1960s, the broader "neighborhood movement" of the 1970s, and the rapid increase in Community Development Corporations operating in disadvantaged communities. The most immediate antecedent of the housing movement was the spate of anti-Reaganomics coalitions that sprouted up around the country in 1981–83. Compared with its predecessors, the local housing movement is more "professionalized," incorporating the ideas of community-based service providers and developers as well as neighborhood volunteers and tenants. It began amorphously, through the simultaneous, uncoordinated activities of a range of actors. Coalescing as a self-conscious housing-oriented movement in the mid-1980s, these groups have become active at state and local levels on a broad range of policies related to housing. The impact of the movement has been nationwide, affecting even those regions (such as the South) that are usually regarded as hostile political environments for progressive and community-based action.[1]

This chapter outlines the origins of the local housing movement, examines its organizational and political strategies, and begins the evaluation (detailed in subsequent chapters) of its impact.

My analysis focuses on the activities of the movement's "peak organizations," which I call "low-income housing advocacy coalitions," LIHACs. These are umbrella organizations that act on a citywide or statewide basis to influence the formation of public policy related to housing. LIHACs are, of course, made up of smaller constituent groups such as neighborhood-based organizations, CDCs, service delivery groups, tenants' rights organizations, or smaller advocacy groups concerned with housing or low-income neighborhoods.[2]

THE ORIGINS OF THE LOCAL HOUSING MOVEMENT

The Tenant Movement

The most important predecessor of the postfederal housing movement is the tenant movement. Tenant activism in the United States has had a long history. Dating back to pre-Civil War times, the tenant movement has been less a continuous phenomenon than a sporadic force, organized and reorganized to respond to the time- and place-specific grievances of renters. In this century the movement has had a number of peaks, occurring in the years immediately after each world war, during the depression, and throughout the 1960–70s.[3] The most recent flurry of tenant activity was sparked by the Harlem rent strike in 1963.[4] At the height of the strike, more than 500 buildings and 15,000 tenants were withholding rent.[5] The experience in Harlem provided the catalyst for tenant action elsewhere. Rent strikes and tenant organizing spread to other cities and expanded through the 1960s. In New Jersey the statewide tenant organization formed in 1969 grew to 80,000 members and successfully advocated for rent control in dozens of New Jersey communities.[6] The movement became nationwide with the formation of the National Tenants' Organization, founded in 1969 by organizers of the Harlem action and the Chicago Tenants' Union.[7]

During the 1970s, tenant activism continued. In New York City a new round of rent strikes protested modifications in the city's rent control program.[8] State proposals to remove rent control authority from local governments in New York State prompted tenants to organize statewide and apply pressure in Albany. Similar action in California prompted the formation of a statewide tenants' organization there in 1977.[9] In 1975 tenant leaders began a national publication on housing and tenant issues. Tenant organizing spread to become one of the methods used by the neighborhood movement of the 1970s to build community-based solidarity.[10] Rent control and tenant activism exploded in California after the passage of Proposition 13 in 1978. After being led to believe that property tax relief would result in direct rent reductions, tenants organized in outrage over sizable rent increases in the proposition's aftermath.[11] The late 1970s also saw a tenant organizing response to widespread conversion of rental apartments into condominiums and the consequent threat of displacement.[12] By the beginning of the Reagan administration, tenant organizing activity was significant. According to the National Multi-Housing Coalition, "momentum for rent control existed in cities in at least 26 states," and tenant activism had been steadily growing throughout the 1970s.[13] Tenants continued to play an active role in the postfederal housing movement of the 1980s, both as members of larger housing coalitions and as an important independent force.[14]

Urban Activism in the 1960s

In some ways the tenant movement was part of a general increase in activism.[15] Increasing activism on issues of urban poverty during the 1960s revealed that housing was a major component of the poor conditions faced by low-income people in the nation's ghettos. Indeed, poor housing conditions were cited as a primary cause of many ghetto uprisings during the decade.[16] The struggle for civil rights and the tenants' movement were often intermingled. For example, the Southern Christian Leadership Council (SCLC) promoted tenant organizing in a number of northern cities during the 1960s, as did Students for a Democratic Society (SDS).[17]

The urban renewal practices of most major cities provided impetus for further neighborhood and tenant organizing.[18] The demolition of low-income housing and the threatened destruction of viable low-income neighborhoods in countless cities mobilized residents into organizations aimed at preserving their neighborhoods and fighting displacement. As Hartman argues in his history of housing advocacy in San Francisco, the community groups that organized tenants and low-income owners against the redevelopment plans of the city constituted the original participants of that city's housing movement.[19] The urban activism in the 1960s over civil rights, urban renewal, citizen participation, and community control of antipoverty programs intersected often with tenants' efforts to organize against rent increases, demolition, conversion, abandonment, disinvestment, and poor living conditions.[20] In that context, the struggle of neighborhoods and low-income tenants in the 1980s to preserve their housing against speculation, gentrification, and urban revitalization is directly tied to previous struggles over similar issues in the 1960s, making the housing groups of the 1980s direct descendants of the tenants' organizations of the 1960s.

The Neighborhood Movement

Another legacy of the community struggles of the 1960s was the "neighborhood movement." Lasting, voluntary neighborhood organizations became the modal expression of community-based concerns about the future of urban neighborhoods during the 1970s. Their concerns were sometimes related to government-sponsored development projects that threatened to substantially change (and sometimes eliminate) low-income neighborhoods. Just as important in the development of the neighborhood movement, however, was the neglect of neighborhoods shown by lending institutions. Redlining—the denial of credit to entire neighborhoods on the basis of their demographic profiles—provided a rallying point for the neighborhood activists. At national conferences on the issue held in the early 1970s, a national coalition of neighborhood organizations was formed. That coalition was instrumental in forcing passage of the 1975 Home Mortgage Disclosure Act and the 1977 Community Reinvestment Act, both designed to heighten the accountability of lending institutions to their host communities.[21] The dimensions of the movement were such that one observer called it a "backyard revolution" fueled by an ideology of "new populism."[22] Whether or not it in fact constituted a revolution, the neighborhood movement of the 1970s was a significant phenomenon. In 1979 the National Commission on Neighborhoods counted 8,000 community groups across the nation. Another observer estimated that more than twenty million citizens were active in hundreds of thousands of smaller neighborhood-based groups across the nation.[23] This new populism had its roots in the antipoverty and civil rights activism of the 1960s; several notable leaders of the neighborhood movement were previously active in antipoverty and civil rights struggles.[24]

In the latter part of the 1970s the neighborhood movement

underwent a split of sorts. On the one hand, some organizations maintained their voluntaristic structure and strategy of grassroots mobilization and advocacy.[25] On the other hand, the movement was incorporating itself into formal nonprofit corporations with the capacity to undertake community development projects ranging from social service delivery to housing development and business assistance. The CDC as a strategy for neighborhood empowerment dates back to the 1960s and the efforts of antipoverty leaders to create community-based alternatives to the service delivery and development initiatives of bureaucratic city agencies.[26] Community development corporations generally provide direct social or development services to their communities and engage in community planning efforts. The CDC model also typically provides for community-based control of service delivery or development; that is, CDCs see themselves as agents of the community. During the 1970s they began to grow quickly in number, and local governments began to incorporate them into their service delivery strategies.

The trend toward incorporation meant a change in the strategy of neighborhood-based groups. Instead of fighting with local government to direct resources into neighborhood areas, CDCs see themselves as capable of creating development and attracting the resources necessary to stabilize their own communities. The shift from advocacy to production took root during an era of public retrenchment, and this too has added to the logic of self-help that drives the CDC movement. "In the neighborhood politics of Chicago, as in most American cities, the era of 'baiting the establishment' is ending. To many activists, it is no longer clear who the establishment is, or whether it exists. Mass protests are giving way to collaboration as neighborhood groups seek partners to provide some of the services and development projects that their communities need and that government is hard-pressed to provide on its own."[27] The CDC movement and the orientation toward technical solutions to neighborhood problems accounts for a great deal of the "professional" character of the postfederal housing movement.

The Local Housing Movement of the 1980s

The initial organizing response to Reagan policies in the 1980s was a broad-based effort on the part of coalitions of organizations and advocates concerned with human services and the social needs of low-income households. Across the country, statewide coalitions organized to fight the general thrust of Reagan budget cuts in domestic social programs.[28] As the decade wore on and the affordable housing crisis grew, groups devoted specifically to the issue of housing emerged as important local interest groups. Whereas before the Reagan budget cuts low-income housing advocates had generally focused their attention on federal legislation, the newest generation comprised groups that were locally based and locally focused. This was a result of changes in both local and national conditions. Local and state governments had simply never been the source of programs designed to meet the housing needs of low-income households and had therefore not attracted the attention of advocates, who felt that policy for their constituents was being set at the federal level. But the dramatic policy changes introduced by the Reagan administration signaled to housing advocates that Washington would no longer be receptive to lobbying efforts on behalf of low-income housing. As it became clear that housing programs, if they happened at all, would happen at state and local levels, housing advocates began to organize at these levels to pursue their objectives.

Another reason for the new local orientation of housing advocates had to do with the changing conditions in urban areas during the 1980s. Like the 1960s, when community activists were struggling to improve conditions in urban ghettos, the 1980s—despite the so-called Reagan recovery—saw conditions in many marginal neighborhoods deteriorating.[29] Even as the downtown areas of many U.S. cities were experiencing a renaissance, low-income residential neighborhoods adjacent to downtown and in peripheral areas were rapidly deteriorating or being eliminated. The unemployment rate for the residents of many inner-city neighborhoods never recovered from the levels reached during the 1982 recession. The jobs generated for blue-collar and lower-income workers during the recovery were increasingly low-paying, low-status, and informal or part time. Investment in the infrastructure of neighborhoods was neglected by local government officials, who were more interested in directing investment to downtown areas. Some low-income neighborhoods near downtown areas did experience "revitalization": that is, they were made unlivable for low-income people. Publicly sponsored gentrification and redevelopment projects eliminated low-cost housing in favor of up-scale commercial, entertainment, and residential facilities in city after city. The disappearance of low-cost housing, coupled with rising real estate prices fueled by downtown development, contributed to an escalating housing crisis throughout the 1980s. Cuts in public benefits and the diminished purchasing power of many households resulted in severe housing affordability problems, leaving an ever larger percentage of the population without homes at all.

As was the case in the 1960s, then, there were growing problems in lower-income neighborhoods at the same time that the rest of the city seemed to be prospering. Unlike the 1960s case, not only was there no supportive federal involvement in attempting to correct the problem of low-income neighborhoods, but local governments seemed to be doing their best to underwrite the very forces that were creating crisis conditions in low-income neighborhoods. Much of the downtown revitalization that occurred during this time was publicly subsidized. The millions of dollars that went to creating up-scale offices and playgrounds for the professional class were destroying residential neighborhoods for the poor. This collusion of local governments in the process of neighborhood deterioration, and the enthusiasm with which local officials engaged in " public/private partnerships" that seemed to benefit the private partner disproportionately,[30]—as much as the inhospitality of the federal government—made local governments the logical focal point for the collective action of housing advocates. The nature of local government involvement in revitalization projects with detrimental impact on neighborhoods also accounts for some of the content of the new housing policy agenda offered by the postfederal housing movement. The emphasis on land-use regulations to channel development benefits to low-income neighborhoods was a direct response to the excesses of development subsidies during the 1980s.[31]

Thus, the housing movement in the postfederal era shifted emphasis from political action at the national level to a decentralized effort to influence the land-use and housing policy of hundreds of separate local governments. The reorientation has been so pervasive that even national lobbyist groups such as the National Coalition for the Homeless (NCH) have turned their attention to the local arena. In 1989, NCH developed model legislation, called the State Homeless Persons' Assistance Act of 1989, aimed at creating more affordable housing, preventing homelessness through rental and mortgage assistance, and providing emergency relief through shelter, education, and social services at the state level.[32] The national coalition distributed the model to local advocates and state legislators in acknowledgment of the important role being played by local governments. As another example of the local orientation of national lobbyists, the National Low Income Housing Coalition (NLIHC), together with the National Housing Law Project, established a support center in 1986 for the purpose of aiding local advocates in forming or further developing statewide housing coalitions. Though both NCH and NLIHC retain a predominantly federal focus in their advocacy, they have both formally recognized the importance of local activism in the postfederal era.

GROUP FORMATION

The housing movement, though recent, is widespread. Housing advocacy coalitions operate in thirty-four states (68 percent) and in eighty-five of the cities responding to the survey questionnaire (64 percent). Figure 3.1 highlights those states that have active housing coalitions. As the map shows, they are concentrated in states east of the Mississippi River; in fact, only one state east of the Mississippi is without an active housing coalition, compared with fifteen of the twenty-four states west of the river.

Figures on the formation of local housing advocacy groups reflect the fact that they are recent phenomena. Table 3.1 shows when the groups in the thirty-four states and eighty-five cities were formed. Fully 61 percent were formed after 1984, and 76 percent since 1980. Given the three- to four-year lag between federal budget cuts and local impact, Table 3.1 shows that most of these groups were formed after the worst of the Reagan budget cuts were felt at the local level. Indeed, in all likelihood another, shorter political lag occurs, during which local advocates begin the process of consolidating their efforts and creating coalitional strategies. Figures 3.2 and 3.3 show the dramatic increase in the number of LIHACs active in the fifty states and one hundred thirty-three cities in the survey sample.

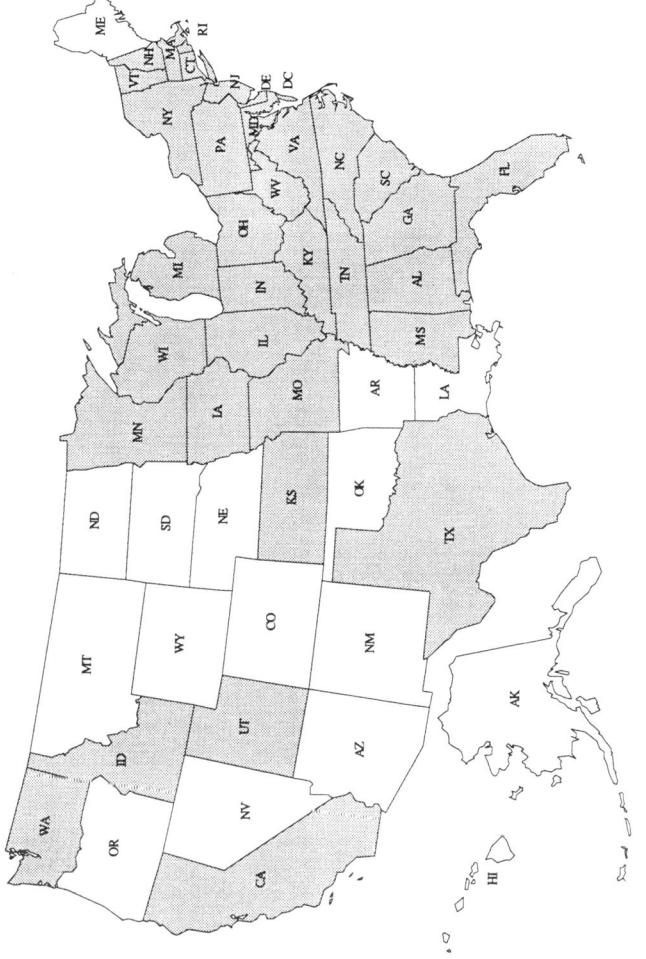

FIGURE 3.1
States with low-income housing coalitions, 1991

53

TABLE 3.1
Local housing advocacy groups by time of formation

	City Groups		State Groups	
	N	%	N	%
Before 1970	5	6.7	3	8.8
1970 to 1979	15	20.3	3	8.8
1980 to 1984	10	13.5	6	17.6
1985 to 1990	44	59.5	22	64.7
Missing cases	11			

The accounts of group formation also reinforce the notion that coalitions were organized in reaction to Reagan reforms. Most commonly, they were formed as local housing advocates or service providers recognized a need to organize at the state level in order to influence or initiate debate on housing issues. Sometimes, as in New Hampshire and Michigan, the organization resulted from specific political battles in which the participants recognized a need for an ongoing voice statewide. In New Hampshire the coalition formed in opposition to the conversion of a large, low-income housing development from rental units to condominiums. The tenant organization that initiated the action against conversion still constitutes the backbone of the state coalition. Similarly, Hartman argues, individual events that helped to mobilize activists and publicize the cause of affordable housing were important precursors to the development of a housing movement in San Francisco.[33] Thus, the "critical event" has played a role in the formation of some of the coalitions active in the local housing movement.

More often, however, mobilization was the result of a steadily increasing awareness that housing policymaking had indeed devolved to local governments and that low-income advocates needed to organize locally to influence that process. In Massachusetts, state government action on housing predated the formation of the state coalition. The administration of Governor Michael Dukakis made substantial amounts of money available for housing purposes between 1982 and 1984, and the Massachusetts coalition formed, in part, to influence the disposition of those funds and the implementation of state housing programs.[34] In Maryland, Delaware, and South

The Local Housing Movement 55

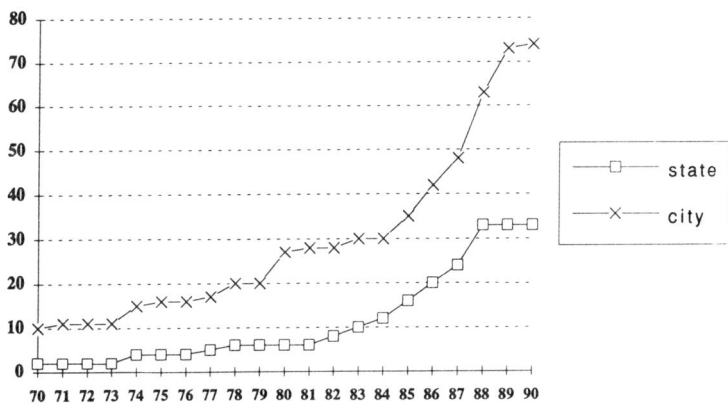

FIGURE 3.2
Number of states and larger cities with housing coalitions, 1970–90
Note: The year of formation is missing for 11 cities in the sample.

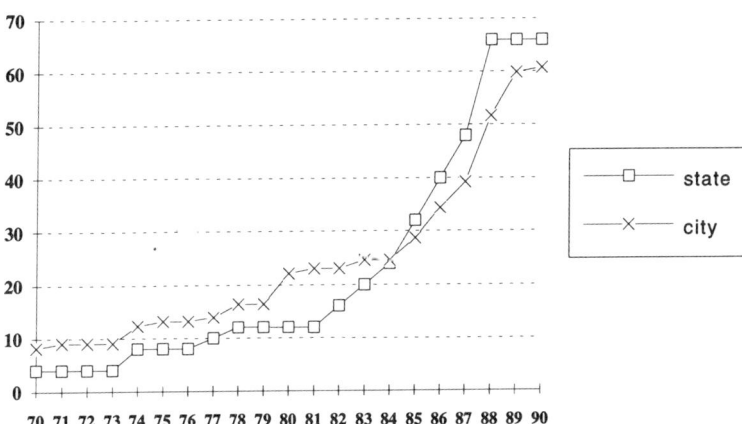

FIGURE 3.3
Percentage of states and larger cities with housing coalitions, 1970–90
Note: The year of formation is missing for 11 cities with housing coalitions.

Carolina as well, the state government played an important role in spurring the formation of housing coalitions: officials sponsored hearings or conferences on housing problems that helped to stimulate the creation of ongoing statewide advocacy groups.

As I have argued, the local housing movement tends to be more professional than its predecessors. The organizers of many coalitions tend to be low-income housing advocates such as poverty lawyers or social service providers, and/or housing providers such as nonprofit housing developers, transitional housing providers or housing assistance counselors. The exceptions to this rule are few, the main ones being those groups formed by tenant unions (New York and New Hampshire).

Often, these coalitions are simply more formal manifestations of a preexisting movement structure. A common occurrence is for a single advocacy group to call a conference or meeting that groups from around the state (or city) attend. Once the common mission is identified, an organizational entity is formed to provide a regular forum for information exchange and strategic planning. For example, in November 1985 the Topeka Housing Information Center hosted the Kansas Conference on Housing. Over 300 people showed up for the three-day event, from which more continuous advocacy on housing has stemmed.[35]

Many of the organizations received funds or in-kind contributions to aid in their formation. In some instances, grants were specifically designed as "capacity-building" funds, as was the case for the statewide groups in Georgia, Iowa, and South Carolina. Other funds were received from public, private, and foundation grants. In-kind contributions helped as well. In California, for example, the Housing Assistance Council (HAC), a national organization involved in rural housing advocacy, supplied personnel in the early years to ensure the viability of the California LIHAC. The national council was also instrumental in the formation of the coalition in North Carolina. Almost an equal number of statewide organizations, however, got started without outside financial help. Citywide groups were and are less dependent upon start-up assistance than statewide groups because they simply do not face the logistical problems associated with creating a coalition and keeping it active and viable over a broad geographical area. The tasks of maintaining a working coalition—

regular communication, conference meetings, emergency sessions, and the like—can be carried out more easily when members are in proximity to each other.

Organizational Structure

Local housing advocacy coalitions can take a number of forms. They usually involve social service and other human service actors, sometimes legal aid attorneys, nonprofit housing developers, and neighborhood-based organizations. Though nonprofit developers may also have an organization or coalition of their own, they generally remain part of a larger advocacy coalition.

Table 3.2 shows the different types of citywide housing advocacy coalitions as named by the survey respondents. The most common form is the coalition of local groups, or the umbrella organization. The Stamford Housing Coalition, the Community Housing Partnership of Phoenix, and the Louisville Metro Housing Coalition are examples. Each one represents a coalition of local advocates and organizations dedicated to housing issues. Sometimes the issues covered are broader than simply housing, as is the case with Community Action against Poverty in Indianapolis.

The second category listed in Table 3.2 is different from the first in that it is a single organization that plays the role of the housing advocate. In Tucson, for example, the Community Housing Corporation was listed as the city's housing advocate, and Housing Opportunities, Inc., is the housing advocate in Rochester, New York. This pattern is, of course, most likely in cities where the community-based housing sector is not as well developed as elsewhere.

TABLE 3.2
Types of low-income housing advocacy coalitions in U.S. cities

Type	N	%
Coalition of local groups	47	60.3
Local organization	7	9.0
Tenant organization	6	7.7
Government-sponsored group	7	9.0
Local chapter of national organization	11	14.0
Missing cases	7	

Tenant groups remain the leaders of the housing movement in close to 8 percent of the cities. In Philadelphia, for example, the Tenants' Action Group (TAG) has had a long history of activism on tenant and housing issues. But like the tenant movement in general, TAG has greatly expanded its role and the scope of its activities since its formation in 1973; it has "grown from a totally volunteer organization, based on two Philadelphia neighborhoods, to a citywide group with a full time staff of eight, and a subsidiary corporation operating three financial assistance programs designed to prevent homelessness."[36]

Sometimes government-sponsored or -related organizations play the advocacy role. The Jackson (Mississippi) Housing Commission was listed as the local housing advocacy group by the respondent from that city, as was the Topeka (Kansas) Community Development Advisory Committee. Both organizations are institutionally attached to the local government in one capacity or another, yet also spearhead housing advocacy.

Finally, local chapters of national organizations are the lead actors in housing advocacy in some cities. Legal Aid plays this role in Long Beach, California; in Little Rock, Arkansas, the local chapter of ACORN is the lead advocate for housing; and in Pittsburgh the Urban League was named.

Often the institutional structure of low-income housing advocacy groups can become complex as different organizations play separate but complementary roles. In the city of Minneapolis the Twin Cities Affordable Housing Collaborative—a coalition of organizations providing affordable housing in the region—is abetted by the Consortium of Nonprofit Housing Developers, the Alliance for the Streets, the Low Income Housing Committee, the Homeless Coalition, and an advocacy group called Up and Out of Poverty Now. Each of these groups specializes in different aspects of the housing situation, and each provides policy and programmatic input to local officials. There is also a great deal of membership overlap between these organizations. Organizational density is quite evident in other cities such as New York. With a history of tenant organizing, the New York housing movement is very strong and visible. Tenants' organizations are said to "number in the hundreds"; every borough is layered with them. In addition, a number of umbrella organizations—including the Metropolitan

Council on Housing, the New York State Tenant and Neighborhood Coalition, the Union of City Tenants, and the Association for Neighborhood and Housing Development—serve to organize and channel the political clout of the individual groups.[37]

In many states there are additional peak associations dealing with housing issues. The problems of the homeless play a large part in the formation and activity of many LIHACs, and many states have organizations devoted specifically to the issue of homelessness. In five states the homeless coalition serves a second function as the state's LIHAC. In these states the group was originally formed as a homeless coalition and is still referred to as such, though it is working broadly for low-income housing opportunities. In other states the homeless coalition is a separate organization advocating primarily emergency and transitional shelter. As of 1991 there were thirty-two statewide homeless coalitions (see Figure 3.4), but the relationship between LIHACs and homeless coalitions remains close. In California and Massachusetts the LIHAC helped to create the homeless coalition that is now active in each of those states. In Missouri the housing coalition originally "focused on homelessness and . . . the root causes of homelessness. The group has evolved into a more general housing task force on the premise that the lack of affordable housing is the major cause of the problem of homelessness."[38]

Because of the similarity in objectives between LIHACs and homeless coalitions, the existence of the two groups can create competition for scarce resources. The director of the Utah housing coalition reported that "housing providers (non-profit developers) felt that they were in competition with homeless advocates for resources." This tension persisted until the state enacted an income tax check-off to fund homeless programs. This dedicated revenue source relieved the pressure on more traditional funding sources. In some other states, however, advocates maintain that there is very little competition between homeless and housing interests.[39]

Community development corporations are another important component of the local housing movement in the United States. These groups, too, often organize among themselves as a separate advocacy group, further adding to the density of the housing movement. In fact, statewide coalitions for nonprofit housing exist in seventeen states (34 percent; See figure 3.5). Among the larger

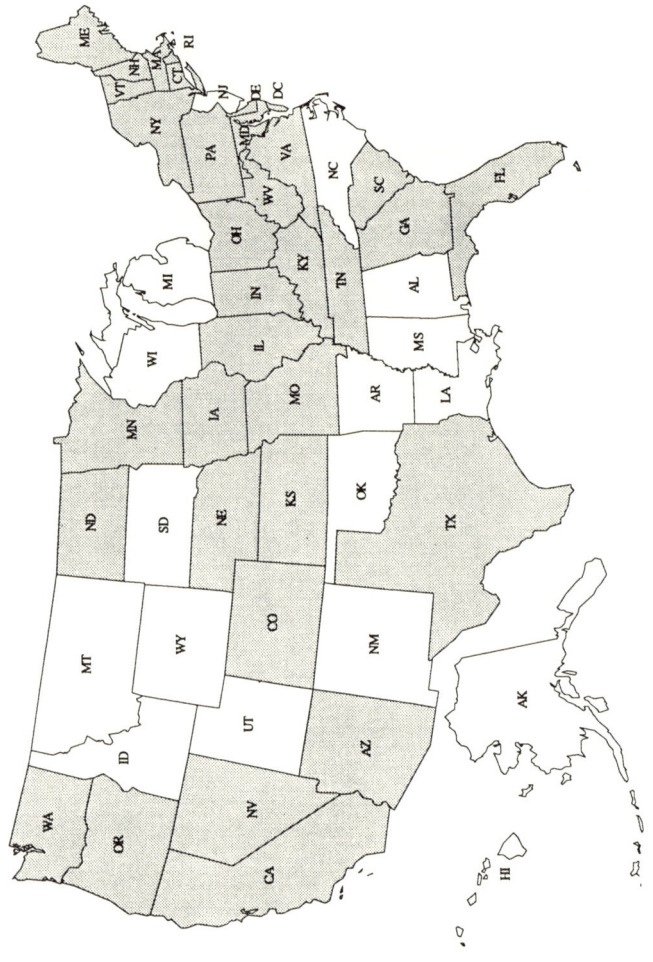

FIGURE 3.4
States with homeless coalitions, 1991

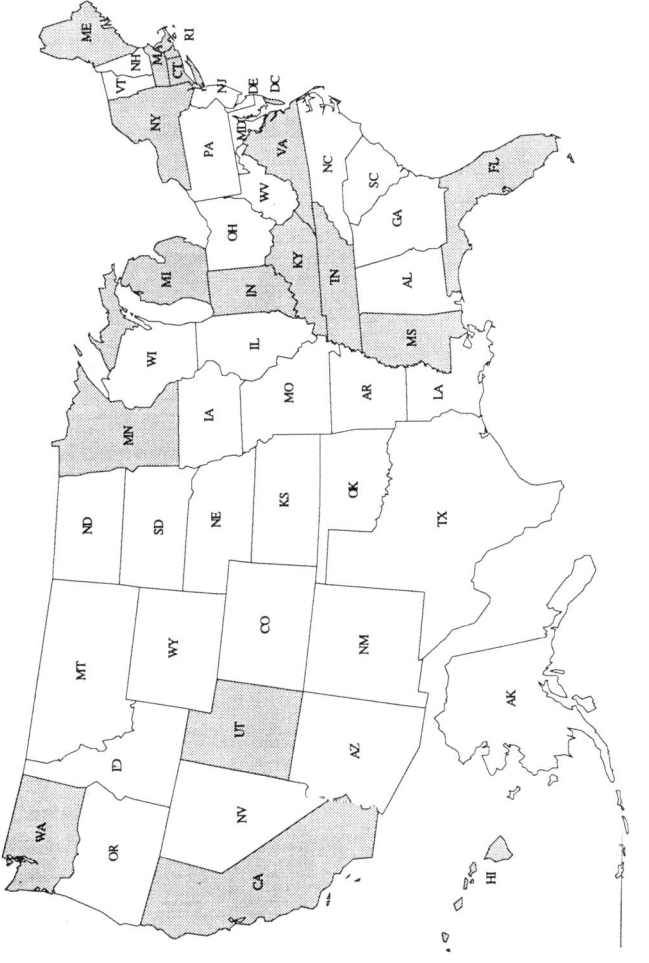

FIGURE 3.5
States with nonprofit housing development coalitions, 1991

cities surveyed, just over one-quarter (26 percent) reported having an organized coalition of nonprofit housing developers.

Combining these elements—LIHACs, homeless coalitions, and nonprofit housing coalitions—allows us to create a composite index of organizing activity at the state level on housing issues (variable name: ACTIVISM) ranging in value from 0 to 3, reflecting the number of such peak organizations in each state. The degree of housing activism is greater in larger states (in terms of 1985 population, $r = .37$), more densely inhabited states ($r = .34$), more urbanized states ($r = .42$), states with higher per capita incomes ($r = .26$) or larger percentages of the population receiving public assistance ($r = .23$), and conversely, states with lower rates of poverty ($r = .21$). Activism at the state level is not significantly correlated with population growth or political culture.

Unfortunately, data on homeless coalitions at the city level are not available, and thus the ACTIVISM index for cities reflects only the existence of LIHACs and nonprofit coalitions. Activism at the city level is positively correlated with the size of the city ($r = .36$) and the percentage of a city's population under the poverty level in 1980 ($r = .21$), and negatively correlated with population growth ($r = -.27$). That is, larger, more slowly growing cities and cities with greater levels of poverty tend to have a more organized housing movement. The regional variation is small, though cities in the Midwest and Northeast are slightly overrepresented among those cities with a high degree of housing mobilization. Local activism is not significantly correlated with political culture or per capita income.

Organizational Resources

These organizations vary considerably in their resource base. The coalitions in New Hampshire, Vermont, and Kansas, for example, are informal coalitions that have no outside funding or any staff. At the other end of the continuum, the coalition in California has an annual budget of $200,000, maintains a mailing list of 22,000 individuals and organizations, publishes a newsletter, and employs full-time paid staff. Similarly, the Michigan Housing Coalition has a budget of over $175,000 and a staff of six people in three different cities. The majority of groups lie between these extremes.

Most of the coalitions are incorporated as 501(c)(3) or

501(c)(4) "nonprofit" or "charitable nonprofit" corporations.[40] Seventeen of the thirty-two groups contacted have paid staff; the others rely on volunteers, though many hire staff when they can locate money to do so and resort to volunteer activity when the funding runs out. The Delaware Housing Coalition, for example, has had a paid director for only two of the years since 1982. In Washington, the coalition was initially funded by a grant. As that funding ran out, the organization relied on volunteers until a grant from the state legislature allowed them to hire a staff person. This sort of irregular funding is fairly commonplace. The Pennsylvania coalition director maintains that financial survival is the major challenge the organization faces from year to year.[41] The West Virginia Coalition for the Homeless stands out in its relationship to outside funding: local organizers in that state received a grant and then decided to use it to create a LIHAC. In this instance the coalition was truly a creature of outside funding. In many states, however, organizational funding is a luxury that, though coveted, is not absolutely necessary for organizational activity to continue.

A coalition's funding base and organizational structure have negligible implications for its political activity. Nonprofit corporations organized under 501(c)(3) and organizations receiving large amounts of public funding are not as free to advocate and lobby for specific legislative or public action; they tend to devote themselves to public information and service delivery to other constituent organizations. Nevertheless, their political activity remains significant as they walk a fine line between advocacy and "public education" campaigns. The Georgia Housing Coalition is an example of a group that claims it is primarily involved in public education rather than legislative advocacy. According to its director:

> We are a 501(c)(3), so we are not legally allowed to initiate or lobby for legislation. So we don't. But we do [provide] education on issues such as the housing trust fund. . . . We are heavily involved in the development of the housing trust fund. We were the impetus for the trust fund study, and we helped document the statewide need for housing. You see, in Georgia, housing has been perceived as only an urban problem. Our education programs have changed that. We helped educate the legislators about the types of affordable housing that would be assisted with the help of a trust fund by conducting tours of affordable units developed by nonprofits.[42]

The Pennsylvania Low Income Housing Coalition has solved this particular problem through the creation of a "sister organization," the Pennsylvania Low Income Housing Corporation, which shares the same office and staff. As a 501(c)(4), the *coalition* can lobby legislators; as a 501(c)(3), the *corporation* can solicit tax-deductible contributions for the development of nonprofit housing projects.[43] For unincorporated groups or those incorporated under 501(c)(4), the charade of maintaining a distinction between public education and lobbying is not necessary.

One strain on the internal structure of statewide organizations is the need to accommodate both urban and rural housing agendas. Generally, the concern for low-income housing during the last decade has focused on urban housing problems; however, coalitions in Georgia and Utah, for example, have released research studies documenting lasting housing problems in rural areas. Many coalitions have attempted to bridge a potential urban-rural gap in their organizing and advocacy. In Illinois, for example, distrust between Chicago and "downstate" has been a long-standing feature of state politics.[44] That antagonism was a major obstacle to organizing, according to a staff member of the Illinois Statewide Housing Action Coalition (SHAC). Because the group's major legislative achievement, the establishment of a housing trust fund, was originally perceived by some legislators as "another trick to channel money to Chicago," SHAC had to overcome this perception before the proposal gained wider acceptance.[45] Coalitions in Georgia, Virginia, Missouri, and Iowa also report urban-rural tensions. The Georgia Housing Coalition is attempting to ease that tension through public information campaigns that stress the commonality of problems in the two areas. In other states the interests of urban and rural housing advocates are self-consciously balanced. The Massachusetts coalition has two coordinators, one urban and the other rural. For many years the Utah LIHAC had two standing committees, one devoted to urban issues and one to rural issues. The Minnesota Housing Partnership reported that the legislation it pursues "is broad in focus and flexible" enough to address both urban and rural problems.[46] In Ohio the coalition is attempting to add greater rural representation in order to bring about better balance.

Organizational Mission

Organizational mission is defined as both the objectives of the organization and the means by which it chooses to achieve those objectives. Coalitions at both state and city levels primarily provide three types of services. First, they are explicitly formed in order to advocate for low-income housing: that is, they are primarily political interest groups. Second, the organizations provide "public education" on housing and low-income issues. Third, these groups often provide technical assistance and training to their membership. This may involve assistance related to the use of tax credits or to grant writing, or merely information on local, state, and federal legislation.

By definition the groups in this study have similar issue agendas; their focus is on the creation, maintenance, and preservation of better housing for lower-income households. Within that category, however, an organization may focus on rental housing and the problems of tenants, or on homelessness, or on rural housing issues—depending upon the nature of local housing problems. Furthermore, coalitions attempt to achieve their objectives in different ways: through political advocacy, through the provision of technical assistance to nonprofit service agencies, or through public information efforts.

Most groups have evolved in their organizational objectives. The coalitions change in one of two ways: they either widen their issue focus, or they change the method they use to achieve their goals. As examples of the former, many groups created in response to specific housing issues subsequently broadened their focus. The New Hampshire example provides an illustration of a group formed initially to achieve a singular and specific goal—the preservation of one low-income housing development in danger of conversion to condominiums—which eventually evolved into an ongoing, permanent advocacy group active on a range of state issues. The California LIHAC emerged from a statewide conference on farmworker housing. The organization soon integrated urban housing issues as a strategy to increase its political base and better achieve its goals. As the director said: "Our focus is on rural issues, but you can't do anything in the legislature without involving the urban legislators. So we ask for bills funded at, say, $250 million and ask that one-fourth go to rural areas. We do better that way than asking only for the rural portion."⁴⁷

The political agenda of the housing movement changes, of course, as the housing policy environment changes. The provision in the 1990 National Affordable Housing Act requiring states and localities to create a Comprehensive Housing Affordability Strategy (CHAS) created a new focus for state and local groups. The Maryland Low Income Housing Coalition used the CHAS process to hold training sessions across the state and increased its membership as a result.⁴⁸ The CHAS process provided one of the main reasons for the formation of the Idaho Housing Coalition.⁴⁹ In Illinois the Statewide Housing Action Coalition ran regional organizing efforts aimed at influencing the form of both the state CHAS and CHAS documents in cities across the state. The Chicago Rehab Network held meetings throughout 1991 to develop proposals for the Chicago CHAS. In some cities, access to CHAS formulation has been relatively easy.⁵⁰ In St. Paul, Minnesota, the city department in charge of creating the document undertook an extensive outreach effort designed to solicit input from a variety of community-based organizations as well as real estate industry spokespersons.

Besides altering organizational objectives, coalitions have on occasion altered the way in which they pursue their objectives. In Ohio, for example, the group was originally created to acquire, rehabilitate, and construct affordable housing but has largely abandoned that approach to focus on advocacy and public education. The Florida LIHAC was the result of the same dynamic. The original organization, a development corporation, felt the need for greater advocacy and spun off a sister group that performs lobbying duties and serves as an information clearinghouse for state activists. In North Carolina the movement of the organization was away from advocacy and toward the provision of technical assistance to nonprofits, assistance to local coalitional efforts, and public education.

The provision of services to local member groups is a strong emphasis of many LIHACs. As pointed out previously, member organizations in most LIHACs are local service agencies (nonprofit housing developers, transitional shelter providers, and the like), local coalitions, and community groups. The organizational mission of many umbrella groups includes a strong component of direct services to nonprofits or local coalitions. The Illinois and South Carolina LIHACs provide organizing and technical assistance to local coalitions in their states; these activities increase support for the groups' legislative activity as well as organizational membership and resources. Since 1987 the Florida coalition has sponsored a series of informational statewide conferences that have attracted local advocates and representatives from financial institutions. Conference workshops focused on the needs of nonprofit housing developers, housing finance issues, and community reinvestment strategies. The group has also sponsored smaller workshops for lenders across the state.[51]

It is not uncommon for these groups to undertake studies of local housing conditions, to create public forums for the discussion of housing problems, and to disseminate literature related to the condition of housing in the local jurisdiction. The Georgia Housing Coalition has been heavily involved in providing legislators with information on the state's housing needs. In 1986 the Connecticut Housing Coalition declared a "Connecticut Housing Week" and promoted a series of events aimed at increasing the level of public awareness of housing problems in the state. The coalition sponsored a series of op-ed articles and editorials, public displays and ceremonies, and a variety of media events. The week was capped by a statewide conference on housing and homelessness issues.[52] Much of the more recent activity of the housing movement involves providing state and municipal governments with information about housing needs that they can plug into their CHAS planning documents.

Policymaking Environment

Most observers of state politics agree that since the 1960s, state legislatures have become more serious and powerful policymaking bodies.[53] That is, legislatures have begun to exert their own policy preferences more often, and the legislature is increasingly an arena of meaningful debate on public policy issues. Housing can be added to the list of issues receiving more considered debate at the state level. The local housing movement has targeted state legislatures for intensified lobbying on behalf of housing assistance programs, with varying degrees of success. Coalition leaders in states across the country mentioned budgetary constraints and the difficulty of passing legislation "that costs money." As the director of the Tennessee coalition reported, "nothing is easy to pass if it involves money."[54] Throughout the 1980s the sluggish economies of West Virginia, South Carolina, and Delaware dominated political discourse and left advocates little hope that funds would be allocated for housing assistance programs.

The budgetary pressures have a temporal dimension as well, since they reflect larger business cycle patterns. Nathan points out that one reason for the "paradox of devolution" was that the economic recovery of the mid-1980s occurred after states had increased taxes in an attempt to deal with the recession of 1981–82. The recovery, coupled with higher tax rates, produced unanticipated budget surpluses in a number of states.[55] The recession of 1990–92, however, forced many states to reduce social spending dramatically; in fact more than half experienced serious budget problems during fiscal years 1990 and 1991.[56] Even relatively generous states under liberal governors (such as New York) have cut funding for social programs and community services because of budget problems.[57]

In some states other issues dominate the scene and push housing from the agenda. In New Jersey the governor was occupied during 1990 and 1991 by the issues of automobile insurance and raising taxes to meet a budget deficit. The LIHAC in that state is not optimistic about presenting a housing agenda in the near future. During the 1989 legislative session in Kentucky, housing was crowded out by educational concerns, as a representative of the homelessness coalition explained: "The state was facing a lawsuit against it for its education system—we rank forty-eighth in the country in education and fiftieth in social services. Everyone's attention was focused on that issue. So we had a hard time getting the press, let alone the legislators to listen to concerns about housing."[58]

In Massachusetts, Michigan, California, and New York, by contrast, government has been very active and generally supportive of expanding state involvement in housing issues. Yet even in those states, passage of housing legislation is not without obstacles. Though the housing movement in California reported success in getting twenty-five bills signed in the 1989 legislative session, the construction and rehabilitation programs it considered most important have not been funded by the governor in recent years. Hence, the coalition has altered its strategy to focus more on the referendum and initiative process. In 1988 it pushed two initiatives that together provided $450 million for housing assistance. In June 1990 the voters of California passed another $150 million housing initiative introduced by the coalition. In 1991 the California ballot included yet another $165 million initiative for housing assistance, which was defeated by the voters.

Most of the thirty-two state coalitions interviewed have been successful in bringing housing to the policymaking agenda. For example, only four reported no lobbying activity during the 1989–90 legislative session. The rest of the LIHACs either actively sponsored legislation or supported particular housing bills. Most active was the coalition in California, which introduced thirty-five bills on a wide range of topics. The Virginia Housing Coalition had twelve items on its legislative list, primarily concerning rural housing conditions. Most organizations, however, dealt with significantly fewer legislative issues, generally from two to six bills.

Tactics

Though active in advocating for low-income housing, LIHACs have apparently not alienated themselves from either policymakers or state agencies. Rather, in many states the LIHACs seem to have achieved an "insider" status that is unusual for low-income advocacy groups. Some coalitions have insinuated themselves into the administrative structure of housing policy. In Kansas, for example, the LIHAC was instrumental in promoting passage of the 1990 administrative reorganization bill that created an Office of Housing. The Tennessee LIHAC reported achieving a high level of integration and legitimacy among policymakers: "We put together a housing program a couple of years ago, and it attracted the attention of the state housing agency, the Tennessee Housing Development Authority (THDA). They invited us to a series of talks to help shape a housing program. At the same time the Governor's Housing Task Force came up with a set of recommendations for new programs, but their recommendations all cost money. So THDA requested that we sit down with the task force and create a program."⁵⁹ The Texas Low Income Housing Information Service drafted legislation that created a new state housing agency, drafted the outline of the state's housing trust fund, and helped push it through the legislature.⁶⁰

The San Diego Housing Trust Fund Coalition, an alliance of more than fifty community-based groups, was instrumental in pushing through a comprehensive housing trust fund in that city. The coalition was able to succeed by crafting a careful electoral strategy that appealed to middle-class residents, stressing the importance of affordable housing to the city's continued growth and health, and capitalizing on good working relationships with city staff. As one participant argued: "The HTF in San Diego, in many respects, was a direct outcome of the relationship the Coalition was able to build with the City staff and the Housing Trust Fund Task Force. Without this positive relationship, the Coalition may well have been frozen out of the process and City staff would not have had the support they needed to create the HTF."⁶¹

In other cases the professionalism of the housing movement has led to its incorporation in more indirect ways. In Cleveland, Mayor Michael White appointed a long-time neighborhood housing activist as director of community development in 1990.⁶² Similar appointments of leading housing advocates have been made in Los Angeles (see Chapter 6). The movement was able to elect one of its own to the Massachusetts state house in 1991.⁶³ In some cities the housing movement has been part of a larger progressive movement that has resulted in the ascension to power of a progressive governing coalition. The housing movement was an important part of the Art Agnos coalition during his term as mayor of San Francisco and the Raymond Flynn administration in Boston.⁶⁴ The election of Peter Clavelle as mayor of Burlington, Vermont, is a prime example of this growing electoral success. Clavelle campaigned aggressively on the issue of housing and presented a housing platform that included support for inclusionary zoning, the construction of single-room-occupancy (SRO) hotel rooms for those with very low income, alternative models of land and housing ownership such as land trusts, and an ordinance that would require private developers to replace demolished or converted housing units on a one-for-one basis. His election assures the housing movement in that city of continued access and influence on city policy.[65]

The director of the Pennsylvania coalition provides an apt summary of the political strategy of a group's ingratiating itself into the administrative structure: "We are a polite coalition and that has paid off."[66] Close relationships with the housing apparatus of state governments, in addition to reflecting nonconfrontational political strategies, may also be a function of the largely professional makeup of most coalitions. As mentioned earlier, most LIHACs are coalitions of local service providers and housing developers. To the extent that they are sophisticated in housing development, finance, and management, they are able to converse with state officials as coprofessionals in the housing field. This has quite possibly gained them a relationship with policymakers not available to groups with fewer professional ties. Such legitimacy has allowed many of these organizations unique access to policymaking.

Their success with "polite" political persuasion, however, does not mean that they have abandoned more old-fashioned advocacy techniques. The housing movement is still very active in litigation, protest rallies, rent strikes, and more innovative forms of public pressure. Advocates for the homeless in Miami, Los Angeles, and New York—to name just a few cities—have successfully litigated the rights of homeless persons.[67] In Washington, D.C., and other cities, advocates have staged sit-ins and demonstrations to publicize the plight of low-income residents and the homeless.[68] In North Carolina the statewide coalition staged a "sleep-out" outside the capitol building to dramatize the state's housing problems.[69] In some cases the combined strategy of different actors in the housing movement seems to be a (perhaps unplanned) version of "good cop, bad cop" in which one or more groups engage in highly visible acts of protest to publicize housing problems, while other groups work in a more cooperative mode with local officials to enact and implement policy changes. One such example occurred in Minneapolis and St. Paul, where the group Up and Out of Poverty Now (like other groups across the country) staged a number of highly visible and publicized "occupations" of HUD-foreclosed homes and placed homeless residents there as squatters.[70] This group has been confrontational in its approach to changing current policies for homeless assistance.

Quite on the other end of the spectrum is the Minnesota Coalition for the Homeless, which works more closely with local officials through special task forces, an annual survey of homelessness in the state, and its own more conventional programs for homeless assistance.

Two Profiles: California and Maryland

The California housing coalition was initiated in 1978 with a conference on farmworker housing. From that conference was born the California Coalition for Rural Housing, which served as the primary statewide organization until the California Housing and Homeless Coalition was formalized in 1991.

> Our initial agenda was to improve farmworker housing and to improve rural housing conditions in general. The agenda has expanded greatly since then. As the problem has gotten worse, our scope of activities has increased. Eight years ago, [1982] we did a few bills . . . designed to help the state get federal money. As the feds left the arena, we created our own programs. [In 1988] we were instrumental in getting two initiatives passed by the voters for a total of $450 million for housing assistance.[71]

During the 1989 legislative session the group introduced thirty-five bills related to nonprofit housing, tax credits, land use, landlord-tenant relations, farmworkers, and fair housing issues, and another $150 million proposition was passed. It was because then Governor George Deukmejian was a strong opponent of housing assistance, vetoing new programs and refusing to fund older ones, that the coalition took housing issues straight to the voters through the initiative process. The coalition fights on an annual basis to keep the developers' and real estate lobbies from successfully pushing a rent control preemption bill that would override local authority on rent control ordinances.

To accomplish its tasks, the California coalition has an impressive array of organizational resources.[72] A staff of five coordinates its activities. Telemarketing campaigns three times a year have produced a donor base of 16,000 individuals plus foundations, churches, and local organizations. The coalition has formed a political action committee that has raised close to $500,000. Four full-time lobbyists handle its legislative agenda. Each year a coalition scorecard rates the performance of state legislators on important housing issues. The coalition's work is supported by a network of local activists (organized into regions and areas within the regions) and a mailing list of 23,000 groups and individuals. A monthly newsletter, *Capitol Gains*, is sent to 10,000 readers, including members of the media and public officials.

The Maryland Low Income Housing Coalition was formed in 1985 as an outgrowth of a statewide conference sponsored by the state.[73] The conference served the ultimate purpose of organizing local advocates around the need for a statewide advocacy group. The group's initial agenda was to work with the governor on housing initiatives aimed at providing safe, decent, and affordable housing to all state residents. It was especially interested in monitoring the Department of Housing and helping to increase the capacity of nonprofit housing developers through the provision of technical assistance. By 1990 the coalition had an official membership of 30 organizations and 150 individuals, a mailing list of over 900, a staff of one, and an advisory board of 35. In 1987 the coalition created the Information Service and staffed it with two people. The core budget for both organizations is around $30,000. The Information Service puts on three regional workshops each year relating to housing issues and supports seminars at Johns Hopkins University in Baltimore.

In 1989 the state enacted a Housing Preservation Act that protects tenants if the owner of subsidized buildings attempts to convert the project to market rate—an accomplishment for which the coalition takes credit. Since then, however, budgetary restrictions have reduced the willingness of state legislators to fund housing assistance programs. Further, the governor requested the Department of Housing not to spend a portion of its allocation for 1989 and proposed a further reduction in funding for the following year.[74] Through 1990 and 1991 the coalition was forced to focus its efforts on restoring previous levels of housing assistance.

NATIONAL IMPLICATIONS OF A "LOCAL" HOUSING MOVEMENT

The explosion of advocacy at state and local levels does not mean that low-income advocates have abandoned Washington. A number of groups still lobby at the federal level for low-income housing, most notable among them the National Low Income Housing Coalition (NLIHC) and the National Coalition for the Homeless (NCH). These groups, extremely active in pursuing federal legislation, influenced the content of the Housing and Community Development Act of 1987, and the National Affordable Housing Act of 1990. A recent study showed NLIHC to be one of the five most influential lobbying organizations in the nation on housing policy issues.[75] Though state coalitions routinely monitor national housing issues and lend support to national advocacy campaigns, only two (in Michigan and Georgia) mentioned advocacy at the national level as one of their primary political activities. In general, state coalitions have left that arena to NLIHC, which is in fact their own umbrella organization.

The local housing movement connects with the national movement in three ways. First, local groups often aim their advocacy at HUD and other federal agencies when the issue warrants. Second, the national movement may provide the structure of a campaign strategy into which local groups insert themselves. Third, the local housing movement has been at times aided and abetted by national advocacy organizations such as NCH, NLICH and the National Housing Law Project.

The potential expiration of public subsidies and rent restrictions on thousands of federally subsidized, privately owned housing units has provided the local housing movement with a major national issue of immediate relevance to local supporters. Groups around the nation have organized in the cities where the threat of prepayment is greatest to publicize the potential loss of affordable housing units and to pressure federal agencies into action.[76] The housing movement has also directed pressure at state and local officials across the country to enact legislation aimed at preserving the existing stock of subsidized housing.

In 1987–88 the National Low Income Housing Coalition and the National Housing Law Project began a venture aimed at fostering the development of local advocacy coalitions. The resulting National Support Center for Low Income Housing has conducted a number of conferences around the country since 1989 in an attempt to create new statewide coalitions or provide support to existing ones. In fact, few coalitions owe their formation to these organizing efforts, but the National Support Center has provided an important source of networking for state groups.[77] Typically, it provides local groups with updated information on federal legislation and HUD regulations, and assists information exchange between state coalition members.

Finally, national organizations have occasionally provided the strategy for a coordinated nationwide advocacy campaign. The first and most successful of these was the Housing Now! march on Washington in October 1989. National groups—NLIHC, NHC, the Union of the Homeless, the Community for Creative Non-Violence—combined forces to organize the march, which was coordinated with local events around the country. Two days before the event, October 5, marchers from across the country took part in a "Lobby Day" that involved briefings and meetings with members of Congress. On that day advocates received a pledge from congressional leaders to pursue national legislation to restore the housing budget cuts made by the Reagan administration. On the following day, part of the Housing Now! delegation met with the HUD secretary, Jack Kemp. On the day of the march, more than 200,000 people rallied on the mall in Washington. According to the National Low Income Housing Coalition, "never before had so many people been brought together in one event to press the cause of low-income housing."[78] As a follow-up, NLIHC initiated the "Two Cents for Housing" campaign, a mass letter-writing effort to advocate more federal spending on housing equivalent to two cents for every dollar of federal spending. With local advocates coordinating the write-in campaign, postcards began to flow from all over the country with two pennies attached. On the anniversary of the Housing Now! march, similar events aimed at influencing local policy (dubbed "Housing Now! Hometown") were staged in forty-four states and more than fifty cities across the nation.[79]

SUMMARY

The local housing movement in the United States is one of the political by-products of the Reagan federalism reforms. The overwhelming majority of the coalitional advocacy groups at both city and state levels have been formed since 1980. The groups themselves attribute their formation to the need to initiate, monitor, or participate in the housing policymaking taking place in their respective state capitols or city halls. The movement has established these peak organizations in over two-thirds of the states and larger cities in the country. Organizationally, they are primarily coalitions of local housing service delivery professionals. Representatives of nonprofit housing developers, social service providers, and community groups dominate most coalitions, though a small percentage evolved from "user" groups such as tenant associations. Because of the organizational makeup of these groups they are influenced by both top-down concerns (related to state policy and the program implementation of state agencies) and bottom-up pressures (from constituent organizations looking for concrete services). The groups show a good deal of flux in the specific issues they pursue and the methods they use to achieve their objectives, probably because of the variation in housing issues across the country and the relative youth of the organizations.

Despite this variety, the constituent groups in the housing movement present a generally unified agenda. The types of programs they advocate have common characteristics that identify a new way to provide affordable housing to low-income households. The "new paradigm" of progressive housing policy and its widespread influence on local housing policy at both state and local levels are examined in the next chapter.

4
Housing Policy Innovation in U.S. Cities and States

THE EXISTENCE of a local housing movement, by itself, is insufficient to characterize the current period as a "postfederal" era in housing policy. The 1960s, as we have seen, also saw an increase in local mobilization around housing, community development, and poverty issues. The crucial difference between the two periods is that beginning in the 1980s, local governments have significantly increased their commitment to providing low-income housing. They have done so in a variety of ways that, taken together, indicate a fundamental relocation of leadership on housing issues from the federal to the local level. The vitality of the local housing movement described in the preceding chapter is a reflection of the centrality of local governments in U.S. housing policy formation. This chapter presents further evidence of the assumption by local governments of policymaking initiative in housing and attempts to describe fully the progressive nature of postfederal housing policy.

STATE AND LOCAL SPENDING FOR HOUSING

The most graphic way to illustrate the increased state and local commitment to housing is to examine expenditure levels. The involvement of state governments in the support of low-income housing is a recent phenomenon. According to the Council of State Community Affairs Agencies (COSCAA), only forty-four state-funded housing programs existed prior to 1980, the bulk of these in just three states: California, Connecticut, and Massachusetts.[1] Generally, states have played an intermediary role, funneling federal aid to local governments and coordinating local activities and planning functions.[2] During the federal era very few states took the initiative to create their own programs of housing assistance.

But beginning slowly during the early years of the 1980s, and accelerating from 1984 on, state governments across the country have introduced housing programs to serve low-income households. Between 1983 and 1987, ninety-two new state programs were established, some in states that had never before been involved in subsidized housing.[3] The breadth of programs was also considerable. Those initiated by state governments during these years ranged from replications of federal programs to new and unique initiatives, including a good part of the progressive housing agenda set forth by the new housing movement. One survey of state housing agencies, for example, found that state housing programs in 1988 were most commonly oriented toward nonprofit developers.[4]

The amount of money that state governments spend for housing-related purposes has skyrocketed since 1965, with almost 80 percent of the increase occurring since 1980. In 1965 the fifty states were spending a total of $80 million on housing and community development.[5] The figure rose to $631.6 million in 1975, mostly on the basis of increased spending in the state of New York.[6] By 1980, states were spending $621.6 million. Between 1980 and 1990, state spending for housing and community development increased to $2.9 billion. As the graph in Figure 4.1 shows, there

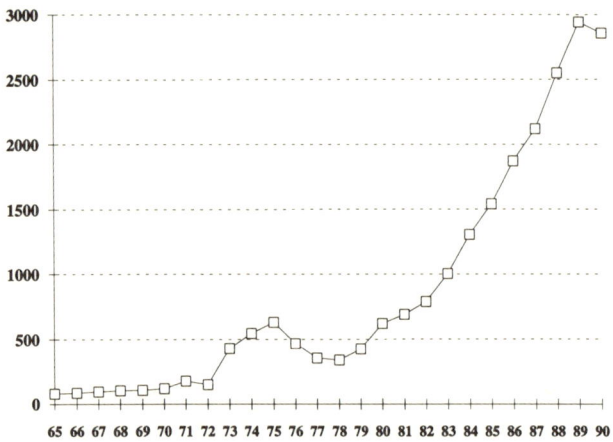

FIGURE 4.1
Spending for housing and community development in the fifty states, 1965–90 (in millions of dollars)

was a modest increase in state spending during the 1970s (confined primarily to one state); however, beginning in the early 1980s and escalating at mid-decade, state spending for housing increased dramatically.

During the federal era it was equally unusual for a city to spend its own money for housing assistance. The volume of housing assistance flowing from the federal government during this time supported most local programs. If the amount of federal assistance was not enough to deal with local problems, the best remedy was thought to be lobbying for greater federal resources rather than enlisting local sources. Since 1980 this practice has changed. Cities have utilized general revenue sources and general obligation bonding authority to fund housing assistance programs. Sometimes the assistance is made available temporarily, or is subordinated to local fiscal conditions. In 1984, for example, San Francisco Mayor Dianne Feinstein made $10 million available for low-income housing and then a year later froze the funds to help make up a budget deficit. More often, however, city governments have used two mechanisms, the general obligation bond and the housing trust fund, to set aside resources for locally funded housing assistance.

A 1989 study found that one-half of the fifty-one largest cities in the United States were using their own funds to support low-income housing.[7] New York City is far and away the most prolific spender. In fact, in 1989 New York spent 3.7 times as much as the next fifty cities combined. New York devotes over $100 per capita to housing assistance, far more than the $74 per capita spent by the second-place city, Honolulu. The most common sources for these funds (in 55 percent of the cities) are the general fund, special taxes, and fees. Somewhat less common is the use of general obligation bonds (by 45 percent of the cities).

My own survey of cities with populations over 100,000 shows that 44 percent of larger U.S. cities are spending their own resources on housing assistance.[8] Twenty-five of the fifty-eight respondents (43 percent) reporting the expenditure of local resources named general fund revenue as the source for housing assistance. Other sources include special taxes, general obligation bonds, developer fees, Urban Development Action Grant (UDAG) repayments, and redevelopment agency funds.[9] In Seattle, for example, where state law forbids the use of tax increment financing, voters approved a

$50 million Housing Levy Program in 1986. The program is designed to last eight years and produce 1,000 units of housing. The levy is funded through an addition to the property tax assessment of Seattle property owners.

Increased expenditures reveal a heightened awareness of housing problems on the part of local governments and a greater effort to deal with those problems. But the postfederal era is not defined by expenditure levels; the spending levels examined in Chapter 1 demonstrate that in the aggregate, local spending for housing has not made up for federal budget cuts, nor does it match current federal budget levels. The postfederal era is defined, rather, by the emergence of a new policy paradigm in housing.

PROGRESSIVE POLICY

During the 1980s the local housing movement produced its own progressive policy agenda and began to successfully articulate that agenda in front of local officials.[10] The alternative paradigm is based on an analysis of urban development that stresses the social and class-based distribution of benefits and costs in urban development.[11] As Chapter 3 indicated, conditions in many communities were getting precipitously worse even as some sectors of the economy were benefiting from economic growth. Specifically, urban development during the 1980s tended to accentuate the uneven distribution of wealth and income produced by the economy. As just one example, though perhaps the one most relevant to this discussion, the pattern of gentrification typically produced by a revitalized downtown brings significant benefits to the city in the form of increased tax revenue, property rehabilitation, and enhanced economic activity. At the same time, of course, gentrification means that low-income households lose their homes and their neighborhoods, and experience significant disruption in informal networks of support and interaction. The progressive policy paradigm identifies the uneven nature of urban development as a primary cause of increased housing problems in the past two decades. Therefore, much of the new paradigm is concerned with altering private market relationships and development practices to better serve the housing needs of low-income households.

A growing number of U.S. cities began in the 1980s to engage in a set of activities related to housing and economic development which is being described by various observers as *progressive* or even *neoprogressive* policy.[12] The striking characteristic of such policy is that it runs counter to the assumptions about growth and the constraints on local policy that underlie the economic-constraints model. As described in Chapter 1, the economic-constraints model suggests that redistributive policies are generally avoided by local governments. The model implies that restrictive market regulations will also be avoided because they infringe on the freedom of market actors. Further, according to the model, state and municipal governments are loath to interfere with the development objectives of private capital; indeed, they are obliged (because of their need to foster a healthy local economy and because of interjurisdictional competition for mobile capital) to facilitate development, usually through the provision of public incentives and subsidies. Policies in the progressive paradigm do not, however, provide incentives or subsidies to private capital in return for investment, nor are they characterized by a flow of public resources to support private residential, commercial, or industrial development, nor do they give greater reign to the private market in determining urban fortunes.[13]

Progressive policy is identified by the opposites of those prescriptions and is characterized by both its techniques and its objectives. The objective of progressive development policy is a wider distribution of benefits from urban development. The economic-constraints paradigm assumes an already wide dispersion of development benefits in the form of jobs, tax revenues, and enhanced community viability.[14] The progressive policy model observes the opposite: that the benefits of urban development have typically been focused in downtown neighborhoods and among large property owners and corporate interests. Indeed, the issue of equity has rarely concerned local officials as they have pursued economic revitalization.[15] Progressive policy attempts to achieve greater equity by channeling benefits to targeted social and economic groups. Policies such as office-housing linkage or first-source hiring, for example, mandate the distribution of benefits to groups that are typically excluded in mainstream development schemes: low-income households in the case of linkage, and inner-city or minority unemployed workers in the case of first-source hiring. Progressive development policy departs from typical growth politics by *directing* the benefits of development to specific groups.

Inherent in the directive nature of progressive policy is a mistrust of the market's ability to distribute the benefits of development equitably. Thus, the progressive model achieves its objectives through the use of nonmarket mechanisms and market restrictions. Clavel's definition of progressive municipal policy therefore involves the following elements: (1) the expanded public regulation of private property; (2) the promotion of alternatives to the private market; and (3) the increased participation of citizens and community-based interests.[16] To that list should be added (4) the identification of specific community-based or other politically defined interest groups toward which to channel the benefits of development.

Alternatively, the new paradigm can be thought of as reflecting more "autonomous" local policy. Clarke writes of differing degrees of decisional independence for local officials, specifically, independence from the pressure to maximize business interests and to respond exclusively to economic imperatives.[17] At the end of the continuum of decisional independence are those cities in which officials "resist economic pressures and are able to alter the economic and political terms of private investment."[18] Thus, a set of policies that have been termed "entrepreneurial" can be added to the defining list of progressive policies. In such entrepreneurial policies, local governments have insisted on a wide range of partnership agreements in return for public assistance in development.[19] These policies go beyond the provision of public resources for private development to make local governments more intimately involved in development through, for example, shared equity arrangements.

The progressive model is based on a set of assumptions about the relationship between capital and community different from those of conventional development policy.[20] Particularly, progressive policy supports social ownership and management of land and capital, and it seeks to acknowledge the socially produced value in each of those factors. Often, what is referred to as "community-based development" is that set of policies which tries to capture the benefits of development for specific neighborhoods or social groups by "democratizing" land, labor, and capital.[21] The progressive policy movement has focused on attempts to reconcile the global nature of capital and capital mobility with local control.[22] Thus, progressive development policy includes programs that regulate private market activity, such as development moratoria to prevent the demolition of affordable housing; or the local enforcement of banking regulations, such as the Community Reinvestment Act, that require community-based lending.

In addition, progressive policy relies more heavily on nonmarket actors and nonmarket alternatives in the provision of goods and services; the most prominent example is the growing importance of nonprofit CDCs. This is especially true in areas where the market has failed to provide sufficient affordable housing for low-income households. Close to 95 percent of U.S. cities over 100,000 have CDCs active in affordable housing production (see Chapter 5). The attractiveness of CDCs is in their greater knowledge of community needs but also in their nonmarket orientation. The imminent "prepayment" crisis—in which up to 1.5 million units of privately owned, publicly subsidized housing units may revert to market rate (see below)—has highlighted the need for housing that is made affordable in perpetuity and therefore kept off the private market forever.[23] The cornerstone of this strategy is not simply everlasting subsidies but the stable operation of a nonprofit sector to produce and manage affordable housing units. Community development corporations also form the basis for a nonmarket economic development strategy.[24]

Another way in which the progressive model alters market relationships is through alternative ownership models. Land trusts for housing and economic development put land ownership in the hands of a community-based trust and eliminate land speculation as an element of development.[25] Such land trusts are in place in Burlington, Vermont, and in the Seattle area, among other places. Community-based ownership of financial institutions and worker-owned businesses also alter traditional market-based ownership patterns and replace traditional market-based incentives with motivations that emphasize democratizing the benefits of ownership and development.[26]

Finally, progressive policy has altered market processes by inserting the state firmly in the center of development and industrial strategy. For example, the administration of the late Mayor Harold

Washington in Chicago was extremely interventionist in creating alternative development models for the city's industrial base. The city's task force on the steel industry, made up of business, labor, academic, and government representatives, analyzed the steel industry and created a set of policy recommendations for the revitalization and continued use of the city's steel infrastructure.[27] The city also created an industrial antidisplacement strategy that relied on heavy governmental intervention to maintain the viability of local light industry.[28]

Progressive policy is often implemented through the imposition of specific social obligations on private-sector developers. The linkage policies of San Francisco, Miami, Boston, and other cities, for example, require office developers to provide affordable housing. Inclusionary zoning, popular in New Jersey and California, requires housing developers to set aside a percentage of their units for low-income occupancy. Other exactions require of developers a range of direct and indirect social services and public benefits.

Progressive policy is achieved and implemented by opening up the policymaking process to include such traditionally excluded groups as representatives of low-income neighborhoods, social service providers, and community-based organizations. Often, the community sector has had to pry open the policymaking process through organized resistance to development and persistent social action in the areas of housing and neighborhood preservation. As the preceding chapter suggested, however, the housing movement is becoming more sophisticated through the establishment of nonprofit development corporations and the creation of effective lobbying organizations for affordable housing. These groups have established themselves as significant political actors and important elements of governing coalitions in many localities. Progressive policy, as a characteristic of what governments do, is often accomplished through the purposive inclusion of community-based organizations in policy formation and implementation. An example, again, is the Chicago industrial policy under Harold Washington, which was part of a large-scale effort that ultimately brought more than 100 neighborhood groups into the policymaking process.[29] Similarly, the housing partnerships that have emerged in a number of cities (and at least two states) are conscious attempts to coordinate the implementation of housing policy through the work of CDCs.

In one sense it might be argued that all affordable housing programs could be called progressive in that they are ultimately designed to provide benefits directly to needy households. However, as the review in Chapter 2 indicated, housing policy in the past was anything but significantly redistributive. The use of zoning powers and the reliance on homeownership programs for middle-income households put a very middle-class tint on previous state and local housing policy, while federal housing programs typically served the interests of either the construction or the financial industry before those of low-income households. In addition, previous policy relied to a great extent on the private sector to produce and manage low-cost housing.

The new housing paradigm, as presented by the local housing movement in the United States, attempts to change these characteristics by adhering to the progressive criteria described above. For example, regulation has been put to use to support rather than hinder low-income housing, and to a large extent the relationship between public objectives and the private sector has been reversed. Instead of inducing private actors to produce and manage low-cost housing with the help of public funds (as in most of the subsidy programs utilized since 1960), the new policy paradigm increasingly leverages private-sector funds (through investment in tax credit investment pools or pools designed to facilitate compliance with the Community Reinvestment Act, or through linkage requirements) for the purpose of assisting housing to be produced and managed by public or nonprofit actors. Though, in fact, it is possible to argue that postfederal policies are more progressive in terms of policy outcomes (that is, they are more redistributive than those of the federal era), "progressive" as it is used here refers more fundamentally to a set of techniques for achieving policy objectives rather than to policy outcomes themselves.

More precisely, the elements of the progressive housing paradigm are these:

1. *Reliance on nonmarket relationships for the production, management, and ownership of land and housing.* The growth of the nonprofit development sector is perhaps the most important element of this strategy. The trend toward nonmarket mechanisms

is also seen in the utilization of alternative means of land ownership through community land trusts, the design of alternative models of tenancy such as the housing co-op and the leasehold cooperative, and the implementation of alternative management strategies such as tenant management.

2. *Greater regulation of the private sector in ways that promote the production or preservation of low-income housing.* The regulation of the private sector in the area of land development follows from an analysis that identifies the source of many housing problems, particularly the lack of affordable housing, in the development practices of the private sector. A significant portion of housing problems—the displacement of low-income residents, rent escalation (even where vacancy rates remain steady or are rising), and poor conditions—can be traced to such development practices as condominium conversion, the replacement of affordable units with luxury apartments, and disinvestment in low-income neighborhoods. An array of regulatory responses has been used during the postfederal era by local governments attempting to control the negative impacts of private-sector development on affordable housing. Policies have been designed to control displacement, or provide one-for-one replacement of demolished or converted units. Demolition moratoria have been imposed, housing linkage programs initiated to make office developers more responsive to housing needs, and rent control introduced in some areas and strengthened in others. Community action designed to make lending institutions more responsive to neighborhood needs has also occurred. The thrust of each of these programs is to regulate more closely the private development process and manipulate it to support low-income housing objectives.

3. *Taxing the private development process to provide financial resources for low income housing.* Beyond regulating the private development process, the progressive paradigm makes use of various methods of taxing developers and those involved in real estate transactions. Transfer taxes, document recording fees, escrow fees, and the like have been used in many areas to fund housing trust funds (HTFs) devoted to low-income housing production. There is a good deal of overlap between these kinds of fees and the linkage programs that I have previously classified as regulatory techniques. Indeed, the similarities are perhaps greater than the

differences, in that both rechannel the profits (social surplus) from private, for-profit land development and real estate transactions into low-income housing uses. The difference between the two approaches is that one is based on a regulatory mechanism, while the other is a form of taxation.

4. *A reversal or mitigation of the impacts of downtown development and the subsequent re-use of inner-city land for low-income housing.* In some cities, housing advocates have attempted to reclaim or preserve parts of downtown areas for low-income housing. An important element in this strategy is the preservation and production of single-room occupancy (SRO) hotels. The recent history of most downtown areas in the United States is one of diminishing opportunities for low-income residency. In fact, the defining characteristic of most downtown areas is increased gentrification: the replacement of low-income housing with upper-income housing units or commercial land uses catering to the professional class. The new housing paradigm incorporates a conscious attempt to reverse the destructive impact of downtown development on low-income housing opportunities.

5. *Community-based planning on housing issues.* The progressive housing movement has successfully utilized planning and research both to establish the justification for a local housing policy and to influence the form of the policy response. As the evidence on housing advocacy groups shows, a common strategy among these groups is the sponsorship of housing studies or needs assessments to document the nature of local housing problems.

THE USE OF PROGRESSIVE HOUSING POLICIES

Nonmarket Production, Ownership, and Management

The progressive housing model emphasizes alternative forms of land ownership, housing production, and property management. The most important element in this strategy is the emergence of nonprofit community development corporations as the primary producers and owners of affordable low-income housing. An outgrowth of the 1960s struggle for community control of federal urban programs,[30] CDCs have matured along with the housing movement. Their growth in number was greatest during the 1980s, and CDCs are now active in the construction and rehabilitation of housing, property management, housing and tenant counseling, and housing design. They have grown in importance as serious flaws emerged in the practice of providing public subsidies to private owners. The progressive argument criticizes these subsidies because they do not provide for continued affordability. Private owners are bound to provide units at affordable rents only for the length of the public subsidy; after the expiration or (p)repayment of the subsidy the private owner has the option of converting units to market rate. Thus, the current crisis over the potential loss of 1.5 million affordable units is rooted in the reliance on the private sector to produce and provide low-income housing. The ready alternative to private development is the development of a viable nonprofit sector that can better ensure the continued affordability of the housing stock. Nonprofits, in the business of providing affordable housing, would not plan to convert units after the expiration of government contracts. Chapter 5 contains a full examination of CDCs, their role in the postfederal housing paradigm, and the technical and political resources they offer to local governments.

Alternative modes of ownership are also promoted by the new housing paradigm. Community land trusts are community-owned and -managed corporations that acquire and permanently hold property in the community's name to be used for housing or other purposes. Community ownership reduces inflation in the cost of housing by eliminating land speculation. Community land trusts are in operation in more than sixty locations in eighteen states across the country, including Burlington (Vermont), Atlanta, and New York City. The Burlington Community Land Trust, initiated in 1983 by then Mayor Bernie Sanders and his progressive coalition, received direct local government support; it was capitalized with a $200,000 grant from the city's general fund.[31] The South Atlanta Land Trust (SALT) was established in 1982, created by residents and supported by the United Methodist Church. In an effort to fight city plans to "revitalize" the South Atlanta neighborhood through the demolition of low-cost housing, SALT purchases and rehabilitates homes in the neighborhood with funds from the city's CDBG program. By 1989 community land trusts had assisted over 1,000 units nationwide.[32]

Another ownership alternative is the limited-equity cooperative. A housing cooperative is a nonprofit association of members who jointly own the building in which they live. Members purchase "shares" that convey the right to occupy a particular unit. Limited-equity co-ops are attempts to control escalating housing costs by eliminating speculation, reducing financing costs, and controlling equity appreciation.[33] The federal government funded limited-equity cooperatives for a short time through the Section 221(d)(3) program. The idea has taken hold in some cities such as Minneapolis and Cambridge, Massachusetts. By some estimates, there were over 300,000 units in low-income cooperative housing in the United States by 1981.[34]

Local Land-Use Controls and Market Regulations

Historically, the focus of housing policy at the urban level, beginning in the 1920s, has been on land-use controls.[35] For the most part they have been characterized by exclusionary intent and regressive effect. Zoning restrictions and subdivision regulations have been established by local governments as a means of guarding or enhancing the local treasury.[36] By restricting land uses that generate high levels of service demand relative to tax value (in practice, that means limiting rental or low-income housing), localities avoid fiscal problems, safeguard property tax values, and control the types of development occurring within jurisdictional boundaries. The effects of such land-use regulations have been well documented.[37] Restrictive land-use zoning has limited the availability of multifamily housing in many suburban areas, has excluded low-cost housing for minorities and low-income families, has led to the concentration of low-income housing in central cities, and has contributed to urban sprawl.[38]

Despite their most common use as means of restricting the residential access of lower-income families, land-use regulations were originally part of a progressive package of reforms pursued around the end of the nineteenth century.[39] They were in fact promoted as a "middle way" between unfettered market processes and a burgeoning "radical" response to the social problems of early capitalism. The growing practice in the 1980s and 1990s of applying land-use regulations to mitigate negative impacts of urban development thus brings these regulations back to their conceptual roots.

Unlike conventional housing programs that provide tax or financial inducements to the private sector for new housing production, these regulatory programs impose restrictions or controls on the land-market activity of private actors. In addition, they impose at least opportunity costs and, more often, real financial costs on private-sector investors for the purpose of producing or preserving affordable housing for lower-income households.

Seven methods of regulation are examined here. Two of these—rent control and inclusionary zoning—predate the Reagan era's budget cutbacks. The other five—linkage, preservation, replacement, conversion restrictions, and community lending regulations—are largely postfederal solutions to low-income housing needs. Housing preservation, one-for-one replacement, and linkage are terms often used interchangeably and sometimes confused with inclusionary housing programs. They are used here to denote separate but related regulatory approaches to supporting low-income housing. Preservation ordinances are those that protect against the conversion or demolition of low-income housing. These take the form of outright moratoria or limits on the number of units that can be removed from the affordable stock. Replacement programs require the one-for-one replacement of units that are removed from the stock. Replacement provisions are often (though not necessarily) a part of preservation laws. Linkage programs require the developers of nonresidential property to produce affordable housing as well. Conversion restrictions limit the options of private owners of subsidized housing in converting such properties to market rate. Community lending regulations monitor the amount of (residential and commercial) credit that financial institutions provide to lower-income city neighborhoods. Inclusionary housing programs require developers of market-rate residential property to produce affordable housing. The most conceptually distinct program considered here is rent control, the limiting of return from existing residential rental property.

Table 4.1 lists the number of cities and states that reported using regulatory mechanisms to support low-income housing. Preservation programs are used in 14 percent of the larger cities surveyed and 10 percent of the states (California, Massachusetts, Minnesota, New Jersey, and Vermont). Replacement programs

TABLE 4.1
Use of regulatory housing programs by cities and states

	Cities		States	
Program	N	% of 133	N	% of 48[a]
Preservation	19	14	5	11
Replacement	10	8	2	4
Linkage	13	10		
Inclusionary zoning	12	9		
Rent control	14	11		
Conversion restrictions			10	21
Other			8	17

[a]Excluding Oklahoma and Arizona

exist in 8 percent of the cities and in two states (Minnesota and California). Five states reported having moratoria on the demolition or conversion of low-income housing units; two states have replacement legislation requiring the production of one unit of affordable housing for every one demolished or converted; and eight other states report some form of regulation of commercial or residential development designed to support the production or preservation of low-income housing. The states have not resorted to restrictive land-use regulations to the extent that cities have, because most land-use control is vested in local, not state, governments; thus, inclusionary zoning, linkage, and rent control are primarily local remedies.

Housing preservation programs developed in response to the fact that as U.S. inner-city areas continue to revitalize, developers are quick to convert low-rent housing into "higher uses." A large portion of downtown and historically significant residential structures are giving way to new commercial development. As a result, an increasing number of cities are using their land-use control to stop the wholesale conversion of lower-income residential uses. Notable among these are moratoria on the conversion of SRO hotel units in cities such as San Francisco and New York, which have seen their stock of such units decline dramatically since 1970.

Nineteen of the cities surveyed (14 percent) utilize some form of housing preservation regulation. Preservation programs can be general in scope, applying to all rental housing, or more specific to a certain type of housing (SRO or mobile home).⁴⁰ Fully one-half of the cities reporting preservation programs have general protections against the demolition or conversion of rental housing. One-third of the cities preserve SRO units, one-third limit condominium conversion, and one-sixth preserve mobile homes (based on $N = 18$; one missing case). Most of the moratoria reported here are permanent. Those most likely to be temporary are the general moratoria.

In San Francisco, for example, the city imposed a temporary moratorium on SRO conversion in 1979 to allow the city a chance to study the extent of SRO demolition. In 1980, the city's planning department published a study that estimated a loss of over 5,000 units during a four-year period (1975–1980). As a result, the city established a permanent moratorium on conversion and demolition of SROs and provided for replacement housing for those units approved for demolition. New York City passed a more restrictive SRO preservation law in 1985, which prohibited owners from demolishing, keeping vacant, or converting SRO units. This law was ruled unconstitutional by the New York State Supreme Court in 1989 for depriving "owners of the right to determine how their properties would be used."⁴¹ Homeless advocates immediately initiated an effort to urge the new mayor, David Dinkins, to step up the city's programs of new construction and purchase and rehabilitation of SRO hotels.⁴²

The moratoria imposed at the state level are similar to those used by city governments. In 1990, for example, Governor Michael Dukakis signed a bill, initiated by the Massachusetts Coalition for the Homeless, which created an eighteen-month moratorium on the demolition and conversion of 5,000 SRO units across the state.⁴³

One-for-one replacement programs require that housing units demolished or converted to other uses as a result of urban revitalization be replaced so as to preserve the existing stock of affordable housing. These programs, like outright moratoria, have been in part a response to the growing loss of low-cost downtown housing. The replacement programs apply to either publicly sponsored redevelopment or private projects but not usually to both. The idea has made its way into federal legislation via the Barney Frank amendment to the 1987 Housing and Community Development Act, which requires replacement housing for units demolished with CDBG or UDAG funds. Replacement requirements were also attached to the demolition of public housing units.

Replacement programs are in place in 8 percent of the reporting cities. These programs, like linkage and preservation, are of recent vintage and uncertain legal status. In 1981 the city of Seattle initiated a replacement policy for units demolished in the downtown area. In 1987 the program was struck down by the Washington State Supreme Court.[44] A similar policy in Hartford, Connecticut, however, has not been invalidated by the courts. The Hartford Housing Preservation and Replacement Ordinance emerged from the advocacy of the Hartford Neighborhood Housing Coalition. The coalition studied construction and demolition patterns in the city and found that "for every new housing unit built, 2½ housing units were demolished or converted" during the years prior to the adoption of the Ordinance.[45] The coalition offered the preservation and replacement program as a solution to this loss of low-cost housing, and the ordinance was enacted in January 1985.

Two of the replacement programs reported in the Midwest place the obligation on the public-sector development partner. In Minneapolis and St. Paul the replacement requirements apply only to units destroyed in developments with public-sector participation, and the responsibility lies with the public-sector partner to replace the units. Although there is no burden on the private developer in these programs, they nevertheless represent an attempt to mitigate the negative impacts of urban development on low-income housing.

Housing linkage programs involve a requirement made of private (usually commercial) developers, as a condition of permit approval, to construct or provide financial assistance for the production of affordable housing.[46] The rationale for this requirement is that the increased demand for housing resulting from commercial space development displaces the low-income households that are least able to compete in the market.[47]

Ordinarily, the linkage requirements apply to developers of commercial space in the downtown district.[48] These developers are obliged to make an in-lieu payment to a housing trust fund (as in Boston) or are allowed either to build the housing themselves or to provide gap financing to other housing developments (as in San Francisco). Linkage programs are sometimes mandatory requirements and sometimes incentives programs. Many cities use linkage irregularly, as part of negotiated development agreements.

Ann Bowman reports that 18 percent of the cities in her national sample use housing linkage at least occasionally.[49] In an earlier study I reported linkage in 17 percent of the cities and 10 percent of the counties in a national sample.[50] Herrero identifies fifteen formal linkage programs operating in U.S. cities.[51] The data from this survey show that thirteen cities use linkage (10 percent of respondent cities). Over one-half (54 percent) of these programs were implemented on an ad hoc basis through negotiations with developers; 31 percent involved incentives; and 15 percent were mandatory.

Cities on both coasts, including Boston, Hartford, Miami, Santa Monica, Los Angeles, and Sacramento have adopted linkage programs in one form or another. Providence, Rhode Island, and Washington, D.C., use linkage on an ad hoc basis, negotiating specific agreements with developers case by case. Local housing advocates have been instrumental in the spread of the linkage concept. In San Francisco, the idea of linking downtown development to housing production originated with community housing advocates. The policy was eventually negotiated by these advocates, city officials, and representatives of the development community.[52] The linkage policies in Boston, Hartford, and Los Angeles have also resulted directly from the pressure of community-based housing advocates.[53]

Inclusionary zoning means "a zoning scheme under which prospective developers are required by a municipality or county to provide, as a condition of approval, or alternatively, are given incentives to provide, low- and moderate-income housing as a part of, or in conjunction with, their proposed development projects."[54] Inclusionary zoning is implemented through "set-asides" that establish the percentage of units in a development to be reserved for low- and moderate-income use. These programs became more commonplace in the 1970s as an explicit reaction to the exclusionary aspects of local land-use regulations and the lack of affordable housing alternatives for low-income households.

The Mount Laurel II court ruling by the New Jersey State Supreme Court in 1983 went beyond restricting exclusionary zoning to affirm an obligation on the part of localities to share in the provision of affordable housing.[55] Inclusionary zoning laws can either require the set-aside or provide incentives (usually in the form of density bonuses) for low-income production. The amount of the set-aside—that is, the percentage of units made affordable to lower-income households—is also variable, generally ranging from a low of 5 percent to as much as 40 percent.[56] The largest study of inclusionary zoning found sporadic use, with the adoption of most ordinances clustered between the years 1977 and 1982.[57] Further, most of the active programs are in California and New Jersey. Both states have passed laws that create an administrative or planning process by which to determine the "fair share" contribution of low-income housing by local governments. In California, regional planning bodies advise localities on their fair-share requirements as part of the statewide planning process. Each locality's general plan must have a housing element that outlines its needs for affordable housing. In New Jersey, the Fair Housing Act of 1985 created the Council on Affordable Housing, which oversees the process of determining fair share in that state.

Twelve (9 percent) of the cities responding to the survey reported having some inclusionary zoning program. Of those, nine (75 percent) have incentive programs in which the housing requirements are activated only in exchange for a development break such as a density bonus.

Rent control is the regulatory limiting of rents, rent increases, and evictions. Controls are usually applied with flexibility regarding the landlord's rate of return and the application of controls to vacant or newly constructed units.[58] The operation of such programs is generally overseen by rent control boards on which both real estate and tenant interests are represented. European countries have used rent controls on a national basis since experiencing acute housing shortages created by World War II. In the United States adoption of rent controls has been confined to the local level and has inspired passionate political debate. Opponents of the mechanism charge it with contributing to disinvestment and abandonment, deflating real estate markets, discouraging new construction, and even contributing to homelessness.[59] Defenders dispute each of those claims and argue that rent control helps prevent rent gouging in heated markets and protects against poor maintenance and unjust evictions.[60] One study indicates that roughly 10 percent of the rental housing stock in the United States is currently rent regulated, and that roughly 130 cities and counties across the country have rent control.[61] Eleven percent of the cities responding to this survey reported using some form of rent control. These ordinances tend to be moderate; 42 percent allow increases set at a fixed rate; 33 percent are pegged to an index such as the consumer price index. Over half of the programs have provisions that allow rent increases up to market rate when a vacancy occurs.

Only four of the rent control programs were initiated after 1980, and these are of the weakest form, merely providing a rent board to adjudicate unfair increases. This suggests that little new activity is taking place with regard to rent control, the movement having lost momentum since the late 1970s.[62] The issue has not disappeared from local political agendas, however. Washington, D.C., for example, extended its 1975 rent control policy in 1985 and ordered a study of the impact of the ordinance on the availability of affordable housing in the district. The Urban Institute conducted the study and found significant cost savings to renters and an acceptable return on investment to owners.[63] The Detroit Organization of Tenants won a 1988 ballot initiative on the issue of rent control. Though subsequently invalidated by state law prohibiting local communities from enacting such controls, it was the first such ordinance ever enacted in a city where renters are not the majority.[64]

In California, developers and real estate interests continue to lobby at the state level for revocation of the legislation enabling rent control. Each year housing advocates from across the state also lobby, to defeat the revocation and retain local authority over rent control.[65] Like their counterparts in California, the Illinois Statewide Housing Action Coalition mounted a lobbying effort in 1987 to respond to a real estate bill that would have preempted local tenants' rights provisions and replaced them with much weaker statewide legislation.[66] As California and Illinois show, despite the fact that most land-use regulations originate at the local level, the state legislature can be the venue for considerable regulatory conflict.

Conversion restrictions constitute attempts to prevent the massive conversion of subsidized housing to market-rate property. The potential loss of hundreds of thousands of units of publicly subsidized, privately owned units through prepayment of public subsidies and the expiration of subsidy contracts with the federal government have led a number of states to enact legislation locally to preserve their stock of affordable housing. After the issue first emerged in 1986, a number of studies showed that the dimensions of the problem were such that it could have a devastating impact on the nation's stock of subsidized housing, with most of the losses occurring between 1993 and 2005.[67] At the federal level Congress passed the Emergency Low Income Housing Preservation Act in 1987, which temporarily limited the prepayment options of private owners until a more lasting solution to the problem could be devised. Since the 1987 act was self-consciously temporary and the housing movement was uncertain about what, if any, permanent action Congress might take, activists directed their attention to local arenas.[68] It was this threat of massive displacement of low-income households that activated the housing movement in many states. State-level studies of "at-risk" housing were conducted in Minnesota and Massachusetts; a model predicting the rate of prepayment was established in Rhode Island; and tenant and housing movement activists organized around the issue in a number of other states.[69]

Ten of the states responding to the survey indicated that they had some program in place to address the problem of expiring use restrictions. Most of the states with such programs are in the Northeast: Maine, Massachusetts, New York, Pennsylvania, Rhode Island, and Vermont. There are three common elements of the legislation and restrictions aimed at preserving the existing stock of subsidized housing:

a. Prepayment notice. Often, owners of subsidized housing are required to post notice of their intent to prepay or opt out of government contracts well in advance of their action (usually nine to twelve months). This helps avoid the emergency eviction and displacement of lower-income households, while also giving tenants, nonprofits, and local governments time to prepare a plan for purchase or relocation.
b. Relocation assistance. Owners may be required to provide relocation benefits to tenants forced to move as a result of conversion to market-rate operation.

c. Right of first refusal. Local governments or their authorities, nonprofits, and sometimes tenant groups are allowed the first chance to purchase buildings whose owners wish to prepay government contracts.

The Massachusetts Housing Partnership stimulated discussion of preservation in 1987 when it created a task force to study the issue.[70] While the partnership was amassing a database on the potential loss of subsidized housing, tenant groups were sponsoring a bill in the legislature that would have restricted prepayments of all federally insured and subsidized rental projects. The Maryland legislature passed legislation in 1988 to restrict and regulate prepayment. The Maryland Low Income Housing Coalition, residents of at-risk housing, and other groups successfully lobbied for the right of first refusal for resident groups, nonprofit organizations, and local government; twelve month's notice of prepayment; and owner-paid relocation benefits for the disabled, the elderly, and family households with children.[71] Also in 1988, Maine and Illinois passed laws requiring notice of intent to prepay.[72] The Maine legislation also grants the state housing authority the right of first refusal.

The *community reinvestment* movement began in the mid-1970s as neighborhood organizers in poor and minority communities became concerned about the lending practices of local financial institutions. This regulatory approach within the new housing paradigm attempts to make local lending institutions more accountable to low-income housing needs and the needs of low-income neighborhoods. Though regulations regarding community reinvestment by savings institutions were adopted by the federal government in 1977, many states and some cities have passed their own legislation to add to and strengthen federal mandates. The 1977 Community Reinvestment Act[73] allows community groups or other agents to challenge a financial institution on its record of reinvesting in its community. The federal legislation was pushed by neighborhood groups as a means of reversing neighborhood decay and disinvestment.

Chicago adopted the first mortgage disclosure law in 1974.[74] The law required lending institutions to provide information on loan practices if they wished to be depositories for city funds. In

1975 a national movement of neighborhood-based organizations succeeded in getting the national Home Mortgage Disclosure Act (HMDA) passed. Two years later this coalition pushed successfully for the Community Reinvestment Act (CRA), which requires banks and S&Ls to meet the credit needs of their communities, and provides a process whereby community organizations can challenge banks on their lending record. An example of such a challenge came from the Chicago Reinvestment Alliance, comprising more than thirty community organizations. Through the last half of 1983 and into early 1984 the Alliance used the leverage of the CRA to negotiate an agreement with three separate banks to commit a total of $153 million in loans for housing and small business development. In its first six years this Neighborhood Lending Program, as it was called, generated $117.5 million to assist close to 5,000 housing units.[75]

The city of Tampa, Florida, has made community reinvestment the linchpin of its affordable housing policy. Its Community Reinvestment Challenge Fund, created in 1987, organizes the CRA participation of lending institutions in a program of loans at below-market interest rate for owners and investors. Twelve lending institutions have made available over $13 million in rehabilitation financing. The city provides loan application and review services, construction monitoring, and mortgage servicing for the program.[76]

By 1990 twenty-eight states had enacted policies related to the investment practices of savings institutions. In fact, the federal legislation in 1977 actually followed action by the state of New York in monitoring and regulating reinvestment.[77] New York also set a precedent for establishing public ratings of financial institutions, a feature that the federal government incorporated into the 1989 Financial Institutions Reform and Recovery Act (FIRREA).

State legislation falls into three categories: reinvestment regulations that mirror the national legislation; standards for interstate banking that evaluate the community record of banks wishing to enter the local market; and linked deposit programs that condition the deposit of state government funds on the community lending record of the financial institution.[78] The states using these tools for making lending institutions accountable are listed in Table 4.2

TABLE 4.2
Use of community lending regulations by state governments

Program	N	States
State CRA laws	10	CT, IA, MD, MA, MI, MO, NY, OH, WA, WV
Interstate banking regulations	20	AR, HI, IL, IN, IA, ME, MD, MA, MI, MN, NV, NH, NY, OK, PA, UT, VT, WA, WV, WY
Linked deposit programs	17	AL, AZ, CO, IL, IA, IN, KS, LA, ME, MA, MI, MO, MT, OH, PA, WV, WY

Source: Robert Stumberg, *State Reinvestment Policy* (Washington, D.C.: Center for Policy Alternatives, 1990).

The majority of these programs have been enacted since 1980, placing them in the mainstream of postfederal solutions to housing problems. In fact, the majority of the post-1980 laws have been developed since 1984, which is consistent with the political lag seen in most postfederal policy initiatives. State-level reinvestment laws generally strengthen federal requirements by adding state enforcement, additional disclosure and reporting requirements, and linkage of performance to public depositing and state approval of acquisitions.[79] The interstate banking regulations take advantage of the powers of state governments over the expansion of out-of-state financial institutions into the local market. The standards for approval in most cases involve a CRA-like review of past performance.[80] Finally, linked deposit programs are underway in seventeen states. States use the vast amounts of money they deposit in financial institutions (estimated at over $100 billion annually) as leverage to improve the community lending practices of local banks.

Other regulatory approaches are used by some states. Legislation in Florida mandates that large-scale developments be reviewed for any adverse effect on the ability of people to find adequate housing that is reasonably accessible to their places of employment. Vermont requires relocation assistance for displaced residents of mobile home parks. Both Florida and Hawaii are becoming more actively involved in managing the patterns of growth within their boundaries.[81] Hawaii is using developer exactions to produce affordable housing. Developers wishing to reclassify land from agricultural to urban uses must set aside at affordable rates 50 to 60 percent of the units they produce. The state supports this land-use control mechanism with a $200 million fund to provide infrastructure in such areas.[82]

The central role of regulatory mechanisms in the new housing policy paradigm is notable because it seems to fly in the face of conventional wisdom about the impact of housing regulation. Conventional wisdom holds that building and land regulations generally increase the cost of housing and thus reduce the amount of affordable housing. This is the so-called "overregulation hypothesis."[83] Indeed, a recent HUD commission report suggests that "regulatory barriers" to affordable housing are significant and proposes conditioning federal assistance on the willingness of local governments to remove such barriers.[84] From the progressive standpoint the issue is more complicated. First, the new housing movement has been able to argue successfully for the application of new regulations, such as replacement and linkage, designed to increase the availability of affordable housing. Second, the movement has defended older regulations such as rent control against claims that it actually inhibited the development of affordable units and even contributed to homelessness.[85] Third, the housing movement has acknowledged that some zoning, building, and construction regulations might make certain kinds of housing units more expensive to produce. The new paradigm has therefore worked for a selective adjustment of such practices, such as the replacement of exclusionary zoning with inclusionary programs and the revision of building codes to provide for greater flexibility in low-cost housing construction. California, for example, has created a new category of housing residence, called the "living unit," which revises minimum building standards and makes the creation of new residential hotel units financially feasible.[86] Thus, in the new policy paradigm, regulations are not treated as a single type of policy with a common impact on housing affordability. Rather, the new paradigm considers the impact on affordability to be variable and argues that policy should be flexible to reflect that variation.

Taxing the Private Development Process

The establishment of a housing trust fund (HTF) is a common way to earmark funds for affordable housing. Housing trust funds have certain common characteristics. First, they are a renewable or continuous source of funds for low-income housing. Whatever mechanisms provide the resources for the trust fund, such as development fees or taxes, they are not a one-time commitment; rather, they act as a revenue stream for the continued support of the trust fund. Second, HTFs are dedicated to housing; that is, they are not used for other purposes, nor can they be diverted to other purposes. This characteristic insulates them from whatever other budgetary demands may be faced by local governments. Finally, most trust fund programs attempt to allocate a large percentage of their assistance to low- and very low-income households.[87] What defines HTFs as a progressive response is the source of funding. Most are funded through real estate transfer fees, or escrow fees, or even interest from tenant security deposits. Thus HTFs are another example of using the private development process to create funds for affordable housing. In Gunn and Gunn's terms, it is the employment of social surplus in the effort to improve housing conditions for low-income people.[88]

In the face of continued budget pressures, the HTF approach is perhaps the most promising long-term solution to state financing. Between 1985 and 1991 nineteen states adopted HTFs (see Figure 4.2) in one form or another. (Though they are more common at the state level, a number of cities too have implemented trust funds. Thirteen percent of the cities surveyed reporting having some form of dedicated revenue stream for housing.) Housing trust funds insulate housing resources from the vagaries and periodic crises of state budgets. A number of statewide housing coalitions have made the trust fund a centerpiece of their strategy. This is true in Illinois, where the Statewide Housing Action Coalition (SHAC) organized in 1986 and pushed for three years until the Illinois Affordable Housing Act was passed in 1989.

The coalition was formed in response to efforts by the Illinois state legislature to put together a Select Committee on Housing. This committee was itself formed as a result of pressure applied by housing advocates statewide, and SHAC organized to ensure that continued housing advocacy would take place and that housing groups would have a part in the emerging housing policy debate. After initial efforts to improve the performance of the Illinois Housing Development Authority, SHAC leaders decided to organize around the development of a trust fund devoted to low-income housing assistance. The coalition engaged in extensive grassroots

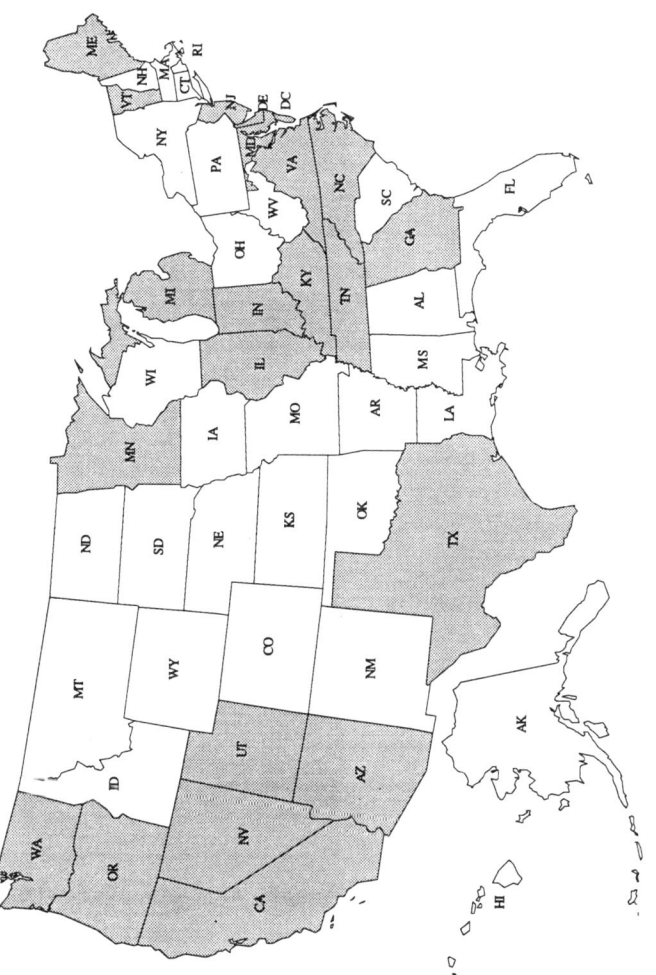

FIGURE 4.2
States with housing trust funds, 1990
Sources: "Survey of State and Local Housing Trust Fund Programs," Center for Policy Alternatives, January 1991 (mimeo); *Housing Trust Fund Project Newsletter*, Center for Community Change, July 1991.

organizing throughout the state, drafted the legislation in 1987, and finally succeeded in getting the trust fund through the legislature in 1989. The HTF is funded by a real estate transfer tax. The trust fund took so much of the organization's effort and was such a singular objective that after its passage, a group spokesperson indicated, the coalition went into a transitional period to decide what its future efforts would be.[89]

Not all HTFs are funded by real estate transaction taxes. Other sources include loan repayments and general fund appropriations. In these cases, the trust fund is simply another means of spending local public funds. In San Antonio, for example, the HTF was initially funded through the sale of the city's part interest in a cable television franchise and subsequently through UDAG repayments. These funding sources represent what is politically possible in a city such as San Antonio. Development fees and real estate transaction fees are strongly opposed by the local real estate lobby. As one San Antonio trust fund official put it, "Ever since the first 163 real estate developers went down in the Alamo, it has been difficult to get anything like impact fees enacted around here."[90]

Nevertheless, even HTFs not funded by real estate fees retain elements of the progressive paradigm. The San Antonio program allots 30 percent of its assistance to projects that provide affordable housing in the downtown area. In addition, the HTF in San Antonio intersects with other elements of the progressive agenda by offering assistance to nonprofit CDCs and by leveraging funds from local financial institutions. In 1990 the city established a nonprofit organization, the San Antonio Housing Trust Foundation, Inc., to administer the program. The foundation is pledged to direct assistance to low-income neighborhoods, leverage financing from local financial institutions, and channel support to nonprofit organizations (CDCs) for the development, rehabilitation, or preservation of affordable housing.[91]

Other HTFs operate in similar manner. Pittsburgh's housing trust fund offers technical assistance to nonprofit, community-based organizations for housing projects.[92] The Cambridge, Massachusetts, fund—developed in 1988—provides financing for multi-family rehabilitation and the establishment of limited-equity cooperatives. The program is funded by various means, including incentive zoning and linkage. The Community Development Department, which runs the programs, gives priority to nonprofit organizations in order to ensure the long-term affordability of the units assisted.

Downtown Housing

Publicly subsidized urban redevelopment originated with the federal urban renewal program enacted in 1949. The program was initially characterized by large-scale demolition of "blighted" neighborhoods, clearance of the land, and its resale to private investors and developers. Very early on, local and national officials discovered that low-income residents generally objected to the destruction of their homes and neighborhoods. Opposition was most vocal in those cases where the "new" neighborhoods created by redevelopment were unaffordable or inhospitable to the previous residents. As the urban renewal program progressed, project area residents increasingly organized against large-scale demolition plans. Advocates fought the displacement of lower-income residents and the lack of relocation assistance by local authorities. Though local redevelopment agencies never fully embraced comprehensive relocation assistance, the urban renewal program did shift from large-scale clearance to rehabilitation, partially in response to displacement controversies.[93] The 1970 Uniform Relocation Act (URA) was an attempt at the federal level to deal with the large-scale displacement of lower-income residents caused by public improvement and revitalization projects.

As the urban renewal program wound down and revitalization moved into the private sector, neighborhoods in and near the downtown core became gentrified, and the problem of the displacement of low-cost housing units reemerged. Though public intervention in redevelopment has matured beyond the clearance strategies of urban renewal, public subsidies and tax incentives still encourage the "higher use" of low-cost residential property. New York City's J-51 tax program, for example, was introduced in 1956 to provide incentives for investment in market-rate rental housing. The extension of that program's tax benefits to residential hotels has resulted in the conversion to luxury housing of a large portion of that city's affordable stock.[94]

New York City officials estimate that one city block of SRO hotels produces $100,000 in annual property taxes while a

250,000-square-foot office building on the same site might bring as much as $3 million.[95] In sum, low-cost inner-city housing has consistently lost out in the competition with so-called "higher uses" of land that provide property owners and managers with larger profit margins, employ more people, increase the tax base of the city, improve the aesthetic condition of the area, and promote an impression of economic vitality.

Residential hotels once constituted a significant portion of the low-cost housing stock in most urban cores. These hotels were typically situated in or near downtown locations and thus became candidates for redevelopment. Redevelopment projects rarely incorporated plans to provide new housing opportunities for hotel residents, who were typically seen as disenfranchised substance abusers more in need of treatment facilities than replacement housing units. According to Hoch and Slayton, professional planners and housing reformers led the attack on SROs, identifying in them the source of a host of social problems.[96]

Compared with residents of other redevelopment project areas, hotel residents have generally had fewer political and economic resources with which to fight demolition and displacement. Consequently, SRO units have been demolished in great numbers. By one estimate, the SRO stock in New York City shrank from 127,000 units in 1971 to less than 14,000 in 1985, an 89 percent reduction.[97] Chicago lost 80 percent of its SRO skid row units between 1960 and 1980, and close to half of its SRO stock citywide between 1973 and 1984.[98] The Gateway Center urban renewal project in Minneapolis eliminated that city's skid row and replaced it with luxury housing and office buildings. The project destroyed seventy SRO hotels with 2,272 units between 1959 and 1964.[99] In Los Angeles the number of SRO units in the skid row area near downtown declined by 26 percent between 1969 and 1987.[100] San Francisco lost 17 percent of its stock in just five years from 1975 to 1980.[101] Portland, Oregon, estimates that it lost 59 percent of its SRO stock between 1970 and 1986.[102] Seattle, Cincinnati, San Diego, and Denver have lost significant portions of their stock as well.[103]

Housing advocates began to notice the SRO hotel only by its increasing absence. As these units disappeared in ever greater numbers, many U.S. cities began to experience acute shortages at the low end of the housing market. As the last rung on the ladder of housing opportunities, SROs provided the very poor with the cheapest available accommodations. The disappearance of this stock has thus contributed to a precipitous increase in the number of homeless persons in the United States.[104]

Cities have generally approached the problem of the disappearance of low-cost downtown housing in two ways. Depending on the size of the existing stock, cities will either aim to create new affordable housing downtown or preserve the existing stock. Many cities pursue both strategies. Survey respondents were asked whether or not their city had programs either to create or to preserve lower-income housing in the downtown area, and also given the same pair of questions related to SRO housing specifically. The results are listed in Table 4.3.

Nearly half of the responding cities (48 percent) reported having programs in place to preserve lower-income housing downtown, and almost as many (45 percent) have programs to create new lower-income housing in or near their downtowns. Fewer cities reported programs specifically for SRO housing, though the number is still substantial. Close to one-fourth of the responding cities have programs aimed at creating SROs, and 18 percent are preserving their existing stock of residential hotels. State governments are less active than cities in promoting SRO housing for very low-income households. The survey respondents indicated that eleven states have programs for creating new SRO hotels, and five have programs for preserving them.

TABLE 4.3
Use of policies to preserve and create low-cost downtown housing by cities and states

Policy	Cities		States	
	N	% of 133	N	% of 48[a]
Create housing downtown	60	45		
Preserve housing downtown	64	48		
Create SRO housing	31	23	11	22
Preserve SRO housing	24	18	5	10

[a]Excluding Oklahoma and Arizona

It is somewhat surprising that more jurisdictions are actually creating new SROs than are preserving existing ones. This might suggest either that SROs have disappeared altogether in some cities and so to focus on such units means to build anew, or perhaps that the conditions in existing SROs are such that new construction is the least expensive or most feasible option. The development of new SROs is remarkable, given the fact that these units were generally regarded as obsolete and undesirable as recently as 1980.

The city of Cincinnati has made the production of SRO units part of its strategy for meeting the problem of homelessness.[105] The west coast cities of Portland, Los Angeles, and San Diego have the most developed SRO production programs. Portland's housing advisory committee officially urged the city council in 1986 to make SRO units a policy priority. Earlier, the Burnside Consortium, a neighborhood-based organization of community groups, public agencies, and private businesses formed in 1979, had contracted with the city of Portland to manage residential hotels in the neighborhood and to begin rehabilitation of SRO units.

In Los Angeles, where the downtown housing stock is typically constructed of non-reinforced masonry, one estimate suggests that over 50 percent of the buildings are in need of substantial rehabilitation to meet code requirements.[106] Compliance in many California cities is made more expensive by seismic safety requirements. Diane Suchman estimates the cost of bringing SRO units into full compliance with earthquake and building codes at $10,000 per unit.[107] Preservation of low-cost housing in the Los Angeles central business district, therefore, requires programs aimed at substantial rehabilitation. The Community Redevelopment Agency of Los Angeles (CRALA) provided $35.2 in financing for seismic and other rehabilitation to central city residential hotels.[108] The agency in 1983 formed and supported SRO Housing Corporation, a non-profit developer that has purchased fifteen hotels, completed rehabilitation on over a thousand units, and plans to begin construction of a new SRO hotel. Between 1976 and 1987 the agency committed over $43 million to the purchase and rehabilitation of some 1,450 SRO units and 1,300 shelter beds in the downtown Los Angeles area.[109]

In San Diego, the city provides infrastructure subsidies and low-interest loans to private developers of SRO housing. As of early

1990 the city had assisted in making available over 1,000 SRO units, more than 90 percent of which were newly constructed. Another 1,000 units were to be completed in the downtown area in 1990, though in the future the city plans to locate some in a neighborhood immediately north of the downtown.[110]

The SRO idea is one that has percolated up to the federal level. In 1987 the Section 8 SRO program was made part of the McKinney Homeless Act, though it was funded at the token level of $35 million. This program provides Section 8 rental subsidies to tenants in newly rehabilitated SRO units. In its first year it produced 1,000 units of SRO housing, with another 2,000 in the pipeline.

Community-Based Planning

The postfederal era has been characterized thus far by a great deal of research and planning on housing issues at the local level. With the devolution of program responsibility, most local officials were faced with meeting housing needs they had never planned for or documented. The federal government had required a minimum of local needs documentation or research-based planning through the CDBG program. Once local officials began to consider devoting their own resources to housing, however, they became interested in knowing more exactly the contours of the problem.[111] This has led to the proliferation of what can be generically called "housing advisory task forces." The formation of such a body is often the first step in a local response to de facto devolution. Besides the practical advantage of providing policy-relevant information, the formation of a consultative committee can represent the beginning of a political acceptance of responsibility for housing assistance.

As shown in Chapter 3, a common strategy for groups in the local housing movement has been to mobilize research and public education campaigns. These campaigns can serve four interrelated purposes. First, they can legitimize demands for greater housing assistance. In Minneapolis, for example, advocates disputed the city planning department's figures on the availability of low-cost housing in the downtown area and sponsored a more rigorous survey of their own.[112] Ultimately, the planning department backed off its position and accepted the figures in the community study. Second, research and public education can represent an important method of lobbying for housing advocacy groups. Housing advocates on the community newspaper the *Tenderloin Times* in San Francisco conduct an annual study of the number of homeless people who have died on the streets of that city.[113] The survey has become a powerful tool for activating greater resources for the homeless in that city. Third, public reports can marshal "allies" in the fight for low-income housing. Many prospective private-sector partners and foundations will not act until the need for assistance is duly documented. For example, in 1988 the newly formed Rochester (Minnesota) Housing Partnership spent its first $30,000 on a needs assessment documenting housing problems in the city and its surrounding area. Organizers believed they needed to make the case to potential funders in the foundation community and the private sector that even in one of the wealthier counties of Minnesota severe housing problems existed.[114]

Finally, studies and the activities of task forces can help to build consensus, or create a community of concern around the issue of housing. As Stegman and Holden point out in the case of Austin, Texas, the work of the city council's housing task force helped "the community . . . [raise] its level of consciousness regarding local housing conditions and needs. Public debate now reflects a common interest in providing for affordable housing."[115]

Case Example: Ohio

The campaign in Ohio to increase that state's commitment to low-income housing assistance provides a good example of the awakening of state and local governments to housing needs. As was the case nationally, Ohio experienced an increase in housing problems through the 1970s and 1980s. Between 1980 and 1989 median gross rents jumped 87 percent, while median renter income increased only 54 percent.[116] The increase in median renter income, however, masks a steep increase in the number of low-income renter households. During the 1980s the state gained 63,000 low-income renter households. This was coupled with the statewide loss of an estimated 90,000 affordable units. In addition, the state was experiencing a different kind of housing problem in rural areas. Rural Ohio, even more than the urban areas of the state, had a significant problem with poor-quality housing. In all, state planners felt that by 1989 they would face a gap of 200,000 affordable housing units.[117] Yet the state and all its local governments were seriously constrained in their ability to deal with housing needs because the state constitution did not recognize housing as a public purpose. Because of this, state and local governments were prohibited from making loans to private or nonprofit organizations or borrowing (in the form of revenue bonds) from private individuals for the purpose of supporting low-income housing. (Only Arizona and Alabama have similarly restrictive constitutions.)[118]

In response to this growing housing problem and the lack of a statewide response, nonprofit housing developers, social service providers, and advocates for the poor created the Ohio Housing Coalition. Formally organized in 1988, the coalition immediately began a campaign for a constitutional amendment to have housing identified as a public purpose and allow public entities to issue bonds to fund low-income housing.

Governor Richard Celeste appointed the Governor's Housing Commission in January 1989 to research the crisis and recommend solutions. Among other recommendations, the commission called for an amendment to the state constitution to make housing a public purpose. The bill to establish such an amendment was passed out of the legislature and put to the voters in 1990. Since similar measures had failed in 1975, 1978, and 1980, advocates formed Ohioans for Affordable Housing (OAH), a political action committee that campaigned intensely across the state.[119] Working in sixty five of the eighty-eight counties, OAH organized the support of major newspapers, community organizations, and the business community. The only significant opponents were the Ohio Chamber of Commerce and the Ohio Mortgage Bankers Association.[120] In November of that year, Ohio voters passed the constitutional amendment to establish housing as a public purpose by a margin of 53 to 47 percent.

Other recommendations made by the Governor's Housing Commission included elements of the progressive agenda: the creation of a housing trust fund to serve as an ongoing source of financing for low-income housing, the establishment of a "Community Housing Partnership Program" to direct resources to localities with demonstrated housing needs, and the expansion of support for nonprofit and CDC-based housing development. Support for low-income housing assistance increased in the state legislature as well. In 1989, $20 million was allocated for new housing initiatives, including $2.5 million in incentives for the preservation and development of rental and migrant-worker housing, $1.5 million for assistance to the homeless, and $4.35 million for nonprofit housing and economic development projects.[121]

SUMMARY

This chapter has attempted to outline the nature of the progressive housing paradigm and to document its widespread and growing acceptance in cities and states across the United States. Two features of housing policy in the postfederal era especially distinguish it from the preceding policy. First, rather than supporting the private sector and relying on private development to serve policy objectives, the progressive paradigm identifies the source of many housing problems in the private development process and attempts to create nonmarket mechanisms and nonmarket actors to implement housing policy. The private development process is more likely to be regulated, taxed, or replaced under the progressive paradigm than relied upon to serve low-income housing objectives. The second defining characteristic of the postfederal era is the initiative of local governments and the displacement of housing politics to a significant extent from the federal to the local level.

The progressive paradigm reassesses the assumed relationship between growth imperatives and redistributive policy. By more tightly regulating the private development process and by fostering nonmarket alternatives for housing production and ownership, the new paradigm attempts to restructure and negotiate the urban development process in order to direct benefits more equitably. Following close to thirty years of systematic destruction of low-cost housing and the pursuit of growth coalition objectives, these steps constitute only a beginning. Given the symbolic importance of, for example, downtown areas to city civic leaders, it is doubtful that downtowns will soon again see large concentrations of affordable housing. One can anticipate that in most cities the commitment to low-cost housing in the urban cores as advocated by housing activists will be carefully weighed against the continuing desire to make the city attractive to international capital and middle-income residents. It is exactly this political battle that the local housing movement has joined. As Varady and Birdsell point out: "Low-income housing advocates are faced with the dilemma of how to persuade policymakers to retain low-income housing while demonstrating that such housing preservation will not harm economic growth."[122]

To date, these two policy objectives have stood in opposition to each other. In some cities, however, the link between affordable housing and the continued growth of the economy is a positive one. One study of Boston, for example, found that the lack of affordable housing options for workers could cause Boston's economic boom to falter.[123] Given the continuation of this country's urban housing crisis and increasing housing advocacy at the local level, it may be that urban revitalization will take on a new character: a careful balance of low-income housing needs with commercial revitalization objectives. Given the evidence presented here, it seems likely that at a minimum the continued economic development of urban areas will be forced to accommodate a greater level of lower-income housing uses than has historically been the case.

The dual objectives of growth and equity in development are pursued primarily through the regulation of the private sector and through greater reliance on a nonprofit sector.[124] This chapter has focused on the regulatory aspects of the new housing paradigm; however, the establishment of sufficient capacity within the nonprofit housing sector to carry the burden of this country's low-income housing production goals is an equally important tenet of the progressive approach. The following chapter examines this issue.

5
The Role of Nonprofit Housing Developers

THE CENTERPIECE of the new housing paradigm is the establishment of a nonprofit housing sector that is dedicated to the production and maintenance of a stock of permanently affordable low-income housing.[1] The basic premise of the progressive approach to housing is that the past reliance on the private sector to provide affordable housing has simply not worked. On the one hand, the private sector does not produce affordable housing on its own; it has been many years since the private market produced low-cost units without substantial government subsidy. On the other hand, the new housing paradigm sees flaws in the subsidy and incentive programs that have been designed to attract private developers to low-income housing. Instead, the development of a nonprofit sector that is capable of large-scale production and ownership is seen as the mechanism by which a "social housing sector" in the United States might be developed.[2] The social housing sector is housing that is neither resold as a commodity for speculation nor managed for profit taking. Ownership is vested in public authorities or nonprofit, community-based organizations.[3]

Nonprofit and voluntary associations have historically played an important role in the delivery system for human and social services in the United States.[4] Governments at all levels have looked to nonprofit organizations to provide a range of government-funded services such as community health care, education, and social services. As a result, the nonprofit sector has grown over the past fifty years, in step with the increasing responsibilities of the welfare state.[5] Despite the contraction in government activity during the 1980s, nonprofits continue to play large roles in delivering basic human and social services. The nonprofit community development corporation implements government housing assistance programs by purchasing and rehabilitating housing for lower-income households. In doing so, the CDC fits firmly into the historical tradition of nonprofit service delivery.

But CDCs also have historical antecedents in the antipoverty and community-based movements of the 1960s and 1970s. Born in the midst of President Lyndon Johnson's Great Society antipoverty programs in the early 1960s, the CDC was seen as the means by which poor neighborhoods might achieve a greater measure of political and economic power.[6] The CDC was a vehicle of social change, both manifestation of and agent for community empowerment. The CDC was envisioned as a truly community-based expression of priorities and needs that would guide neighborhood development in ways that would serve the needs of residents. Rooted in a fundamental political and economic struggle by disadvantaged neighborhoods, CDCs were, in fact, the institutional expression of that struggle and proliferated during the 1970s, an era of neighborhood-based activism that led to a "neighborhood movement" in the United States.[7]

This history puts CDCs into a tradition entirely different from the more apolitical, technical service delivery framework mentioned earlier. Yet, both histories are true, both traditions valid. These nonprofits have continually faced the inherent tension between these two missions, tension made more extreme by the close and codependent relationship between CDCs and the state. This chapter provides a profile of the nonprofit sector in housing, presents survey data on the ways in which local and state governments are assisting in the development of nonprofit-sector capacity, evaluates theoretical arguments regarding the politics of CDCs, and provides four models that represent the political and technical relationships formed between nonprofits and local governments.

COMMUNITY DEVELOPMENT CORPORATIONS: A PROFILE

The growth of the nonprofit sector has been very pronounced in the community development arena. Community development corporations have greatly increased in number and in scope since their introduction in the 1960s.[8] A national study of CDCs completed in 1989 put the average age of these organizations at twelve years.

Roughly one-quarter of them were born prior to 1972, over one-half emerged from 1972 to 1980, and about one-fifth since 1980.[9] Though they were clearly not created as a response to governmental cutbacks in social and housing services, CDCs have taken on greater importance since the budgetary retrenchment of the late 1970s and 1980s. The 1980s witnessed significant growth in the size of CDCs and the range of activities undertaken by nonprofit organizations.[10] Only 21 percent of CDCs in a national study reported no growth between 1983 and 1988, whereas 79 percent reported substantial or moderate growth.[11] Though there were fewer than 500 CDCs in operation across the country during the 1970s, there were, by 1991, between 1,500 and 2,000.[12]

Though CDCs undertake a number of different activities, the largest are the production and management of affordable housing. In a national study the National Congress for Community Economic Development (NCCED) found that 87 percent of the CDCs in their survey were performing some housing functions, while one-half of their sample did *only* housing development or management.[13] With growing importance in local efforts, nonprofit CDCs are in many markets the only actors involved in developing low-income housing.[14]

The growing interest in nonprofits is partially an evolutionary change and partially a response to specific contemporary problems. The expiration of the affordability requirements contained in federal subsidy loans to private developers since 1960 has resulted in a potentially sizable loss of low-income housing units. Nonprofit housing corporations are increasingly being looked to as a solution to this problem because they are less likely to convert units to market rate after the expiration of subsidies.[15] Because they offer advantages that for-profit producers do not, CDCs have gained a prominence in affordable housing production: they provide for greater tenant control of housing; they better target lower-income households; they have better access to and relations with low-income communities; and they generally have a better understanding of local needs.[16]

The NCCED reports that nonprofit CDCs are active in every state.[17] They are mainly though not exclusively an urban phenomenon. Only one in five CDCs in the NCCED study reported a rural base; 15 percent indicated both an urban and a rural constituency. The remaining 65 percent were operating only in urban areas. Among major cities, CDCs are almost universal. In my survey sample, 95 percent of the cities reported having nonprofit CDCs working on affordable housing (see Table 5.1). In 45 percent of the cities there were fewer than five CDCs; 35 percent had five to ten nonprofit housing developers; the remaining 16 percent reported more than ten such organizations.[18]

Production

The number of units produced by the nonprofit CDCs in 1989 (see Table 5.1) varies widely from 0 (in eighteen cities, including the seven cities that reported having no CDCs) to a high of 2,200 (in Nashville). Thirty-six cities (28 percent) reported that nonprofits produced over 100 units in 1989, and in nine of those cities CDCs produced more than 500 units. The number of units produced is also positively correlated with city size (r .42, $p < .001$). The cities in this sample report some 17,000 units developed by CDCs in

TABLE 5.1
Number of nonprofit housing developers and number of housing units produced by nonprofits in responding cities, 1989

	Cities	
	N	%
CDCs		
0	7	5
1–4	59	45
5–10	45	35
11	20	16
Missing cases	2	
Units Produced		
0–10	38	29
11–50	39	30
51–100	17	13
101–500	27	21
501	9	7
Missing cases	3	

1989. Extrapolated to all 177 U.S. cities with populations greater than 100,000, the production figure for CDCs in 1989 stands at over 23,000 units. Thousands more are produced in smaller cities and rural areas. The NCCED survey found an output of 23,120 units produced by the CDCs in its sample over a two-year period, 1986 and 1987.[19] The New School survey (based on 1989 rates of production) estimates that nationally, CDCs produce close to 45,000 units per year.[20] For the *two-year* period 1986–87, HUD-subsidized housing completions totaled 77,364, or 38,682 per year (excluding vouchers and Section 8 rental certificates for existing housing).[21] Thus, according to the figures in the New School study, nonprofit developers were producing new and rehabilitated units of affordable housing at roughly the same rate as HUD during this period. Though this says nothing about the level of production relative to need, the figures do indicate that the CDC sector has developed a production capacity roughly equal to the federal government's low-income housing output.

Roles

Housing nonprofits typically engage in one of several major roles. The most sophisticated role for nonprofits is the intermediary model in which the nonprofit acts as a financial agent, collecting the investment capital of private corporations (tax credit investments, for example), private foundations, and the public sector. As an intermediary, the nonprofit then disburses the money (generally through low-interest loans) to the developers who actually produce the housing. This is the manner in which the national nonprofit organization Local Initiatives Support Corporation (LISC) operates; it is also the model used by the Boston and Chicago housing partnerships.

A second role is the developer model, in which the nonprofit actively seeks out property or land to purchase and develop into affordable housing. This is the most common model followed by CDCs. The New School survey revealed that 86 percent of CDCs were developers.[22] The nonprofit developer's main task is finding new and creative ways of developing low-income housing in an era of federal government nonparticipation.

Alternatively, a housing nonprofit can provide nondevelopment housing services. Such services might include managing low-income units (the New School survey showed that 56 percent of housing CDCs provided management services), offering tenant counseling and tenants' rights services, or acting as an information clearinghouse for low-income tenants, homeowners, and home buyers.

Finally, in the advocacy model the nonprofit acts primarily as a political agent advocating for greater low-income housing assistance. Groups fulfill this role by providing citizen education and information as well as by lobbying elected officials. Given their historical roots in community action and antipoverty struggles, most CDCs retain some degree of advocacy; in the New School survey sample, 87 percent engaged in housing advocacy.

Despite the variety of roles played by CDCs and the overlap between them, the developer and advocacy models are the two most important simply because they are the most common. They are also important because of the inherent tension between them. Development and advocacy objectives can conflict in two important ways. First, the technical nature of housing development requires expertise, technical and financial training that is often at odds with the more democratic, neighborhood-based orientation of low-income housing advocacy. The greater the need for technical proficiency and the greater the professionalization of activities, the more likely it is that the CDC will have to rely on personnel who are not rooted in community concerns or neighborhood-based struggles. Second, the close ties of CDCs with local governments through funding can create a tension between the pursuit of development objectives and the pursuit of political objectives. This is especially acute if the object of political action is the local government that substantially funds and supports the nonprofit. These dual tensions between development and advocacy define the politics of CDCs, examined more fully below.

Needs

Nonprofit producers of affordable housing require support in four specific ways; they require ongoing administrative support, predevelopment capital, project capital, and technical assistance.[23]

Nonprofit CDCs cannot rely on project revenues for ongoing administrative funds. Given their mission to produce affordable housing for low-income households, the cash flow from most CDC housing projects is minimal if it exists at all. Finding resources to pay for staff and administrative expenses is therefore a continuing problem for CDCs. Administrative funding was the most-mentioned funding priority in surveys of CDCs in New York City, Minneapolis–St. Paul, Los Angeles, and the state of Minnesota.[24] The typical sources of administrative support are the government and private foundations, but these must be tapped anew each year or two as grants expire. A small percentage of CDCs have regular and reliable sources of support such as a sponsor organization or an endowment fund; the majority, however, are in a continual search for administrative funds to support the office activities of the organization.

A second regular need of CDCs is predevelopment financing, or funding to cover expenses incurred on a project before it is begun. In fact, CDCs in the Los Angeles area mentioned the lack of predevelopment and bridge financing as their largest impediment to greater productivity.[25] Unlike for-profit developers, CDCs do not have a ready reserve or cash balance to cover these predevelopment expenses.

Beyond predevelopment financing, CDCs require project capital: low-interest financing for "hard costs" related to property acquisition and construction. Again, the objective of providing low-cost housing to lower-income households precludes heavy reliance on conventional financing. Nonprofits therefore must seek low-cost financing elsewhere. The most prominent source of project capital is the public sector.[26] As the federal government has reduced the amount of low-income housing assistance it provides, cities and states have attempted to make up some of the difference with innovative local programs. Another source of project capital is foundation money. Sometimes special nonprofit intermediaries, such as LISC and the Enterprise Foundation act to channel low-interest financing to nonprofits.[27] Where this occurs, CDCs have a regular source of project capital.

Finally, CDCs are typically in need of some degree of technical assistance and expertise.[28] Many have small staffs (partly because of the difficulty in obtaining administrative support) and thus have to contract out for design, architectural, engineering, and construction supervision expertise.[29] Legal expertise and assistance in project planning and syndications are also needed by nonprofits, as is property management. By paying for such expertise on a project-by-project basis, the CDC amortizes the cost into the project itself, rather than funding one or more staff positions on a regular basis.

CDCS AND LOCAL HOUSING SERVICE DELIVERY SYSTEMS

Local governments and nonprofit CDCs are in a position of mutual dependence in the pursuit of low-income housing objectives.[30] The nonprofit organizations depend on the government to provide financial support, and government relies upon nonprofit groups to deliver an array of social and human services. Despite this mutual dependence, there is no uniform method by which local governments provide support to nonprofit CDCs. Indeed, the relationship between government and nonprofit CDCs at state and municipal levels, and the ways in which local governments link themselves with CDCs to provide affordable housing, vary significantly. Where most studies of the nonprofit sector have focused on CDCs, here the analysis focuses on the governmental unit (states; cities with populations over 100,000), and the research question relates to how these governments incorporate the nonprofit sector into their local housing delivery systems.

Though nonprofits are increasingly active locally, there is little systematic knowledge about how local governments are incorporating CDCs into housing policy implementation or whether they are providing the assistance necessary for CDCs to operate effectively. Rachel Bratt provides a description and analysis of the state of Massachusetts and its programs in support of community-based housing.[31] Massachusetts has created a well-developed system of support that "includes all of the necessary funding and subsidy mechanisms" to maintain a community-based housing strategy.[32] In Massachusetts and most other locations the ties between nonprofit CDCs and the government are very strong. Nonprofit organizations are reliant upon government for a large portion of their revenues.[33] A study of New York City CDCs found that 76 percent received funding from the state government, 67 percent from the city, and 17 percent from federal sources.[34] A national study found that 92 percent of the surveyed CDCs received federal funds (the largest portion from the Community Development Block Grant, which is allocated locally), 53 percent received state funds, and 42 percent received local government funds.[35] The financial ties between the public sector and CDCs are indeed very strong.

Local Government Support for Nonprofit Developers

My survey respondents were asked to indicate whether their jurisdictions provided each of the four means of support described in the previous section: project capital, predevelopment financing, administrative support, and technical assistance. Table 5.2 provides a summary of the responses.

Funding for nonprofit housing developers' administrative costs is provided by seventy-five of the responding cities (59 percent) and twenty two of the responding states (47 percent). The most common form of support provided by local governments is development capital; 82 percent of the cities reported making project financing available to nonprofit housing developers, as did 63 percent of the states. Even predevelopment financing, the least common form of support in cities, is offered by over one-half (52 percent) of both cities and states. Finally, 56 percent of the cities and 52 percent of the states reported providing technical assistance to nonprofit housing developers operating in their jurisdictions.

The cities that provide funding support for CDCs do so primarily from their CDBG program. Table 5.3 examines the source of funds in those cities that provide predevelopment, development,

TABLE 5.2

Support for nonprofit housing developers provided by responding cities and states, 1989

Form of Support	Cities		States	
	N^a	%	N^b	%
Administrative funding	75	59	22	47
Project financing	104	82	30	63
Predevelopment financing	65	52	25	52
Technical assistance	70	56	25	52

[a] of 124 cities that reported having nonprofit housing developers
[b] of 48 responding states

TABLE 5.3
Sources of funding for support to nonprofit housing developers

	States		Cities		
Source	Admin. Funding	Project Capital	Admin. Funding	Predev. Funding	Project Capital
CDBG	1 (4)	1 (3)	67 (94)	57 (89)	87 (88)
Redevelopment agency			7 (10)	11 (17)	13 (13)
City general funds			6 (8)	4 (6)	5 (5)
State	17 (77)	17 (57)	2 (3)	4 (6)	5 (5)
Other city			1 (1)	3 (5)	15 (14)
Other federal				2 (3)	19 (19)
State bonds	5 (23)	12 (40)			
Housing trust fund	4 (18)	3 (10)			
N	22	30	71	64	99
Missing cases			4	1	5

Note: Figures are the number of cities or states reporting each funding source. Figures in parentheses are percentages of the column's N.

or administrative funding. As the table shows, close to 90 percent of responding cities offering financial support were using CDBG funds for this purpose. The second most common source of funding was the local redevelopment agency, typically through tax increment financing. This source was used for administrative funding by 10 percent of the cities, and for predevelopment financing by 17 percent. General operating funds were used by less than 10 percent of the cities, as were state funds. Other federal funds (usually the rental rehabilitation program) and other local funds were most commonly used as sources of project capital for nonprofit developers. Even then, they were used for those purposes by less than one city in five.

For states, the financing picture is somewhat different. Their reported programs of support for nonprofits were in almost all cases funded by state revenues. Over 77 percent of the states providing administrative support to nonprofits were doing so from state appropriations, another 23 percent from bond revenues or reserves, and 18 percent from their housing trust funds. In fact, only one of the twenty-two states providing administrative support used federal funds for this purpose. Project financing was similarly weighted to own-source expenditures. Only one of the thirty states providing project financing to nonprofits use non-state-generated revenues.

The technical assistance provided by responding cities and states ranged from general organizational planning to architectural design and construction supervision (see Table 5.4). For the most part, the percentage of city and state governments providing each form of assistance was similar. The most common form of assistance from cities, provided by 47 percent, was project-specific financial analysis.[36] States provided this type of assistance somewhat less frequently; it appeared in only 36 percent of the states. Construction monitoring and project supervision was offered by 34 percent of the cities and 32 percent of the states. Design and architectural assistance was provided by 31 percent of the cities and 28 percent of the states. The major difference between cities and states in the technical assistance they offered to CDCs was in the area of general organizational planning. Though very few cities (11 percent) were offering comprehensive organizational planning, this function was by far the most common form of state assistance: a full 68 percent of the states that provided technical assistance included it.

Capacity Building

The provision of these and other forms of support is commonly referred to as "capacity-building" assistance. Several states and localities have recently adopted capacity-building programs that

TABLE 5.4
Technical assistance provided to CDCs by state and local governments

Form of Assistance	Cities (%)	States (%)
Construction management	34	32
Project (financial) feasibility	47	36
Design and architectural	31	28
Construction specs and engineering	25	32
Organizational planning	11	68
N	61	25
Missing cases	9	

incorporate many of the elements described above. In North Carolina, for example, the state's HTF funds a $1.5 million "nonprofit development fund" that provides administrative grants, predevelopment financing, financial packaging assistance, and project financing.[37] The Vermont capacity program offers "broad-based" organizational support via grants of up to $40,000, and "project-specific" assistance with feasibility studies, architectural and engineering services, or predevelopment financing.[38] Pittsburgh has established a city fund for project financing but also contributes to the Pittsburgh Partnership for Neighborhood Development, provides technical assistance and operating funds for nonprofits. The Minnesota Housing Partnership has successfully advocated for a legislatively funded program of capacity building for nonprofits. In addition, the Housing Finance Agency in that state has held a series of meetings with nonprofit developers in an attempt to better incorporate them into the agency's programs.[39]

THE POLITICS OF LOCAL NONPROFIT HOUSING

The mutual dependence of nonprofits and local governments highlights the tension between a technical service delivery orientation and the advocacy of low-income housing and neighborhood issues. Despite the community-based origins of many CDCs, some observers maintain that they tend to be apolitical or too technocratic and nonrepresentative.[40] Indeed, there is evidence that CDCs have become more technical and less oppositional in their approach to neighborhood development issues. The New School survey showed that even though 53 percent of the nonprofits pointed to community-based struggles as the important impetus to their creation, most groups were moving from confrontational to cooperative strategy on neighborhood development.[41] What is clearly driving this change in strategy is the ever greater reliance on government and private-sector funding.[42]

This is, in fact, the very dynamic described by Gittell in her study of citizen participation.[43] Examining sixteen community organizations in three cities, she found that groups in poor and working-class neighborhoods shifted their strategy over time from advocacy to service delivery. "Participants in lower class organizations explained the shift from advocacy and political action and toward a service role as the result of two problems: inability to sustain long-term advocacy efforts which required major investments of time by large numbers of people, and inability to secure financial support to maintain organizational structure."[44] Government funding of services was a way for these groups to solve their funding problem and their organizational maintenance problems. Gittell concludes that the shift to service delivery "raises some serious questions with regard to whether community organizations form a vital mechanism for lower-income groups to gain access to the political system."[45]

In a similar vein, Piven and Cloward argue in *Poor People's Movements* that the essence of insurgent political or social movements exists despite, not because of, the organizational structures created by activists. Organizations that endure, they assert, do so "by abandoning their oppositional politics."[46] This results from the growing demands that organizational maintenance makes of group leaders. In order to compete for the resources necessary to keep the organization viable, they abandon strict oppositional strategies so as not to alienate potential (financial) supporters.

More recently, analysts have directly questioned the political relevance of CDCs. Lenz argues that neighborhood-based development organizations are "ignoring their roots in political protest and organizing" and have thus lost touch with their poor constituents.[47] Organizations that provide technical services such as housing are forced to rely on a cadre of professionally trained workers able to negotiate the complicated process of land and housing development. The ethos of professionalism, according to Lenz, conflicts with the more democratic ethos of community-based political advocacy. Thus, CDCs run the risk of becoming seriously detached from the real political interests of the communities they nominally represent.[48] In sum, these arguments suggest that for reasons related to the conservatizing effects of (1) organizational maintenance, (2) government funding, and (3) the technocratic nature of land development, the advocacy potential of CDCs faces serious limitations. Furthermore, CDCs may even represent a negative potential for housing advocacy to the extent that they divert attention and effort from more mass-based political action.

Maintaining Activism

Those arguments, however, tend to overemphasize the singular role of CDCs in the community housing movement and underemphasize the extent to which they contribute to other organizing efforts that are more overtly political in nature. A common strategy undertaken by CDCs is to contribute to the efforts of other groups that are formed specifically for the purpose of housing and neighborhood advocacy. It is the rare CDC that is cut off from the network of organizations acting at the local and neighborhood level on development and planning issues. Coalition building among CDCs and across housing organizations is likely, however, to require a "critical mass" of organizations. That is, we can expect that the more CDCs there are in a given place, the more likely they are to join a formal coalition to further political and organizational objectives. Such coalitions provide crucial political support and a means of political participation for nonprofit organizations incorporated under the 501(c)(3) statute, which legally prohibits them from directly engaging in political action. In addition, the coalitions often provide technical assistance and informational services to their members.

This expectation is supported by the survey findings. One questionnaire item asked city officials whether CDCs in their city were neighborhood-based or citywide in scope. In only 35 percent of cities with fewer than five CDCs were they characterized as primarily or exclusively neighborhood-based. On the other hand, respondents in 70 percent of the cities with more than ten CDCs indicated they were neighborhood-based ($X^2 = 21.7$, $p < .001$). This means that CDCs were more likely to "carve up" the community and serve neighborhood-based needs in those cities where they were more plentiful. In places where there were few CDCs, they tended to have citywide or regional scope. It is also logical to presume the more CDCs there are in a city, the greater the potential for them to form a coalition among themselves. This hypothesis is borne out by the data: officials in only 10 percent of the cities with fewer than five CDCs reported the existence of a CDC coalition, compared with 84 percent in cities with more than ten CDCs ($X^2 = 39.4$, $p < .001$). Thus, the more CDCs there are, the greater the likelihood that they have created their own coalitional body.

When these data are combined with the information reported in Chapter 3 on citywide low-income housing advocacy groups, the scope of local political action for housing and the role of CDCs in that process becomes clearer. As previously reported, eighty-five cities (64 percent) have an active housing advocacy coalition. The existence of such an advocacy group, combined with the existence of the CDC coalition, creates an index measuring the level of organization of community-based housing interests. That variable, ACTIVISM, ranges in value from 0 to 2 and is strongly and positively correlated with the number of CDCs present in a city ($r = .47$, $p < .001$). Thus, as the number of CDCs grows, so does the likelihood that they are involved in coalitional strategies to support one another and to advocate for low-income housing issues in general.

The weakness of the Lenz and the Piven and Cloward approach is that it does not account for the organizational context within which individual CDCs operate. It may well be true that, individually, CDCs are forced to conservatize themselves somewhat because of financial and organizational imperatives, but they remain supportive of complementary political action taken by other groups organized for that specific purpose. In addition, those arguments tend to overlook the *codependence* in the relationship between local officials and CDCs. The community base of CDCs, their legitimacy in the community, and their expertise in creating and managing affordable housing are each very useful to public officials. The nonprofit corporations represent a political constituency and therefore provide elected officials with an efficient method of reaching that constituency through the provision of technical or financial support. For program officials, CDCs provide an effective means of implementing housing assistance programs. These political resources provide CDCs with a greater entree to local government than might exist otherwise.

Profile: Seattle

The Seattle Housing Development Consortium (SHDC) is an incorporated coalition of nonprofit housing developers.[49] Around 1980 and for a number of years afterward, nonprofit developers and housing advocates in the city met on an informal, ad hoc basis to discuss housing and development issues. Collective action among the groups was slow in coming because for many years the nonprofits looked upon one another as competitors for the same shrinking CDBG pie. In 1985, however, Seattle voters created the Housing Levy Program (see Chapter 4), and the city's support of nonprofit housing began to escalate. Housing advocates felt at that point that they needed a more formal organization in order to influence and shape the way the city government dealt with nonprofits. In 1986 the city awarded a contract to the advocates to assist in a review of Seattle's housing assistance programs. Shortly afterward the advocates incorporated SHDC, whose eighteen member organizations have, among them, developed 4,239 units of low-income housing since 1975.[50] Many of the coalition members work on a regional basis, producing housing throughout much of the Puget Sound and western Washington area. The groups provide housing that ranges from SRO hotel units in the International District near downtown Seattle to renovated and newly built homes for first time home buyers.

The organization's core activities are policy development, fund raising, and the provision of technical assistance. In policy development, SHDC works actively at the local level through the city council as well as through administrative contacts in the city's Community Development Department. The consortium's early agenda was to create a better working relationship with the city government and to disseminate information about nonprofits and the need for low-income housing assistance. In 1989, SHDC proposed that the city adopt standardized loan documents for its rehabilitation programs. The coalition created the first drafts and worked with city attorney's office to come up with the final version of the documents the city now uses. The executive director of SHDC also serves as chair of the statewide low-income housing coalition, which has successfully worked on the passage and funding of a state housing trust fund. SHDC also pursued capacity-building support for CDCs by proposing to the state a system of "peer counseling" in order to provide technical assistance to nonprofits. The state now contracts out to SHDC and other groups for the provision of technical assistance to nonprofits. Thus, the organization plays a role in policy development both at the local level, through assisting the review of city policies and developing program implementation guidelines, and at the state level, through the successful housing trust fund campaign and the provision of technical assistance to local nonprofits.

Like so many of the housing advocacy coalitions described in Chapter 3, SHDC and other nonprofit coalitions play dual roles as advocates and program administrators. They lobby for policy change while simultaneously working with public agencies to implement existing programs. In their status as subcontractors they are agents of the state; in their status as lobbyists, they attempt to alter state policy. Rather than being contradictory, these roles have been made by SHDC and other groups in the housing movement to serve each other. The group's technical development expertise has given credence and authority to its lobbying demands, while its community base makes it indispensable to the state in the implementation of policy that is increasingly aimed in that direction.

As CDCs become more expert at housing development, they strengthen their status as an important element in the local housing service delivery system. Indeed, in those cities in which nonprofits are the major implementer of housing assistance, the distinction between the "success" of the local public agency and the "success" of CDCs becomes blurred. This leads to a much greater integration of CDCs into the entire range of policymaking roles. Public agencies in these cities look to them not only to implement policy but also for advice and input in policy formation.

On the electoral side, CDCs generally represent constituencies of poor communities. The data have shown that where more CDCs exist, they tend to be neighborhood-based. Supporting CDCs is thus a political act for elected officials who might wish to show support for neighborhood constituents.[51] In an important way, then, CDCs offer advantages to both elected officials and local development bureaucrats. This has placed them at the center of the housing development policy process in many U.S. cities. To the extent that they retain their advocacy orientation—and this analysis suggests that they can and do, through support of coalitional strategies—CDCs can achieve increased policy influence without sacrificing advocacy goals.

This is not to suggest that CDCs or the housing movement have in some way "won" the local political battle for low income housing, but only that they are more integral players than ever before. As the Los Angeles case study in Chapter 6 shows, the process of political influence is dynamic, and greater decisionmaking access is not a guarantee of effective policy change.

INCORPORATING CDCS IN LOW-INCOME HOUSING DELIVERY SYSTEMS

The incorporation of CDCs into policy implementation is, at least in part, a political arrangement between local housing advocates and public officials. How these political arrangements are made at the local level, however, is subject to wide variation. As a tentative typology of the arrangements that exist in different jurisdictions between the community-based housing sector and the local government, four models can be isolated. These models differ primarily along dimensions that reflect the basic needs of CDCs: that is, arrangements for administrative funding, availability of project capital, the existence of financial intermediaries, and the provision of technical assistance to CDCs. The models range from (1) government sponsorship of CDCs, in which each of the primary needs is provided for by the local government, through (2) partnership and (3) a community-based network to (4) a condition of pre-organization in which there exists no *systematic* source of support to CDCs in any of the need areas. In addition, the models differ in the extent to which the nonprofit sector is organized and in the nature of local government—CDC relations.

These models exist in varying degrees in localities with active nonprofit housing activity; they may, in fact, exist simultaneously in the same city. Further, there can be a fair degree of fluidity in these arrangements. The typology is meant to characterize the dominant form of relations between public and nonprofit sectors in the housing arena and to isolate relationships among CDCs and between CDCs and the government. The distinctions made in these models are an attempt to capture variations in institutional and programmatic relationships created by local public and nonprofit sectors in low-income housing production.

Model 1: Local Government Sponsorship

In this model the local jurisdiction provides for each of the primary needs of the nonprofit housing sector. It is the regular and ongoing provision of organizational support to nonprofits, plus its source in the local government that sets this model apart from the others. San Francisco provides the best example of this model at the municipal level. Through the Mayor's Office of Housing, the city provides CDBG funds for the ongoing operating expenses of eleven CDCs. These CDCs, acting as regular subgrantees in the city's CDBG program, provide housing development (new construction and rehabilitation), management, architectural, and housing counseling services. The city has funded eight of these nonprofits to produce low- and moderate-income housing in six different target neighborhoods. Since 1980 these CDCs have played the major role in housing rehabilitation and the construction of new affordable housing in the city. The operating expense grants provided by the city in 1990 represented, on the average, 54 percent of the administrative funds utilized by these eight development corporations.[52]

Additionally, the city sets aside $2 to $4 million annually in project capital pools for the exclusive use of the nonprofit developers. The 1989 San Francisco CDBG programs funded a site acquisition pool in the amount of $2.5 million and a community housing rehabilitation program in the amount of $1.9 million. The city also funds the operating expenses of two technical service corporations, which in turn provide "free" assistance to the nonprofit development corporations funded by the city. These technical corporations, their operating expenses underwritten by the city, are able to offer low-cost architectural, engineering, design, and construction expertise to the development corporations, thus reducing the cost of housing production.

The city's CDBG program, which is the source of administrative and program funding for the nonprofits, provides the regular linkage between the local government and CDCs. There are other nonprofits operating in San Francisco outside this government-sponsored network. A regional nonprofit called BRIDGE is the largest of these; the Catholic Archdiocese, through its nonprofit Catholic Charities, is also active in local low-income housing. But these nonprofits represent the minority in both number of CDCs and the amount of housing developed in the city.

Massachusetts approaches the sponsorship model at the state level, with perhaps the most developed set of support systems for nonprofits.[53] The state provides financial assistance through the Massachusetts Housing Finance Agency and the Community Development Finance Corporation. Another quasi-public state agency, the Community Economic Development Assistance Corporation, supplies nonprofit community-based organizations with technical assistance. Finally, the Community Enterprise Economic Development program provides administrative support and startup funds for nonprofit organizations.

True government sponsorship of CDCs implies a depth as well as breadth of support. Besides San Francisco and Massachusetts, in thirty-six cities (28 percent) and 15 states (31 percent) all four forms of assistance are provided by the public sector. What sets San Francisco and Massachusetts apart from many of these others is the depth of their support. The operating support and project capital provided by San Francisco represents the core of financial support for the CDCs in the city. The technical assistance and the predevelopment financing by the city often meet 100 percent of the nonprofits needs in those areas. Because of the level of public subsidy required in such a system, the government sponsorship model is not widespread.

Model 2: Partnership

The partnership model refers to those local governments in which the local public, private, and nonprofit sectors have come together to form institutional and programmatic partnerships to provide low-income housing. Boston and Chicago are the two prominent examples of cities operating under this model. The institutional partnerships play the role that government plays in Model 1—that is, the partnerships channel project capital and technical assistance to nonprofit development corporations—but the partnership model does not provide the same level of ongoing administrative support for nonprofits as does the sponsorship model.

Stegman and Holden call the Chicago and Boston Housing Partnerships "prototypes of a new kind of local institution."[54] These partnerships bring together public, private, and nonprofit actors engaged in housing production. The cities participate by contributing capital for project development; in Boston, both the city and the state government provide capital to the partnership. The private sector is represented by the mortgage financing of local lenders and the investments of insurance companies and other private investors. The nonprofit sector is represented by neighborhood-based housing development corporations. In Chicago, LISC, a national nonprofit housing investor, is a partnership member. The partnership, with representatives from each of these sectors, allocates financing resources to the CDCs, which are the actual project developers.

The partnerships thus serve as locally constituted financial intermediaries, attracting both public and private financing and channeling that capital to nonprofit developers. In addition, the Chicago partnership offers the nonprofit developers various forms of technical assistance, from project feasibility analysis to the assembly of a development team, and the Boston partnership provides its nonprofit developers with predevelopment funds as well as regular project capital. Similar partnerships, acting as intermediaries for local CDCs, exist in other cities such as Tampa, Dallas, and Cleveland.[55]

The Wisconsin Partnership for Housing Development (WPHD) is an example of the partnership model of state-CDC relations. Established in 1985, it was the first statewide housing partnership. Taking the classic partnership role, WPHD is not a housing developer; instead, it acts as a financial and technical intermediary, channeling investment capital and technical assistance to (primarily community-based) housing developers throughout the state. The WPHD was established by the state legislature and given seed funds by the Wisconsin Housing and Economic Development Authority.[56] Since its state-aided start-up, however, WHPD has primarily concentrated on raising capital from private foundations and investors and has also received HUD funds to cover the provision of technical assistance.[57]

Both partnership and sponsorship models involve locally constituted "intermediaries" channeling resources to the nonprofits. In fact, the existence of these intermediaries and the reliability of their support are the primary advantages of these models. In model 1 the intermediary is the local government, and in model 2 it is the partnership. In most cases where the partnership model exists, a strong network of CDCs helped to prompt its formation. For example, it was the Cleveland Housing Network, an organization of inner-city CDCs, that initiated formation of the Cleveland Housing Partnership. Very strong nonprofit housing sectors exist in Chicago and Boston as well.

In the final two models there are neither locally constituted intermediaries nor other regular and reliable sources of development support. In fact, models 3 and 4 are distinguished not by a government-CDC relationship but by the degree of organization within the nonprofit sector.

Model 3: Community-based Network

In cities where the community-based network model exists, there is no formal, systematic, or ongoing relationship between the local government and CDCs. Local CDCs are organized into coalition-like bodies that generally provide two distinct benefits to members: a relatively low level (compared with models 1 and 2 above) of technical assistance and access to financing, and political advocacy on housing and community development issues. Without a locally constituted intermediary to provide and channel project capital, let alone administrative support, CDCs rely on their own organization for political and sometimes technical resources. Infrequently, there may be regular or extensive public- and private-sector involvement in the CDC network.

The survey data have indicated that coalitions of nonprofits are fairly common and more common in cities with a greater number of CDCs. The nonprofit housing coalitions that exist in seventeen states and in two-thirds of large U.S. cities are in line with a more general trend toward "organizing" the nonprofit sector. Associations of nonprofit organizations that cross functional categories such as housing and health and social services are becoming more common in the United States.[58] Their greatest utility to member CDCs is in political advocacy.[59] These coalitions provide nonprofit organizations with a political arm that works for public policies supportive of nonprofit missions.

St. Paul and Minneapolis are examples of the community-based network model. In St. Paul twenty-one organizations, including twelve nonprofit housing developers, make up the Coalition for Community Development. Organized in 1984, the coalition brought together neighborhood-based developers to discuss the basic needs of the organizations and ways to communicate those needs to the local public and private sectors. The coalition's activities have thus been political or advocacy-based from the beginning. For example, it has negotiated Community Reinvestment Act compliance with local lenders and provided assistance in drafting the city's vacant housing policy initiative. The Coalition has been very active in the development of the city's Comprehensive Housing Affordability Strategy (CHAS), mandated by the National Affordable Housing Act of 1990. In addition to this advocacy the coalition offers limited technical assistance to members.

The situation is similar in Minneapolis, where CDCs organized themselves into the Minneapolis Nonprofit Consortium in 1980. The impetus for organizing was a threat on the part of the city to withdraw sponsorship of a number of nonprofits. The consortium traded that administrative support for a regular source of project capital for development projects. As a result of the consortium's lobbying effort, the city sets aside a pool of funds for the rehabilitation of low-income rental housing; nonprofits must compete with for-profits for these funds, however. Currently, the consortium serves primarily as a political and organizational resource for its members.

At the state level, coalitions of nonprofits and statewide housing coalitions often provide services to their members. In Illinois the Statewide Housing Action Coalition receives a contract from the state to provide technical assistance to groups. A similar system operates in Washington, where the state uses a network of consultants, including local coalitions, to provide technical assistance to nonprofit developers.

Model 4: Preorganization

Cities in which CDCs exist and are active but, as of 1991, were not organized are represented in this sample by San Antonio, New Orleans, Omaha, and others. Public support of nonprofit activity is sporadic and dependent mainly on the political resources and initiative of individual CDCs. The public support that is provided is likely to be project-specific rather than program-wide. Private-sector participation is similarly, unorganized. As in the community-network model there is no locally constituted financial intermediary that serves as a clearinghouse for project capital, or source of technical assistance for nonprofit developers. This model is common at the state level, where support for CDCs is less well organized.

These four models represent a rough continuum of support for and integration of CDCs in local governments. Under the sponsorship model, the local government provides for each of the four needs of CDCs, as the partnership does in the second model. Under the community-network and preorganization models, very little is provided to CDCs in any regular or organized fashion. The nonprofits get access to these forms of support only on a project-by-project basis; they must reestablish the connection with funder or technical assistance provider with each new application.

SUMMARY

The data presented here reveal that nonprofit housing development occurs in almost all U.S. cities with populations over 100,000. Further, the practice of local government support for nonprofit housing developers is widespread. Development capital for nonprofit CDCs is offered by 82 percent of the responding cities; 59 percent provide administrative funding; and just over 50 percent provide technical assistance and predevelopment financing. Over 76 percent of the responding cities offer two or more of these benefits to local CDCs. Only 11 percent offer none.

There can be little doubt that CDCs are heavily integrated into the housing policy approach of local governments. What these data do not as readily reveal, however, is the depth of the support provided. As Bratt argues, without deep subsidies government support of community-based housing, "however comprehensive and exemplary, may face serious problems."[60] Without such data an evaluation of government support for CDCs remains incomplete.

A definitive assessment of the forces that lead to the adoption of one model or another awaits further research. Nevertheless, the accommodations between local public and nonprofit actors in low-income housing are, it seems, primarily political in nature. The strength of the community-based movement in general and housing CDCs in particular, the salience of the low-income housing issue, and the existence of public officials sympathetic to community-based housing may all increase the likelihood of an institutionalized (model 1 or model 2) accommodation of CDCs.

Nonprofit CDCs are undeniably important actors in housing policy, partly because of the reduction of tax incentives and subsidies to for-profit developers,[61] and the crisis of expiring use restrictions that has forced a rethinking of housing policy strategy.[62] Yet this chapter also suggests that the devolution of housing policy authority to the local level has played a role in increasing the importance of nonprofit, community-based development. The findings suggest that CDCs offer tangible political benefits to local policymakers. Because of their community base, CDCs represent a potential constituency for local officials. Providing support to nonprofit CDCs is not simply a technical decision about how to implement housing policy; it is also a political decision that gives officials an opportunity to respond to neighborhood-based constituencies. The devolution of housing policy to cities and states has made this political connection stronger now than in the past. Further, the organization of low-income housing advocates and providers helps to solidify their political importance as a constituency, and brings greater local government support for nonprofit housing.

The Politics of Housing in Los Angeles

THE CITY OF Los Angeles presents a prototypical example of the political dynamics of the postfederal era in housing. Before 1980 the city had little in the way of locally funded housing programs. Like most cities, it suffered an increase in housing-related problems during the 1980s and witnessed the birth of an organized movement of community-based advocates for low-income housing. By the end of the decade the city had transformed its meager housing policy into a progressive approach in the tradition described in this book. Previous chapters have presented a national analysis of postfederal housing policy in U.S. cities and states. That analysis has described the nature of the new housing policy paradigm and demonstrated the effectiveness of the community housing movement at the state and local levels. This chapter utilizes a case study of the city of Los Angeles to explore the dynamics of community influence and local policy change.

LOS ANGELES DURING THE FEDERAL ERA

The city of Los Angeles entered the 1980s with a housing policy that was heavily dependent on the federal government and federal programs for assistance. In that sense the city was typical of U.S. cities during the federal era. Aspects of the local political system, however, also contributed to the lack of a policymaking infrastructure. Like most cities in 1980, Los Angeles lacked a critical level of civic organization and public commitment to the provision of low-income housing. The public officials, city agencies, and private interests that might have activated local concern about housing were simply not in place or not predisposed to create a local housing effort.

There are a number of reasons why such a policy infrastructure did not exist. First, as described earlier, prior to 1980 the federal government had taken responsibility for housing, and thus officials looked to Washington for leadership on this issue. Second, there was little in the way of advocacy aimed at pressuring local officials to establish a housing policy. Though neighborhood organizations in Los Angeles (as in other cities) fought political battles with the city's redevelopment agency, these groups stopped short of demanding that city government take the lead on affordable housing issues. The defense of neighborhoods from potential redevelopment had not yet been wedded to the idea that local government might play a proactive role in housing policy design. According to Stegman and Holden: "There was no politically powerful constituency exerting pressures on elected officials to respond to local low-income housing problems; the lack of pressure was matched by a lack of housing expertise in legislative and executive chambers."[1] Finally, such local agencies as did exist for the development of housing were doing little more than implementing federal policy, fulfilling federal mandates, and complying with federal regulations. Thus, as in most U.S. cities, elected officials in Los Angeles were unfamiliar with the issues surrounding the formulation of housing policy; local agencies were unprepared for the development of local programming; and housing advocates were unorganized at the local level, unable to bring new ideas to the public agenda.

These factors were exacerbated by the city's historical political decentralization, which dispersed power and accountability across the political landscape. A number of studies of Los Angeles have noted the extreme fragmentation of political authority in the city and the region.[2] The historical lack of party influence following the advent of the progressive reforms in the early part of this century contributed to a political system heavily dependent on personality and personal financial capacity. The political structure lacked any strong centralizing institution. Indeed, Greenstone and Peterson argue that the "pervasive fragmentation of southern California's civic life [was] fundamental to every interpretation of Los Angeles politics."[3]

Despite operating in a nominally weak-mayor governmental system, the mayor of Los Angeles remained the strongest actor in the political structure of the city because no one else was able to marshal sufficient resources to control the process. In effect, the mayor became the strongest among many weak players.[4] This was manifest in the city's housing policy. Mayor Tom Bradley controlled the housing authority and the redevelopment agency through his appointment power. Their lack of dynamism on low-income housing issues reflected the low priority that Bradley gave the issue. Nor was there any coalition of council members to step forward and offer alternatives.

Fragmented Housing Policy

The fragmentation of political life exhibits itself in the character of public institutions as well as in the formation and activities of interest groups. In 1980 the city's housing functions were nominally set in the Community Development Department (CDD), which implemented the city's CDBG program. At the beginning of the 1980s the city typically spent around 50 percent of its federal block grant on housing functions—a slightly higher percentage than most cities[5]—but a fairly small proportion of that was devoted to low-cost rental housing. Roughly one-half of block grant–funded housing assistance went to homeowner rehabilitation programs that generally benefited middle-income homeowners.[6] In addition, the city spent an inordinately high percentage of its CDBG housing funds on administrative costs, that figure reaching a high of 39 percent in 1988.[7]

The other major source of financing for housing assistance was mortgage revenue bonds (MRBs). The city of Los Angeles, through its CDD, made extensive use of this financing mechanism. Between 1980 and 1988 the city issued $706.3 million in MRBs. But this program, too, failed to target the needs of lower-income residents. Federal regulations required that only 20 percent of multifamily units assisted through bond financing be affordable to lower-income households. The city stuck closely to the minimum, producing only 2,000 low-income units via tax-exempt mortgage revenue bonds through the first eight years of the 1980s.[8] Indeed, as HUD budget cuts were implemented during the early and middle years of the decade, MRBs and CDBG became nearly the only means by which CDD provided assisted housing.

Though CDD was the home for the more traditional housing rehabilitation programs, other agencies were and still are involved in housing issues. The Housing Authority of the City of Los Angeles (HACLA) operates the city's public housing program. Regulatory functions are located in the Building and Safety Department, and planning functions are carried out by the Planning Department. But the major public producer of housing in the city is the Community Redevelopment Agency of Los Angeles (CRALA). California law mandates that 20 percent of the revenues generated in tax increment districts be allocated to affordable housing. The CRALA, sitting on a huge tax increment district in the Bunker Hill and central business district sections of downtown, has spent millions on housing. Another reason for CRALA's housing activities is strong and persistent community pressure; it has been the target of intense community-based lobbying for years.[9] Nevertheless, the agency has not been a net producer of affordable housing. In fact, from 1967 to 1988 it constructed 10,700 units of low-rent housing—540 fewer than it demolished.[10]

Despite the involvement of multiple agencies the city had no comprehensive low-income housing policy throughout most of the 1980s. The CDD provided moderate rehabilitation assistance through the CDBG program, while CRALA essentially ran its own programs of new construction and rehabilitation. There was neither cooperation nor joint planning between the two agencies. By 1988, when Mayor Bradley's Blue Ribbon Committee on Housing made its report (see below), it identified eleven different local agencies involved in housing issues, with virtually no coordination among them.[11] The chair of the committee stated, "We are light years behind other cities" in creating an affordable housing strategy.[12]

The Fragmented Community Movement

The fragmentation and incoherence of the city's housing policymaking infrastructure was matched by equal fragmentation and underdevelopment within the community housing movement. Groups worked in relative isolation from one another, each focusing on issues of neighborhood-level importance. Greenstone and Peterson contend that there is a "high cost of forming a political coalition in a city as geographically dispersed and socially mobile as Los Angeles."[13] This seems to have contributed to the lack of a citywide approach to housing and neighborhood development issues. Community groups were formed or mobilized primarily with the intention of altering or stopping the redevelopment plans of the CRALA. The Coalition for Economic Survival was defending tenants' rights and opposing CRALA clearance and redevelopment strategies primarily in the Hollywood area. Legal Aid lawyers were advocating for the rights of very low-income central city residents against CRALA's plans to redevelop major portions of skid row and areas south of downtown. Neighborhood groups such as the Pico-Union Neighborhood Council were also mobilizing against CRALA redevelopment plans.[14] Thus, although there was a good deal of neighborhood activism, it was essentially defensive in nature (reacting to redevelopment plans) and lacked coordination or unification into a broader movement.

Economic Environment and the Housing Crisis

The city's economy was changing in important ways during the late 1970s and early 1980s. As a number of analysts have pointed out, Los Angeles is the prototypical example of regional economic restructuring.[15] During the 1970s, while most cities were losing manufacturing jobs and converting to a service-based economy, the Los Angeles region actually added 225,000 manufacturing jobs.[16] These statistics, however, mask an underlying and fundamental change in the region's economy. The city lost close to 100,000 jobs in heavy manufacturing such as steel, automobile assembly, and tiremaking—industrial sectors characterized by highly unionized and more highly paid blue-collar workers. The growth in manufacturing in the Los Angeles region has instead been in high-tech electronics-based industries on the one hand and garment industries on the other. These industries are characterized by low-paid, weakly organized assembly workers employed in what are often sweatshop operations.[17] The overall unionization rate for manufacturing in the Los Angeles region fell from 26.4 percent to 10.5 percent during these years.[18]

At the same time the service sector greatly expanded. The downtown area, for example, has been transformed since the mid-1970s into a major financial and corporate headquarters. The "internationalization" of the economy directly affected Los Angeles in two ways: the region experienced an influx of foreign capital feeding its downtown revitalization, and an influx of immigrant labor feeding its reindustrialization.[19] These changes created a more differentiated labor force, one characterized by increasing income polarization with highly paid "high technocracy" and financial management jobs at one end of the scale and low-paid, low-skilled labor on the other.

Additionally, the housing market in the city was undergoing rapid inflation during these years. Rents and home prices were skyrocketing. Median rents in Los Angeles doubled from 1970 to 1980 and again from 1980 to 1988. In 1988 only 17 percent of Los Angeles families could afford the median-priced home.[20] The average rent for a new apartment unit in Los Angeles in 1988 was around $900 per month.[21] Further, in a residential market so heated, landlords and realtors went to great lengths to protect their property values and "tenant profile." The city became increasingly segregated residentially, with identifiable housing submarkets for African-Americans, Asians, and Hispanics.[22] A 1984 study revealed a 60 percent rate of discrimination against nonwhite apartment seekers.[23]

The combination of skyrocketing housing costs and increasing low-wage labor contributed to an explosion in homelessness during the 1980s. In 1984, HUD estimated that Los Angeles had the largest per capita homeless population in the country, the second largest in absolute numbers (behind New York). Estimates put the total of homeless in the region at more than 50,000 persons, 15,000 of whom were located in the central city area. Their presence on downtown streets and the city's beaches belied the image of a thriving, prosperous local economy. Media attention to their increasing numbers and their worsening plight on the streets added to a sense of crisis felt by local officials and advocates for the homeless. In May 1987 the *Los Angeles Times* published the results of its own survey, which indicated that some 200,000 people, mainly immigrants, were living in 50,000 garages throughout Los Angeles County.[24]

Downtown Development and the Homeless Crisis

Despite evidence of a growing crisis in housing, for the first half of the decade Mayor Bradley was preoccupied with other issues. His two gubernatorial races in 1982 and 1986 resulted in narrow defeats. Each campaign took the mayor away from the city a great deal and absorbed much of his attention. Closer to home, his administration was intent upon completion of the city's downtown redevelopment. During these years Bradley was presiding over the complete transformation of the city's downtown from a small regional (though hardly dominant) commercial center into an international center for finance and corporate management. The Bradley administration was very active in attracting corporate investment, especially from the Pacific Rim. In competition with San Francisco to the north, Bradley undertook trade missions to the Far East in search of investors.[25] His success in these missions and the extent of the makeover accomplished in the downtown were remarkable. By 1985 over 75 percent of the major properties in downtown Los Angeles were foreign-owned.[26] As Mike Davis reported in 1987, "Almost $2.5 billion of new investment flowed into Downtown in the decade after Bradley's election [in 1973]. Where there were just five new highrises above the old earthquake limit of thirteen floors in 1976, there are now forty-five. Increasingly the CRA operated a casino as players moved in and out of speculative positions, nearly a third of Downtown exchanging hands between 1976 and 1982."[27]

To make room for expanded corporate centers downtown, CRALA cleared away the residential areas of Bunker Hill and other central city neighborhoods. The redevelopment of Bunker Hill alone resulted in the eviction of 6,000 people.[28] Over 2,200 units of SRO housing were eliminated in the central city area. The demolition of so many units of low-cost housing put increased pressure on the low end of the market. When the private market failed to produce affordable housing of its own, many low-income households were forced into the streets. When the successful redevelopment of downtown was threatened by the large numbers of homeless persons in the skid row area next to downtown, the Bradley administration enlisted the support of the police department and CRALA to contain skid row and thus free investors from the anguish of seeing their properties devalued by street people.[29]

As the problem of homelessness grew and the number of people on the streets of skid row increased, the city responded in a two-pronged fashion. Having agreed, after negotiations with community activists, to spare skid row from demolition, CRALA set about concentrating within the neighborhood a range of housing and social services for the very poor. The agency established a nonprofit developer, SRO Housing Corporation, to rehabilitate residential hotels in the area, and it funded a number of social service agencies in the neighborhood. Over time, CRALA began to assist the relocation of social services from other downtown locations into skid row.[30] This was part of the agency's avowed policy of "containment."[31] Another element in that policy was the design of public and private space in the rest of downtown so that it was inhospitable to homeless persons.[32]

The second prong of the Bradley administration's approach to the homeless problem was the use of the Los Angeles Police Department to keep downtown streets and sidewalks clear and free of temporary encampments and shelters. From 1984 through 1989 the LAPD engaged in a series of street sweeps designed to minimize the establishment of semipermanent dwellings on the streets of skid row and surrounding areas. The police were also active in maintaining containment by more vigorously patrolling downtown areas.[33]

By 1986 and 1987, however, the pressure on city officials to provide shelters for the homeless as alternatives to the streets had mounted to a level that could not be ignored. The city engaged in a number of temporary solutions, including the establishment of an open-air "urban campground" located on unused industrial land just east of skid row. The controversy over this response and the failure of the city to follow up this temporary solution with a more permanent policy brought public concern for homelessness to a peak in the fall of 1987. Homeless advocates (chiefly attorneys with the Legal Aid Society and other public interest organizations) and directors of downtown shelters publicly pressed the Bradley administration to take a more comprehensive and sympathetic stance toward the homeless. Attorneys for the homeless sued the police department for harassment; they sued the city for destruction of private property resulting from the street sweeps; and they joined the city in its suit with the county over the adequacy of the county's homeless programs.

Despite this advocacy, the Bradley administration clearly put the development of downtown and the rights of investors in front of the problems of homeless persons in the city.[34] The maintenance of a healthy real estate market and the continuation of growth politics were the top agenda items for the Bradley administration through the first half of the 1980s.

THE TRANSITIONAL PERIOD

Electoral Pressure

As mentioned earlier, CRALA's development strategies had been opposed by community groups for many years, and especially vocal in that opposition were two organizations: the Coalition for Economic Survival (CES) and the Legal Aid Society. Legal Aid attorneys were constantly criticizing the city's development policy and its treatment of the homeless in the central city area.[35] Nevertheless, the Bradley administration continued to put its greatest efforts and resources into downtown development—until voters, primarily on the city's west side, began to indicate their displeasure with continued growth. In 1986, growth control organizations offered Proposition U, a measure to restrict growth by downzoning a large portion of nondowntown Los Angeles. Bradley opposed the measure and even had his lieutenant on the city council, Council President Pat Russell, introduce legislation that would exempt thirty developers from its impact. But Proposition U passed by a large margin, revealing a fundamental split in the Bradley coalition of working-class African Americans in south central Los Angeles and white liberals on the west side, which had supported the mayor since his first election in 1973. For years Bradley had worked to add the downtown business and investment community to that coalition by subsidizing rapid downtown growth. The passage of Proposition U was the first indication that at least portions of his electoral coalition had come to consider him too cozy with the development community.

Less than a year later Russell, Bradley's closest council ally, was defeated in her reelection bid by a growth control advocate from the west side. At the same time, another west side liberal on the council, Zev Yaroslavsky, hinted broadly that he might run for mayor in 1989. These developments and the growing controversies related to the city's failure to deal with homelessness caused a good deal of concern in the Bradley camp. The major responded with a series of moves intended to shore up his increasingly fragile electoral coalition. Bradley turned around on Proposition U and, with a good deal of fanfare, began to enforce the mandate.[36] He advocated community-based planning to ensure that neighborhood concerns would be incorporated in the city's land-use strategies. He appointed environmentalists and growth control leaders to positions on the Board of Public Works. In the area of housing he took two steps. On September 17, 1987, he created a new position, the Mayor's Housing Coordinator, and appointed to that position Gary Squier, a long-time community-based advocate from the west side community of Santa Monica. That same day Bradley announced that he would appoint a Blue Ribbon Committee to study the city's housing problems and delivery system and make recommendations for improving his administration's housing policy.

The CRALA Cap Proposal

One of Squier's first assignments was to carry to the community Bradley's plan to increase city expenditures on affordable housing to $2.5 billion over a twenty-year period. The money would come from lifting the cap on revenue from the downtown tax-increment financing (TIF) district, which had been imposed through a 1977 court settlement. Los Angeles County (which stood to lose a significant share of tax proceeds from downtown growth if the TIF district were allowed), Councilman Ernani Bernardi, and other activists who were concerned about the way CRALA spent its money had sued to block the creation of the downtown redevelopment project. The court settlement limited to $750 million the amount of TIF revenue that CRALA could receive from the downtown project. In 1987 the agency was nearing its court-imposed limit and predicted that by 1933 or 1994 it would be out of business in the downtown area. Bradley proposed that the cap be lifted to $5 billion and that half of the amount be spent on affordable housing. The other half, the mayor proposed, could be spent as CRALA saw fit to continue downtown revitalization. To Bradley, the proposal seemed a "win-win" proposition; he could appease his housing critics while allowing CRALA to continue its downtown development activities.

Squier presented this proposal to housing activists shortly after taking office. He did not get the response he and the mayor expected. Activists were divided on the issue. Some regarded the

$2.5 billion as a very substantial sum and noted that the fifty-fifty split was 30 percent more than California law mandated. The larger group was not persuaded, however, and demanded that the entire increment be spent on housing and human needs. A number of these activists represented social services agencies serving low-income populations in the downtown and outlying areas. They, along with other professionals in the housing field during this time, were beginning to call for the integration of housing and social services as a more effective way to solve low-income housing problems. They reasoned that the additional $4.25 billion (above the original $750 million) should be spent on housing and social services and that no more downtown revitalization was needed.

Though the issue threatened to tear apart a fragile activist coalition, in the end it accomplished the opposite. In the short space of two years the activists involved in reviewing the CRALA cap proposal coalesced into an effective and important voice for low-income housing in the city. The word "coalition" is perhaps too strong a characterization for what was initially a loose collection of activists. There was little in the way of formal organization. In December 1987 fifty housing and community activists had formed a group called Housing L.A. to discuss housing problems in the city and strategies for dealing with them. This group succeeded a previous entity called LA 1000, a smaller group of developer-activists whose aim had been to produce 1,000 units of low-income housing in the city annually. LA 1000 lasted only a short time and then disappeared without accomplishing much. Many of its participants, however, reappeared as members of Housing L.A.

It was to this group, forming the core of the housing movement, that Squier and the mayor addressed their proposal. There were two fault lines in the community housing movement, however. The first was between the older nonprofit housing developers and the neighborhood-based community groups. The nonprofit developers were generally white and often (whether factually or not) identified with the west side and an almost paternalistic approach to the needs of inner-city residents. Because of their ties to Gary Squier (Squier and some of these nonprofit developers had first formed LA 1000), the older nonprofit organizations had greater entree at City Hall than did the community groups. In 1987 only a handful of CDCs were operating in the Los Angeles area, prominent among them the Los Angeles Community Design Center and the Santa Monica Housing Development Corporation. Though the number of nonprofit housing developers was to grow exponentially in the coming years and become more inclusive, racially as well as geographically, in 1987 they were quite separate from the social services and community-based activists in Housing L.A. The nonprofit development community from which Gary Squier came was inclined to think that the $2.5 billion proposition from the mayor's office was a good idea. The social services providers and community-based organizations were more often people of color, or they represented communities of color, and were not as well integrated into the housing production system. The human services people saw little in the mayor's proposal for them or their constituencies, and thus they argued for more money and for a split between housing and human services.

The second and crosscutting faultline, having more to do with the nature of the mayor's proposal than with the organizations themselves, was between community-based agencies funded by CRALA and those funded by the county. Both types of agencies worked in the downtown area providing housing and human services to low-income people. Yet an informal system had developed in which service agencies received money from either CRALA or the county but rarely from both. On one hand, the lifting of the cap would keep the development agency in business and therefore mean continued funding for one segment. On the other hand, the lifting of the cap would limit future revenues of the county and therefore mean possible budget cuts for the other segment. The County Board of Supervisors in 1987 was controlled by a conservative majority that was against expansion of the human services component of the budget; hence, those service agencies felt certain that their programs would be among the first sacrificed should fiscal strain occur at the county level.

Eager to see the cap lifted, CRALA sponsored a series of community meetings at which activists could listen to the specifics of the proposal and present their suggestions. The agency even hired a well-known public interest law firm to facilitate the meetings. Community opposition was intransigent. Activists demanded data on the number of housing units demolished, the number of truly low-income units produced, the amount of money spent on developer subsidies versus human services, and other indicators of past performance. The relationship between CRALA and the activists soon deteriorated to previous levels of hostility and mistrust. The agency refused to provide the data requested, and the meetings ended. Ultimately, the talks between the mayor's office, CRALA, and the community were inconclusive, and the negotiations between the city and the county on the lifting of the cap moved behind doors.

Though the cap issue itself was unresolved, it did serve as a catalyst for the housing movement in that it established Housing L.A. as the focal point for previously disparate elements of the community-based housing sector. The group filled a void by providing a platform for the discussion of a variety of housing issues and a vehicle for advocacy on a range of housing issues. Throughout 1988, housing activists met to discuss the cap and other housing and social service issues. One such issue was the city's rent control law.

Rent Control

Rent control was first passed in Los Angeles in 1978. The first bill was a six-month freeze that capped two years of organizing and lobbying by tenants. In 1976 the Coalition for Economic Survival had taken on the rent control issue. Rents in the Los Angeles area were rapidly escalating during this time, and a wave of gentrification had made many low-income tenants insecure. The CES began organizing tenants on the west and south sides around the issue of rent control. Its efforts were part of a statewide tenants' movement at that time.[37] A statewide advocacy group for tenants, called CHAIN, had been successful in getting rent control passed in a number of northern California cities.

After presenting to the city council a petition in favor of rent control, with 30,000 signatures, CES tenants' organizations saw their initial attempt fail in committee. In 1978 the same bill made it out of committee but failed on the council floor. Proposition 13 (the property tax limitation initiative) passed in June 1978, and the rent savings and rebates that renters had been led to expect did not occur. The CES and other activists capitalized on renters' anger and mobilized again around rent control. This time the pressure was enough to achieve the six-month freeze in rents. As the freeze expired, the council considered a permanent bill. Significantly, two council members representing the African American communities in south central Los Angeles opposed the 1979 bill because it did not address housing issues in that area: abandonment and disrepair. Once the bill was amended to allow the pass-through of rehabilitation costs, these council members supported the bill, and it was passed.

In 1988 the city council was set to review the 1979 law. Housing L.A. established a rent control and housing preservation committee that began to prepare for the city council battle not only to review the law but to strengthen it considerably. Housing L.A., tenant organizations, and the CES met throughout 1988 and 1989, first to prepare a tenants' rights platform and then to lobby council members heavily with phone calls, postcards, and literature. The work built on the efforts of a number of groups such as Legal Aid and Inquilinos Unidos, a tenants' rights organization focused on slum housing conditions which had been advocating for tenants since 1985. Most of the elements of the tenants' rights platform were incorporated into the legislation proposed by Michael Woo, chair of the council committee considering the rent control review. The Housing L.A. people packed the council chambers during the hearings. Finally, in October 1989 the council approved much of the platform as presented by Woo and Housing L.A. The council strengthened the law in many areas: it eliminated some loopholes, provided for interest on security deposits, restricted capital improvement pass-throughs and other items. The rent control issue served to mobilize tenants and attracted other groups to Housing L.A. Indeed, the rent control fight took place during a period of rapid expansion for the housing movement in general.

Growth of the Nonprofit Housing Development Sector

One important source of growth in the movement can be accounted for by the mushrooming number of groups becoming involved in nonprofit housing development. As mentioned earlier, Los Angeles and the entire southern California area had very few nonprofit housing developers before the mid-1980s. Those that did exist were generally regional in scope. One survey of nonprofit developers in southern California in 1987 identified a pool of sixty developers in the entire five-county region.[38] A 1986 attempt to organize these developers was unsuccessful. The nonprofit community at that time was far behind those of other cities in both size and scope. Jennifer Bigelow, director of the Southern California Association of Non-Profit Developers (SCANPH) in 1991, believes that this institutional underdevelopment was the result of low levels of housing advocacy:

> To do affordable housing, you really have to have advocacy at the local level to build consensus. At least that has been my experience. The first five years I did affordable housing, it was coalition building. We ended up doing a lot of projects, but you really need the cohesion of a lot of people that are in one place and identifying it as a community. Los Angeles is the antithesis of that. I'm not saying there aren't neighborhoods. There are, but I think [organizing is] slower to get up to speed here. People move around. I'm astonished how people even in the housing network here—they're always changing jobs.[39]

As Bigelow suggests, advocacy and institutional development did progress in tandem.[40] At the same time that Housing L.A. was gearing up, the Local Initiatives Support Corporation (LISC), a national nonprofit with an office in Los Angeles, offered a series of development training seminars in southern California. This program provided basic development skills to community members interested in nonprofit development. A second effort at organizing nonprofits was attempted in 1989, and close to 500 people attended a technical assistance training seminar. By then, as Bigelow explains, there was "just an explosion of activity going on around affordable housing in Los Angeles. I think groups were starved for the kind of networking information this kind of meeting provided."[41] By 1991 SCANPH had 235 member organizations; two years earlier it had had only fifty. The new crop of nonprofit housing organizations are different from their regional predecessors in that they are typically community-based organizations with roots in neighborhood politics and social services delivery. Many groups are church-based, and some are tenant organizations that have decided to become involved in housing development. The demand for an umbrella organization like SCANPH was a natural outgrowth of the rapid increase in the number of CDCs and their relative inexperience in development issues and techniques. The coalition serves those members by offering a range of technical assistance and information services.

During this time period the CDC movement took off in Los Angeles and substantially changed its character from a few regional nonprofits to growing numbers of neighborhood-based groups with a social service history, rooted in community development. This change, coupled with the involvement of tenants' groups through CES and the rent control issue, gave the housing movement a much greater community base than it had ever previously enjoyed.

Growing City Council Opposition to CRALA

As the group of housing activists grew, so did the momentum of opinion against CRALA. In September 1988 the city council held hearings on the cap issue, and several council members used the opportunity to blast the agency and its past record. Yaroslavksy, in what was widely interpreted as a precampaign address, attacked CRALA and the mayor for their record on low-income housing. At the same time a Legal Aid Society study found that CRALA's claims regarding the number of low-income family units produced were grossly inflated (the agency had counted cots provided in CRALA-funded shelters and CRALA-assisted SRO hotel rooms as "family units"). Furthermore, some social service agencies funded by CRALA revealed that they had been pressured into testifying in favor of lifting the cap. Much to the mayor's dismay, he found that far from placating his critics on the housing issue, his offer of $2.5 billion had ultimately emboldened and helped to mobilize them.

Other events conspired to accelerate criticism of the city's housing effort. In November 1988 the *Los Angeles Times* published a series of articles focusing on the housing crisis in the city and describing at some length the controversies surrounding CRALA and its housing record. The three-part series made the front page and stated, among other things: "Remarkably, for a city its size, Los Angeles has no agency or person in charge of construction or rehabilitation of low-cost rental housing.... 'God, don't tell anyone I said this, but there is no [housing] plan,' said one high-ranking city official."[42]

Meanwhile, criticism of CRALA was increasing on the city council among a cadre of four and sometimes five members. The council had changed between 1985 and 1987 to include more members with a progressive background and with fewer ties to the Bradley administration.[43] For many years Pat Russell had been able to hold together a loose coalition that supported the mayor on most issues and routinely approved CRALA work plans and redevelopment projects. But the election of Michael Woo to the council in 1985, former State Assemblywoman Gloria Molina's victory in 1987, and growth control activist Ruth Galanter's upset win over Russell in 1987 marked a dramatic change in the composition of the council. Molina, especially, was a vocal supporter of low-income housing. A fourth newcomer, Nate Holden, defeated a Bradley candidate in yet another district in 1987, compounding the likelihood that the council would be a more independent force than in the past. These new members, along with west side liberal Yaroslavsky, constituted the core of the opposition to status quo development politics in Los Angeles, with other council members entering the picture on specific issues such as growth restrictions, rent control, and downtown redevelopment.[44] The city council in 1987–90 was much less reluctant to criticize the CRALA and the mayor's downtown development strategy and more likely to review agency budgets and work plans seriously than it had ever been in Bradley's previous three terms.

In December 1988 the Mayor's Blue Ribbon Committee on Affordable Housing released its report. It had been formed a year earlier with significant representation of community-based interests, including several members of Housing L.A. The committee charged the city with negligence in the housing arena, finding that the housing element of the city's general plan was years out of date. There was no citywide housing policy document, no formalized process to monitor the housing market or to determine housing needs and programming and budgetary levels. There were no performance goals for housing or any procedures to evaluate the housing assistance delivery system.

To rectify the situation the committee offered recommendations in five areas. First, it recommended institutional reforms centered on the creation of a commission to oversee the housing functions in each of the agencies with housing-related responsibilities and to supervise a new centralized housing department. Second, the committee recommended devoting new resources to housing; among its suggestions were the lifting of the CRALA cap, issuance of a $100 million bond for affordable housing, an office-housing linkage program, a housing trust fund financed by a document transfer tax, and a series of incentives for the production of affordable housing. Third, the committee recommended new housing programs, including the transfer of slum properties to nonprofits, the establishment of a housing partnership modeled after those in Chicago and Boston (see Chapter 5), the preservation of assisted housing at risk for prepayment, rehabilitation programs, and the reinforcement of brick buildings to earthquake standards. Fourth, the committee recommended the creation of a new city policy document for housing, to include a review of all city policy in order to determine its impact on affordable housing, and the establishment of building permit priority for low-income housing production and preservation. Finally, the committee suggested that existing housing policy should be changed to target the lowest-income groups and place emphasis on long-term affordability.

The movement to overhaul the city's housing delivery system, as proposed by the Blue Ribbon Committee, and the process of deemphasizing CRALA's role received some unintentional impetus in 1989 from the agency itself. In May 1989, Legal Aid lawyers accused CRALA of secretly negotiating with Los Angeles County over a proposed two-million-square-foot real estate project that the county planned in downtown Los Angeles. In 1986 the CRALA had cut a deal to allow the expansion of the county's office development by ten stories, or 200,000 additional square feet; in exchange the county had agreed not to oppose CRALA's Hollywood redevelopment project. As insurance against the possibility that the city council might disapprove, CRALA agreed to pay the county $600,000 per year in damages for every year the council opposed the deal. Council members were outraged by an arrangement that essentially left them no option but to approve the expansion of the county's office building. Officials from CRALA maintained that they had notified the council at the time the deal was struck, but not a single council member recalled being notified.[45]

In 1990, with controversy swirling about CRALA, Executive Director John Tuite, having survived a criminal investigation the year before, was persuaded to step down. Yet even his resignation caused a furor, because the agency's board bought out his contract for over three-quarters of a million dollars. Again, members of the city council were furious. Having failed in its earlier attempt, the council tried once more to assert some control over the agency and its operations. This time it was successful in creating an oversight

Housing Politics in Los Angeles 157

committee and shifting the agency's financial and legal dealings to the city comptroller and the city attorney. In this way the council hoped to hear about CRALA "deals" before they occurred.

By this time the analysis of CRALA offered by critics in the housing movement had reached its greatest level of acceptance. The agency's heavy-handed approach to development and its arrogance in dealings with the council and critics were apparent as they had never been before. Referring to the Tuite buyout and the related political fallout, one housing advocate remarked, "It's funny, you spend ten years organizing and then you watch these people very slowly and carefully shoot themselves in both of their feet. And you can't take credit for it, but everything that you have been asking for for ten years starts to happen."[46]

POSTFEDERAL HOUSING POLICY IN LOS ANGELES

The recommendations of the Blue Ribbon Committee and the somewhat reduced independence of CRALA constituted a significant remaking of the city's housing policy structure. The policy climate at the end of 1988 was such that the city council moved immediately to endorse (by a unanimous 13–0 vote) the Blue Ribbon Committee's recommendations. By the summer of 1989 all but one of the committee's recommendations had been drawn up in ordinance form and approved by the council. In April 1989 the voters passed a $100 million bond for housing assistance. A linkage task force was formed, and it hired consultants to study the issue and present recommendations for implementation of the program. Only the formation of a commission on affordable housing was delayed. After reviewing this reorganizational proposal, however, the council went forward in 1990 with the creation of the Housing Production and Preservation Department (HPPD) and the Affordable Housing Commission. The department was given responsibility for housing programs that had been located in the CDD, and the commission was charged with the broad review of the housing-related responsibilities of all city agencies. Bradley appointed a number of housing activists to key positions in these newly created bodies. He named Gary Squier director of HPPD and picked Chuck Elsesser—a former Legal Aid attorney and the author of the report exposing the CRALA's inflated family housing claims—to head the housing commission. Another Legal Aid attorney and long-time CRALA-basher, Michael Bodaken, was named as the new Mayor's Housing Coordinator to replace Squier. Finally, three tenant activists were appointed to vacancies on the seven-member Rent Adjustment Commission, which oversees the city's rent control program.

By the end of 1990 Los Angeles had most of the elements of the progressive housing policy paradigm identified in Chapter 4. Proposals for a linkage ordinance had been approved; the mayor had halted demolition of residential hotels in 1987; the city's rent control ordinance and its inclusionary zoning ordinance were well established. Further, pursuant to the recommendations of the Blue Ribbon Committee, the city had established extensive supports for nonprofit developers.

The Housing Department

In August 1990 the Los Angeles Housing Preservation and Production Department was established to run the city's rehabilitation and new construction programs. In addition, the department took over the city's rent control program and housing planning functions. The objective behind the creation of a line department with sole responsibility for housing was that it would also acquire sole authority over the development of affordable housing. That is, the hope was that over time HPPD would become the locus of most if not all of the city's housing assistance programs. Initially, however, CRALA's unwillingness to relinquish its housing component limited the new department's influence. The CRALA budget for housing was more than twice the $25 million budget of HPPD. Nevertheless, the chair of the Affordable Housing Commission, Chuck Elsesser, expressed the hope that HPPD would ultimately be able to centralize housing production in the city.

> I don't think anybody can say that [HPPD] does centralize the housing function. It just hasn't happened. The question is whether this is a step in a process or not. If this is the end result, we haven't done very much, and we certainly didn't need to create a housing department to do it. . . . I think you've got to see this as a process of centralization; whether it is through coordination or actual transfer of funds and

functions, you have one place to go for housing money and housing planning in the city, and that is the housing department. The real question is the extent to which that happens. I think it has to happen slowly.[47]

If the department should be unable to coax its housing budget from CRALA, it might grow on the basis of housing linkage fees. Both Squier and Bodaken hope to see linkage fees channeled into HPPD, though CRALA may want to retain fees collected from developments inside its own redevelopment areas. The lifting of the CRALA cap, should it occur, is another potential source of funds, although CRALA will doubtless attempt to retain control over that pot.

Linkage

At the end of 1991 the Los Angeles housing linkage program was still in the planning stage. The city spent more than $250,000 doing a study to establish the nexus for such a program.[48] The city created a linkage fee task force that included nonprofit community housing developers, for-profit developers, members of the building industry, retailers, and chamber of commerce and public-sector representatives. Meeting regularly throughout 1990 and 1991, the task force established guidelines for pursuing enactment of a linkage policy. Currently the city proposes to create five different areas and four different fees ranging from $2.00 to $7.50 per square foot for developments, depending on their location. A linkage program establishing a fee of $4.20 per square foot has been adopted for the Central City West area.

Los Angeles Housing Partnership

The Los Angeles Housing Partnership was formed as one of the first Blue Ribbon Committee recommendations implemented by the city. The committee envisioned the partnership on the Chicago or Boston model, a public-private entity that would provide financing and technical assistance to nonprofit developers in the city. As HPPD head Gary Squier saw it, "The notion was that the Partnership would be the hub of a wheel . . . being the coordinator, pulling together public capital, lender debt, equity investment, predevelopment funds, at a one-stop shop through which nonprofit developers could get all the support they needed to put together affordable housing deals. The whole idea was to support nonprofit development."[49]

In 1989 the mayor appointed wealthy Republican entrepreneur David Murdoch to chair the partnership and named Squier its executive director. Murdoch's emphasis, however, was on private-sector development rather than on providing services and financing to nonprofits. The partnership began to play the role of developer in a number of projects, and Squier quit his post, claiming that the partnership had not fulfilled its mandate. The housing partnership has continued to play a minor role as a developer of affordable housing, but the more grandiose vision of it as a service, finance, and technical assistance center for nonprofit developers has not emerged.

Support for Nonprofits

In March 1991 the mayor's office stepped up its efforts to assist nonprofit developers. In coordination with the local office of LISC and several private foundations, the city contributed $1.5 million and leveraged over $4.5 million from the private partners for a Community Development Collaborative to provide technical assistance and development support to the area's nonprofit housing sector. In practice, the collaborative is much closer to the "hub of the wheel" model than the Los Angeles Housing Partnership ever has been, in terms of gathering financing from an array of public and private sources and then passing on the financing and assistance to community-based groups.

The collaborative is not the only means by which the city supports nonprofits, however. The HPPD's Innovative Housing Fund provides $2 million in predevelopment loans, construction loans, and technical assistance to nonprofits, and the department subcontracts with SCANPH and other organizations to offer training to community-based organizations. Indeed, Housing Coordinator Michael Bodaken claims that the development of the city's nonprofit housing sector is a policy objective: "The city is trying to replicate in a short period of time the kind of experience that other cities have [had] over the period of a decade. We're trying to do it in two or three years—to bring nascent nonprofits to the table, give them some training, find a piece of property and give them predevelopment financing, and find out which ones work out."[50]

Housing Politics in Los Angeles   161

As the analysis in the preceding chapter indicates, the development of the nonprofit sector is important for political reasons as well as technical reasons related to the development and provision of affordable housing. As in other cities in which the nonprofit sector has become an important political resource for local officials, the new housing regime in Los Angeles is counting on the support of the nonprofit sector. What it hopes for, says Bodaken, is

> the emergence of a number of new community-based nonprofits who will have not only the ability to produce housing but also act as a trade association and interest group, which I think is key to the success of nonprofits in this city. What politicians respond to, frankly, are special interests. For example, I saw on Tuesday night they are having a forum for the eighth and ninth council districts, put on by the neighborhood development corporation. Now that has never happened before. They are bringing in candidates to talk about housing and redevelopment. Once they start doing that and see it in their self-interest to act more like a trade association, I think that they are going to have more clout. I'm very much in support of that notion.[51]

SUMMARY

The transformation of housing policy in Los Angeles since 1980 has been nearly total. With long-time and vocal housing advocates in the three top housing policymaking positions, the city's approach to the issue acquired a pronounced progressive tint. At this writing, the office-housing linkage program is set to begin soon; the Mayor's Housing Coordinator has made support of nonprofits a top priority; the city council recently strengthened its rent control ordinance; a housing trust fund has been established to provide regularized local funding of housing assistance. The city has begun a collaborative effort with LISC and a number of local foundations for ongoing administrative support and technical assistance to nonprofits. The $100 million general obligation bond for housing assistance is set to fund an extensive housing rehabilitation effort.

In 1980 the city of Los Angeles had no housing policy, no local resources devoted to affordable housing except for a state-mandated tax increment set-aside, and no advocacy organized around the issue. Indeed, housing was not even a local issue. In the intervening years the situation has changed markedly. Four factors combined a produce this change: economic changes in the city, media attention and the growing acknowledgment among officials that the city was experiencing a housing crisis, the political pressure of the housing movement, and the electoral vulnerability of the mayor.

The first factor highlights the objective conditions for low-income households in the city. Changes in the labor market have increasingly polarized the distribution of income in Los Angeles. The labor market is characterized by a growing number of informal, low-wage, and irregular jobs filled more and more by a weakly organized and easily disciplined immigrant labor force. The declining earnings produced by such a labor market have been able to purchase less and less housing in a real estate market marked by escalating prices and the diminished availability of low-cost housing. The rapid redevelopment of the downtown area has led to the wide-scale loss of low-cost housing, while the residential market elsewhere has escalated beyond the means of low-income households. The explosion of homelessness and the visibility of homeless people walking the streets of the city's downtown and beach areas have created the awareness of a housing crisis. As Squier noted, "The housing crisis was not a crisis until homeless people started showing up, and then advocacy started occurring that pointed to the city government as part of the problem."[52]

This awareness has been facilitated by local media attention. The local print and electronic media have been covering the homeless problem in the city since the early 1980s. The *Los Angeles Times* survey of "garage dwelling" was pivotal in creating an atmosphere of concern about the housing market. The series of articles in 1988 also came at a crucial time as the Bradley administration was reeling from a series of attacks on CRALA from city council members and housing movement activists. The media played an important role in the elevation of housing to the status of a primary agenda item.

Central to this process, however, were the activities of housing advocates. Both the city's policymaking infrastructure and the community housing movement were underdeveloped in 1980. The city relied almost exclusively on HUD programs to provide housing assistance. There was no central authority for housing, nor was there a city policy. Community-based housing activists were scattered and typically involved in parochial disputes with CRALA over redevelopment plans. Despite growing housing problems, an increased awareness of homelessness, and the impact of Reagan budget cuts, initial organizing attempts were unsuccessful. LA 1000 was unable to articulate an effective community housing agenda. Only when a more broadly based coalition emerged did the housing movement coalesce. Shortly after Housing L.A. was formed, it received the mayor's proposal to lift the CRALA cap. This served to mobilize the group further and orient it toward thinking in broader terms about the future of housing policy in the city. Though the issue also produced strains in the coalition by dividing groups along lines related to service funding, the movement was able to survive and forcefully articulate its position on both the cap and other housing issues such as rent control.

The history of the housing movement in Los Angeles, however, is not entirely or even mainly a history of one organization. In fact, the mayor was moved to appoint Gary Squier and to propose a $2.5 billion fund for housing because of criticism from neighborhood and social service groups prior to the formation of Housing L.A. The Legal Aid Society was the primary source of criticism of the city's redevelopment strategy. The city's homeless advocates, who are pressuring CRALA to be more responsive to low-income housing needs, included a loose coalition of legal assistance and social service agencies. West side liberals on the city council became a threat to Mayor Bradley with the success of growth control measures and growth control candidates in an area of traditional Bradley strength. And even after the formation of Housing L.A., it was the Legal Aid study of CRALA that revealed grossly inflated housing assistance claims; it was the actions of LISC and SCANPH in providing workshops and technical assistance that laid the groundwork for the explosion in the number of housing CDCs; and it was the CES that organized the lobbying effort on behalf of rent control and organized a series of meetings on the potential loss of existing subsidized housing through the expiration of use restrictions. These organizations and their principals formed the nucleus of a movement that would have existed without a formal group called Housing L.A. In essence, the pattern of civic fragmentation identified by Greenstone and Peterson and others endured even through an era of intense mobilization around the issue of housing.

The Los Angeles housing movement grew during this process from a rather small collection of disparate groups attending to parochial issues to a more (though still not strongly) unified movement with broad representation and its former leaders installed in key policymaking posts.

The gains made by the housing movement during these years were the result of separate and distinct acts of advocacy more than of a planned campaign. Indeed, there is a sense among advocates in the city that things just suddenly "fell into place" for them around 1988. Asked to describe the process of change in the city's housing policy, Elsesser said: "The *Times* did a series of articles, and that combined with the Blue Ribbon Committee, though I'm not sure of the timing of that, but a whole bunch of things happened together in one of those opportunistic, semi-planned ways, with people taking advantage of opportunities. It was certainly not a strategy that was laid out beforehand. But the end result was to validate a lot of what housing advocates and others had been saying for a long time."[53]

This sense of serendipity, with unrelated events—the *Los Angeles Times* series, the Tuite buyout (CRALA "shooting itself very carefully in both feet"), the Blue Ribbon Committee recommendations, and so on—occurring together to produce policy change in the city is common among members of the housing movement in Los Angeles. Though the impact of the movement cannot be denied, its influence was not in the form of a planned platform of reform presented by a coherent oppositional coalition. Rather, its impact was the cumulative influence of a wide number of groups pursuing related affordable housing objectives under only the broadest form of organizational unity.

The movement benefited from the mayor's political insecurity. Bradley's perceived electoral vulnerability (though Yaroslavsky ultimately decided not to challenge the mayor, and Bradley won reelection in 1989) predisposed him to a quick response to the criticisms of progressive housing advocates. By 1990 Bradley had incorporated three of the most vocal and high-profile critics into his administration (a strategy he was employing in other areas as well, notably environmentalism). The existence of these critics, engaged in an ongoing public debate primarily with the CRALA, was crucial

Housing Politics in Los Angeles 165

to the city's policy shift. The organization of these advocates, and their mobilization increased the pressure on the administration for a radical reassessment of the city's housing approach. The increased visibility of the city council, primarily through the efforts of Councilwoman Molina, also helped in the transformation of policy. Further, the housing movement seems to have been able to institutionalize itself securely in Los Angeles. The mayor's top three housing appointments are from the movement itself. These appointees are presiding over new programs and administrative directives aimed at increasing the role of nonprofit developers (themselves members of the movement) in the city's housing delivery system, even further entrenching the movement and its goals.

The development of the movement did not occur, however, without exposing two major fault lines. The first fault line derived from the degree (or perceived degree) of community-based orientation of the groups in the movement. The neighborhood-based community organizations that joined the housing movement in the late 1980s had a slightly different agenda for policy reform from that of the more professional development corporations, which initially dominated the movement. The second fault line had to do with the source of funding for the social programs that member groups were implementing. The issue of the CRALA cap threatened to pit CRALA-funded organizations against county-funded groups. The movement was able to produce a unified front on the issue but not without what one participant called "a really frightening divisive debate."[54]

To some extent, these two fault lines in the housing movement support Gittells' and Piven and Cloward's argument that more formalized forms of organization and service delivery can be detrimental to the progress of a social movement. In the first case, community-based organizations and the regional nonprofits did not share political objectives. It can be argued that the more professionalized nonprofits had lost touch with the political and social objectives of the communities they ostensibly served. In the second case, division occurred because organizations in the movement were reliant on government funding. The implications of this for the autonomy of the movement are obvious and foreboding. In the end, however, though these tensions threatened the cohesion of the housing movement in Los Angeles, it has not ruptured or splintered into factions. Indeed, the degree of division between the community-based groups and the more professionalized CDCs began to blur as the number of community-based CDCs began to multiply.

POLITICAL POSTSCRIPT

The gains made by the housing movement in Los Angeles have been impressive but incomplete. Though the mayor's office is now much more receptive to housing advocacy, the city council lost its main housing champion in 1990. Councilwoman Molina won election to the County Board of Supervisors in that year, and no one else on the council has stepped into her shoes as the premier advocate for low-income housing. It appears, in Molina's absence, that Yaroslavksy and the others who supported housing initiatives did so out of opposition to CRALA more than from a strong commitment to low-income housing. As Bodaken put it, "The irony of this is pure. The mayor has indeed turned the corner on housing, but the city council, on the whole, has not."[55]

Without an effective housing advocate on the council, the housing advocates now holding posts in the Bradley administration are faced with an entirely different political challenge. In a weak-mayor form of government with an increasingly independent council, Bodaken, Squier, and the rest now must persuade council members (as well as independent-minded agencies such as CRALA) to cooperate with and support their initiatives. In addition, as government officials they find themselves accountable to a much larger constituency, as evidenced by the controversy created over the mayor's initial draft of the Comprehensive Housing Affordability Strategy. The city's draft CHAS incorporated a strong commitment to the production of affordable multifamily units, reflecting the orientation of the mayor's new advisers, but it also included strongly worded criticism of the exclusionary tendencies of homeowner groups and NIMBYism ("not in my back yard") throughout the city. The response was an overwhelming protest from homeowner groups all over the city, which instantly coalesced around the issue and forced the mayor and his aides into visible retreat.[56]

Finally, though advocates have much greater access to decision-making because of the mayor's appointments, bureaucratic impediments remain. As one community advocate put it, "If the housing staff was unproductive when housing was under CDD, why would they be any different now that the housing function is under HPPD? I don't see where HPPD has had a significant impact. I wish I could say that money is hitting the street faster than it did under CDD, or that, say, 20 percent more housing has been produced under HPPD than we were getting under CDD, but I can't. You still have a situation where the CRA has all of the money, and those turf issues have not been resolved yet."[57]

Thus, despite the enormous gains made by advocates in Los Angeles, there remain significant political and administrative challenges. The assumption of influence by progressive advocates does not mean that opposition to low-income housing has disappeared. In this sense, the struggle of the housing movement is ongoing. The election in 1993 of a conservative businessman to succeed Tom Bradley as mayor will likely present new challenges to the housing movement.

John Walton argues that the current debate over the importance of economic constraints versus local political factors in determining urban policy outcomes is in some ways misguided.[58] Clearly, economic restructuring has affected urban politics in profound ways, but it has not eliminated politics. Cities are affected by global economic trends at different times and in different ways. In Los Angeles, economic restructuring has produced very severe fissures in the social fabric: homeless shelters and make-shift cardboard shanties emerge in the shadow of multimillion-dollar highrises; thousands of immigrant families live in garages next to neighborhoods where median home values are over $400,000; business leaders share the downtown streets with homeless persons. As the case of Los Angeles has shown, the timing and nature of economic change, combined with the organization and distribution of local political resources, create local policy outcomes. Nevertheless, the response of city officials on a wide range of policies has been influenced by the emergence of a housing movement that has helped to bring the issue to the local agenda, framed the discussion of policy alternatives, and participated in the design and implementation of new programs.

7
Explaining the Use of Progressive Housing Policy

CHAPTERS 4 and 5 documented the spread of the new housing policy paradigm, and Chapter 6 illustrated that process in a single city. The evidence presented in those chapters points to the effectiveness of a community-based housing movement in establishing the new policy agenda and forcing action on it by governments at state and local levels. The proliferation of new policies and the apparent efficacy of local political action confounds the conventional understanding of local and state politics. The economic-constraints model predicts that local governments are likely to respond with strong disincentives to redistributive policies and policies that directly encumber private development. Yet the new housing paradigm is characterized by just such techniques. In addition, the constraints model identifies nonpolitical factors as the important determinants of local policies. The widespread adoption of progressive housing programs at state and local levels thus requires a different understanding of local government capacities and the politics of redistributive policy. This chapter provides an assessment of why this new type of housing policy is occurring in some locations. In the process, the chapter presents the findings from a statistical examination of the central thesis of this book: namely, that a locally oriented, community-based housing movement has effectively advocated a new policy paradigm that has significantly altered the nature of housing policy in the United States.

The first section presents a statistical analysis of housing policy in U.S. cities. Survey data are combined with census and economic data in an attempt to create a model that explains the use of progressive housing policy at the municipal level. The second section repeats the analysis at the state level. In the course of this examination, a number of hypotheses about the utilization of more progressive housing policies are tested.

THE IMPACT OF THE HOUSING MOVEMENT IN U.S. CITIES

The impact of community-based political action on housing in U.S. cities is examined here in two ways. An initial analysis presents data on the influence of local housing advocates as perceived by city government officials. The second and more extensive analysis is a multivariate statistical examination of the determinants of progressive housing policy in U.S. cities.

The Perceived Impact of Local Housing Mobilization

Survey respondents were asked the following question: "How influential in policymaking are local housing advocates: influential on a wide range of issues, influential on specific issues, not influential, or not involved in the policymaking process?" Officials in 24 percent of the cities responded that housing advocates were influential on a wide range of issues; in 41 percent responses indicated isolated influence on the part of advocates; in 16 percent local advocates were considered not influential; and in 19 percent they were characterized as not involved in policymaking. Thus, in almost two-thirds of the large cities responding to the survey, city officials perceived local advocates to be at least sporadically influential in policymaking.

Though these findings indicate some support for the notion that the housing movement has been influential, we were more specifically interested in whether the formal organization of advocates into coalitions enhances the impact of the movement. The extent of community mobilization was measured through the combination of responses to two questions: first, "Is there a citywide low-income housing advocacy group in your city?" and later in the questionnaire, "Are nonprofit housing developers organized into a coalition?"

We found a strong relationship between the degree of coalition building within the housing movement and the perceived influence of the movement. Officials in 90 percent of the cities with both housing and nonprofit coalitions regarded the housing movement as influential in policymaking, compared with 72 percent in cities having only one of the two kinds of coalitions and 31 percent in cities with no organized low-income housing advocacy coalition.[1]

But a perception of influence and actual impact on policy choices can be two different matters. Indeed, a high level of organization may simply provide the movement with a higher profile, and local officials may have been responding to this higher profile rather than to a truly enhanced policy impact when they evaluated the influence of housing advocates. So, although the relationship just reported can be argued to support the central hypothesis of the book it cannot be taken as sufficient evidence by itself. For a more extensive analysis of the impact of the housing movement on local housing policy choices we turn to a multivariate statistical examination of the determinants of progressive housing policy.

Multivariate Analysis of Progressive Housing Policy

A more rigorous examination of the impact of the local housing movement can be achieved by testing the relationship between mobilization and actual policy outputs. A multivariate analysis allows us to test for the policy impact of the housing movement while controlling for other possible influences. For competing explanations of the proliferation of new paradigm policies, it is necessary to go both to the literature on economic constraints and to a series of studies of "progressive development policy."[2] These analyses have attempted to describe and explain the emergence of policies that do not follow the assumptions of the economic-constraints framework, and thus they provide a source of alternative explanations.

The central hypothesis argues: *Progressive development policy is associated with higher levels of community-based political mobilization.* Much of the anecdotal evidence presented in the previous chapters points to the importance of political pressure from community-based housing advocates. Indeed, community-based advocates represent the primary source of alternatives to conventional incentive-based housing and development policy.[3] Further, extant analyses of "progressive" cities identify the success of populist, community-based political activity as a common characteristic.[4] Arguments that stress the importance of such political actors as a mobilized community-based movement fundamentally challenge the mechanistic explanations of the economic-constraints model. That is, evidence of effective local political action suggests that nonlocal economic and fiscal constraints are not as binding as the constraints model holds.

The economic-constraints model provides hints regarding why and under what circumstances more redistributive development policies will occur. Peterson and others imply that cities able to expand the boundaries of development policy are those that have sufficient wealth to enhance (1) their bargaining position vis-à-vis the private sector, and (2) their competitive position vis-à-vis other municipalities. Dreier and Keating describe progressive housing policies in Boston as being in large part due to the city's strong economic performance.[5] Analyses of office-housing linkage programs have concluded that they are likely only in cities experiencing a very robust office-based economic boom.[6] One study of the different development policies "possible" in growth and nongrowth cities (using Boston and Detroit as examples) argues that economic performance creates the conditions for policy that is free of external economic constraints.[7] This understanding of local policy establishes economic growth and well-being as necessary conditions for progressive land policy. The second hypothesis is thus taken from the economic-constraints model: *Progressive housing policy will be undertaken only in those cities experiencing relatively favorable economic/fiscal conditions.*

In previous analyses of unconventional development policy, however, the constraints hypothesis has not fared well. A number of studies have found evidence that more policy innovation has taken place in slow-growth cities or that policy innovation follows need.[8] These findings point to an obvious need for additional hypotheses related to the incidence of progressive development policy. Hence, the third hypothesis tested: *Progressive development policy is associated with a concentration of needy populations.* That is, sizable concentrations of poverty or high unemployment can create specific and identifiable needs that require a direct policy response. Swanstrom, for example, argues that the level of neighborhood distress in Cleveland produced a political climate that supported neighborhood-based development planning and strongly opposed tax abatements and corporate handouts.[9]

Though the need hypothesis seems contradictory to the economic-constraints hypothesis, it is not necessarily so. Analyses of economic restructuring and the urban impacts of global economic changes point to a pattern of uneven development within cities that have undergone extensive economic restructuring.[10] Cities such as New York and Los Angeles can benefit from an unprecedented amount of commercial investment (in the form of downtown office highrises or the growth of high-tech industries) and at the same time have a growing population of under- and unemployed because of a loss of unionized manufacturing jobs and an increase in low-wage, irregular, and informal employment.[11] If, in cities such as these, development policy is characterized by a more progressive orientation, then both the constraints and the need hypotheses are supported.

The literature on state-level policy outputs has established "need" as an important determinant of redistributive policy,[12] even though measures of need are often categorized with growth and wealth variables and conceptualized together as measures of "economic development."[13] Postindustrial urban growth has shown, however, that summary measures of wealth and poverty can have distinct trajectories and that the two concepts do not share a simple inverse relationship. This "uneven development" hypothesis states: *Progressive housing policies will occur in cities experiencing relatively high degrees of income polarization.*

The fifth hypothesis relates to the political culture of local areas and the willingness to orient development policy toward equity concerns. Clavel and Kleniewski and, in a separate analysis, Walton suggest that the existence of a historical tradition of innovation and concerns about equity may produce a local political environment conducive to questioning the conventional wisdom and tenets of growth politics.[14] This line of reasoning suggests that local political culture is an important factor in determining urban policy outcomes. As defined by Verba, political culture is "the system of empirical beliefs, expressive symbols, and values which defines the situation in which political action takes place."[15] The most compelling operationalization of political culture comes from the work of Daniel Elazar, who many years ago posited the existence of three distinct political subcultures in the United States: the moralistic, the individualistic, and the traditionalistic.[16] The distribution of these subcultures is determined by settlement patterns and the spatial distribution of "ethnic, socioreligious, and socioeconomic differences which existed among residents of the three main sections of the original thirteen colonies."[17] In the moralistic culture, politics represents the common effort to create a good and just society. Government and participation in politics are seen as means of providing for the public welfare, and therefore governmental intervention in economic and social matters is assumed to be legitimate. By contrast, "the individualistic political culture holds politics to be just another means by which individuals may improve themselves socially and economically."[18] Ideological and moral bases for political action are replaced by a market-oriented, utilitarian concept. Politics and government produce individualistic rewards or favors rather that programmatic ends, resulting in a "tradition of privatism" in government.[19] The traditionalist political culture in Elazar's formulation is based on a hierarchical or paternalistic view of society that discourages broad-based participation in favor of an elite network of power brokers.

Elazar's original formulation of the concept, as scaled by Sharkansky,[20] has proven to be a strong predictor of a variety of policy responses at local and state levels.[21] Sharkansky applied a system that assigns numbers from 1 to 9 for cultures ranking from moralistic to traditionalistic. Thus: *Progressive development policy is more likely to occur in areas characterized by a moralistic political culture.*

The final hypothesis to be tested relates to the bureaucratic experience and capacity of local governments to pursue innovative development policy.[22] It is plausible to expect that officials with experience in development or housing policy—through participation in federal programs, for example—have acquired sufficient expertise to innovate. Clarke and Rich, in their study of local implementation of the Urban Development Action Grant, point to the influence of federal officials in broadening the scope of local development policy options by requiring local officials to be more aggressive in the demands they make of private partners.[23] Thus: *Progressive housing policy is more likely to occur in cities with greater public development experience.*

The multivariate regression analysis uses a number of independent variables that specifically test each of the six hypotheses just described. The independent variables measure political mobilization, fiscal conditions, economic conditions, need, political culture, and bureaucratic experience.[24]

The dependent variable for this analysis, taken from the survey of housing officials, represents the additive combination of answers related to three different areas of policy, each of which fit into the framework of alternative or progressive policy outlined in Chapters 2 through 6. The policy areas are (1) the use of regulations to support low-income housing; (2) the promotion of low-income housing in downtown areas and the promotion of SRO housing; and (3) the support of nonprofit housing through the provision of four types of operating, technical, and financial assistance.

Respondents were asked whether their municipality had the following regulatory devices for the support of low-income housing: rent control, inclusionary zoning, one-for-one replacement requirements, a housing linkage program, a moratorium or limit on the conversion or demolition of affordable housing. Regarding the second area, there were items asking whether the municipality had programs for the production or preservation of affordable housing downtown, and the production or preservation of SRO housing. The third policy cluster is the support of nonprofits. Chapter 5 outlined the nature of nonprofit CDC needs, and the extent to which cities reported providing for those needs. The number of nonprofit supports provided by municipalities ranges from 0 to 4. The summary scale ranges from 0 to 13 and is seen as measuring the progressive orientation of local housing policy. The scale variable, PHOUSING, is the dependent variable in the analysis to follow.

Analysis: The Use of Progressive Housing Policies

The breakdown of the use of the progressive housing policies is shown in Table 7.1. The most widely used policies relate to support for nonprofit housing (items 6 through 9 in the table). Over one-half of the responding cities in the sample were providing each of the supports listed. Downtown and SRO housing policies (items 10–13) were in evidence in one-quarter to one-half of the cities. The regulatory policies (items 1–5) were used more infrequently, showing up in 9 to 14 percent of the sample cities.

The distribution of the PHOUSING variable is shown in Figure 7.1. The PHOUSING variable ranges from a value of 0 (in those cities

Spread of Progressive Housing Policy   175

TABLE 7.1
Use of progressive housing policies by 133 responding cities

Policy	Cities N	%
1. Rent control	14	11
2. Inclusionary zoning	12	9
3. Housing linkage	13	10
4. Demolition/conversion moratoria	19	14
5. One-for-one replacement	10	8
6. Technical assistance to nonprofits	70	56
7. Administrative funding to nonprofits	75	59
8. Project financing to nonprofits	104	82
9. Predevelopment financing to nonprofits	65	52
10. Creation of SRO housing	31	23
11. Preservation of SRO housing	24	18
12. Creation of downtown affordable housing	60	45
13. Preservation of downtown affordable housing	64	48

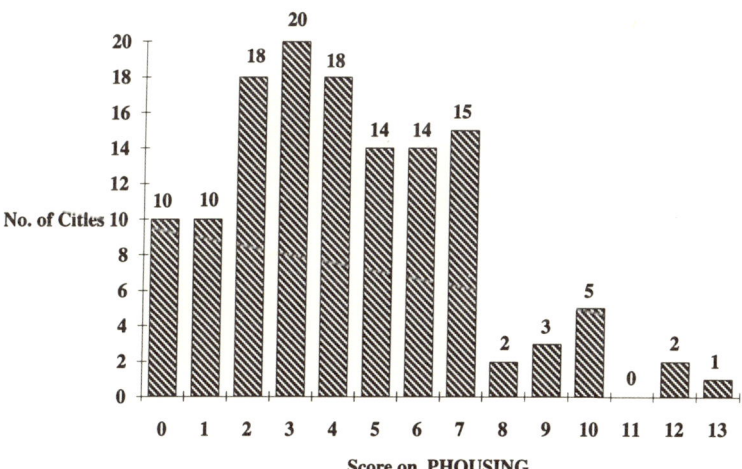

FIGURE 7.1
Distribution of PHOUSING variable among cities

that do not engage in any of the progressive housing policies identified here) to 13 (in those cities having all of the policies listed). Figure 7.1 shows that most of the cities in the sample achieved scores on the PHOUSING variable of seven or less. Only ten cities in the sample engaged in none of the progressive policies explored in this analysis. The mean value of PHOUSING is 4.36.

As Figure 7.1 shows, there are a few cities that use many of the progressive housing programs. These more progressive cities tend to be concentrated on the west coast, especially in the state of California. Nevertheless, there are representative cities from all regions in the list of the most progressive housing cities, including Stamford, Connecticut, and Buffalo, New York, in the East; Cincinnati, Ohio, and Milwaukee, Wisconsin, in the Midwest; and Miami, Florida, and Alexandria, Virginia, in the South (see Table 7.2).

Multiple regression analysis was conducted to determine the relative importance of each of the hypotheses stated above.[25] The analysis reveals support for most of the hypotheses. The degree of community-based housing mobilization is strongly associated with progressive policy response. Cities that have an organized housing movement are significantly more likely to engage in progressive housing than other cities. In addition, net of other factors, cities with better bond ratings and cities with higher per capita incomes also pursue more progressive housing policies. These findings suggest that the economic-constraints model is supported by the

TABLE 7.2

Cities scoring highest on progressive housing scale (PHOUSING)

City	Score	City	Score
Berkeley, Calif.	13	Springfield, Mass.	9
San Francisco, Calif.	12	Sunnyvale, Calif.	9
Los Angeles, Calif.	12	Milwaukee, Wis.	8
Stamford, Conn.	10	Buffalo, N.Y.	8
Seattle, Wash.	10	Miami, Fla.	7
Oakland, Calif.	10	Minneapolis, Minn.	7
San Bernardino, Calif.	10	Alexandria, Va.	7
Cincinnati, Ohio	10	Madison, Wis.	7
Portland, Ore.	9	San Diego, Calif.	7
		Washington, D.C.	7

data, yet at the same time the need hypothesis also finds significant statistical support. In fact, the degree of poverty within a city is the strongest single predictor of progressive housing. Another indicator of need, the existence of housing cost and availability problems, is also significantly associated with the pursuit of progressive policies. The results indicate that both the existence of wealth and the extent of poverty are important determinants of housing policy response. As a result of these findings, another test was made to examine the uneven development hypothesis by combining the income and poverty variables into one indicator that measures the degree of income polarization within the city. The data show that as income polarization becomes greater from one city to the next, the use of progressive housing policies also increases. Political culture is also related to progressive housing in the manner predicted. That is, the more moralistic the local political culture (other things constant), the greater the use of progressive housing programs. The only hypothesis that does not receive support is the bureaucratic experience hypothesis. Officials' previous experience with federal urban programs has little bearing on whether their cities will be innovators in the postfederal era.

THE POLICY IMPACT OF STATEWIDE HOUSING COALITIONS

In order to assess the impact of the housing movement at the state level, I employ a strategy similar to that just used for the analysis of city housing policies. Three separate analyses assess the impact of the housing movement. The first utilizes interviews with the directors of statewide housing coalitions in 32 states. Coalition directors provided information on the scope and success of their advocacy campaigns at the state level. These data relate the self-perceived success of members of the housing movement. The second analysis is based on data from the survey of state housing agency officials. State officials, like their city counterparts, were asked: "How influential have low-income advocates been in the formulation of the state's affordable housing policy?" The analysis of responses to this question mirrors the examination of the same question at the city level. These data provide state officials' perceptions of the influence of the housing movement. The third means by which the impact of the statewide housing movement is tested also echoes the analysis done at the city level; that is, the adoption of progressive housing programs by the states is examined in a multivariate regression analysis. Alternative explanations for the spread of progressive policies are examined along with the impact of the housing movement.

The Legislative Success of State Coalitions

As reported in Chapter 3, state coalitions exhibit a wide range of legislative strategies, from public education campaigns to the active pursuit of specific legislative initiatives. Similarly, coalition directors reported a range of success stories. In California the state coalition was successful in getting twenty-five of thirty-five bills signed in the 1989 legislative session. Additionally, in response to gubernatorial obstruction of existing programs, the coalition successfully switched to a strategy based on voter approval of initiatives to fund housing programs. In Connecticut the coalition reported that it successfully put two bills through against the will of the administration. Some successes were not related to specific legislative action. In Tennessee, for example, the coalition was not active in the legislative session but was able to shape policy significantly through its involvement in governmental planning sessions.[26]

Other groups reported much less success in their respective legislatures. In Iowa and Kentucky the organizations' achievements were limited to "getting people to notice housing issues."[27] Elsewhere, legislative packages supported by state coalitions simply failed. In New Hampshire both portions of the LIHAC's agenda were tabled and ultimately died in committee. In New Jersey all three bills on the group's slate failed. West Virginia reported that it had "not seen a lot of tangible results" from its advocacy efforts.[28]

For summary purposes the coalition directors' responses are categorized as follows:

1. Significant success ($n = 8$): Arkansas, California, Connecticut, Illinois, Kansas, Minnesota, Ohio, Tennessee. These groups reported more than 50 percent of their agenda successfully adopted. They may have also reported success in electoral

campaigns (such as initiatives and referendums) and policymaking influence.
2. Limited success (*n* = 11): Alabama, Georgia, Maryland, Michigan, Missouri, North Carolina, Pennsylvania, Rhode Island, Utah, Virginia, Washington. Groups in this category reported mixed results. Some legislative agenda items were adopted, but typically, little was accomplished relative to the goals of the organization.
3. Little or no success (*n* = 13): Delaware, Florida, Iowa, Indiana, Kentucky, Massachusetts, Mississippi, New Hampshire, New Jersey, New York, South Carolina, Vermont, West Virginia. This category includes groups claiming "moral victories" in "getting people's attention," groups reporting rejection of their legislative agendas, and groups that reported no legislative activity.

Nineteen of the thirty-two organizations interviewed, or 59 percent, reported at least limited success during the 1989 legislative session. Even groups in states with little previous involvement in housing programs, such as Arizona, Kansas, and Tennessee, reported some success in the legislature. Conversely, in states such as Massachusetts, New York, and New Jersey, historically very active in housing assistance, the statewide advocacy group reported little or no success. Though this finding seems anomalous, the self-reported legislative success was limited to the 1989 legislative session and does not reflect the record of these groups (or these legislatures) over the entire postfederal era.

In the second measure of housing movement impact, state housing officials, like their city counterparts, were asked to rate the influence of housing advocates in the policymaking process. Officials in states with organized coalitions were significantly more likely to rate housing advocates as influential. Advocates were rated influential in 55 percent of states with no formal organization, compared with 85 percent and 88 percent of states with one and two housing coalitions.[29] This is the same pattern of response as that shown by city officials. Though the findings indicate an impressive pattern of influence of the organizational manifestations of the housing movement, they remain impressionistic, based as they are on the perceptions of policy officials. The next section attempts to buttress these findings by applying statistical techniques to the aggregate analysis of the policy impact of the community-based housing movement.

Multivariate Analysis of the Impact of Statewide Housing Coalitions

The multivariate analysis of state level housing policy generally follows the format used for the city level analysis. The central objectives of the analysis are twofold: first, to test the importance of community-based mobilization in determining the scope of progressive housing policy at the state level; second, to fashion a more general model of progressive housing policymaking. To that end several hypotheses are examined that closely follow the city-level analysis. The hypotheses regarding the impact of economic conditions, need variables, and political culture on city policies all have their counterparts in the analysis of state policies. In addition, the long-established literature on the determinants of state policy outputs is used to help shape the analysis.[30] Especially useful are the various studies that have examined the impact of "political factors" in determining policy outputs in the states.[31] The most common political factors analyzed in these studies are party competition, voter turnout, and apportionment. Among these factors, voter turnout is generally found to be unrelated to most policy outputs,[32] and the impact of apportionment is inconclusive.[33] In contrast, party competition has been shown to be strongly related to redistributive policy at the state level.[34] As Fenton argues, the impact of party competition on redistribution "is a result of the fact that party competition 'democratizes' politics by paying greater deference to the poor and thereby rendering politics less oligarchical."[35] Thus, the following analysis of state-level housing policy substitutes a party competition hypothesis for the bureaucratic experience hypothesis used in the city level analysis: *States having higher levels of party competition are more likely to engage in progressive development policy.*[36]

As in the city-level analysis, a summary index of progressive housing policy is used as a dependent variable. As explained in Chapter 4, the face of progressive policy is somewhat different at the state level. Land-use regulations, such as linkage and rent control, and spatial strategies that focus housing benefits in downtown areas are either inappropriate at the state level or related to specifically local powers of land-use control. On the other hand, some forms of progressive housing policy are *more* appropriate at the state level. For example, the development of housing trust funds, though in evidence in some municipalities, has occurred in close to half of the fifty states. This is in all likelihood due to the greater potential for funding resources at the state than at the local level. In addition, policy responses to the crisis of expiring use restrictions are generally made at the state level in order to protect previously state-assisted housing projects and provide regional uniformity. Thus, the measure of progressive housing for state governments (PHOUSING) is a simple additive index reflecting the number of the following policies that each state is pursuing:

1. A moratorium on the conversion or demolition of low-income housing.
2. One-for-one replacement of low-income housing units demolished or converted.
3. Restrictions related to the expiration of subsidies to privately owned, publicly assisted housing.
4. Other regulations related to the preservation and support of low-income housing (see Chapter 4).
5. The provision of predevelopment financing for nonprofit housing developers.
6. The provision of administrative support for nonprofit developers.
7. The provision of project financing for nonprofit developers.
8. The provision of technical assistance to nonprofit developers.
9. A program designed to create SRO housing units.
10. A program designed to preserve SRO housing units.
11. A housing trust fund.

Analysis: The Use of Progressive Housing Policies by States

The use of the progressive housing policies by U.S. states is shown in Table 7.3. As in larger U.S. cities, the most widely used policies relate to support for nonprofit housing. Over two-thirds of all states provide at least one of the supports to nonprofits identified earlier,

TABLE 7.3
Use of progressive housing policies by responding states

Policy	States N	%
Demolition/conversion moratoria	5	11
One-for-one replacement	2	4
Other land-use regulations	8	17
Technical assistance to nonprofits	25	52
Administrative funding to nonprofits	22	46
Project financing to nonprofits	30	62
Predevelopment financing to nonprofits	25	52
Creation of SRO housing	11	23
Preservation of SRO housing	5	10
Expiring-use restrictions program	10	21
Housing trust fund	21	44

ᵃ Arizona and Oklahoma missing.

and almost one-third provide all four forms of support. As for the regulations and SRO housing support, less than one-fourth of all states engage in these programs.

The distribution of the PHOUSING variable for states is shown in Figure 7.2. The PHOUSING variable ranges from a value of 0 (in those states that do not engage in any of the progressive housing policies identified here) to 10. None of the fifty states engages in all the progressive housing policies listed above. Figure 7.2 shows a fairly even distribution tailing off at the high range. Eleven of the states engage in none of the progressive policies explored in this analysis. The mean value of PHOUSING for the states is 3.73.

As in the city-level analysis, independent variables were entered into a multiple regression equation to estimate the impact of various explanations while controlling for all the others.[37] The findings from this analysis closely mirror the results at the city level. First, as to the central hypothesis, there is a strong relationship between the existence of a housing movement and the adoption of progressive policy. States that have housing advocacy coalitions are significantly more likely to adopt progressive housing measures even controlling for other factors. This indicates that the community-based advocacy of the housing movement has had a significant

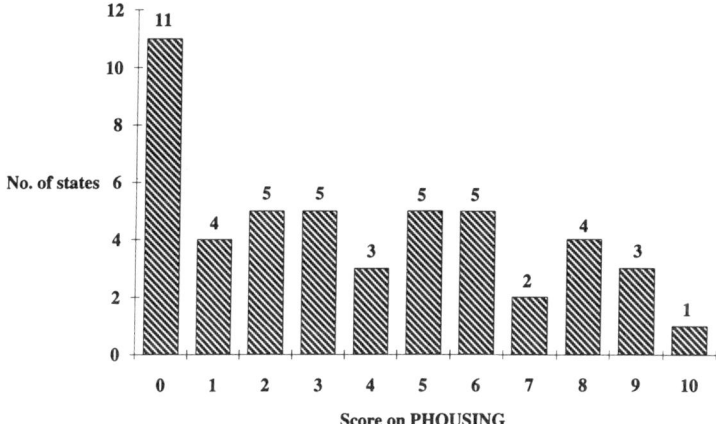

FIGURE 7.2
Distribution of PHOUSING variable among states

impact in shaping housing policy outputs at both the state and local levels.

States with higher per capita income levels are more likely to pursue progressive policies, as are states with higher public assistance rolls. These findings mirror those at the city level which suggest that both wealth and need are important determinants of policy innovation in housing.[38] Political culture plays a less important role at the state level; there is, in fact, no relationship between statewide political culture and the use of progressive housing policies. Finally, the amount of party competition in state politics is also irrelevant to the adoption of the new housing paradigm.

SUMMARY

Two important conclusions emerge from the preceding analyses. First, the importance of community-based political mobilization is supported statistically at both the state and the local level. Mobilized advocacy for the housing needs of low-income households and, equally important, advocacy for a progressive response to those needs have produced a local policy response in the postfederal era. Second, the net impact of the economic variables and the needs indicators suggests that income polarization—the existence of both wealth and poverty—is another important condition leading to housing policy innovation at state and local levels. In contrast, institutional explanations that focus on bureaucratic experience and interparty political competition find no support in the data.

Social Action and Progressive Housing Policy

The analysis presented in these pages validates findings reported elsewhere showing that the existence of active community-based mobilization is necessary for the introduction of alternative development policy. The impact of community mobilization occurs through two channels. First, community-based mobilization has led to electoral success in some cities and occasionally resulted in a governing coalition sympathetic to the demands of neighborhoods, African Americans, the poor, or other traditionally excluded groups. Such governing coalitions characterize the "progressive cities" of Berkeley, Burlington, and Santa Monica. More frequently, however, the control of progressives is less complete and their agenda only partially enacted. Boston and Harold Washington's Chicago are perhaps the best-known examples in this category. Nevertheless, the electoral avenue has been successfully exploited by some local progressive movements.

Second, community-based mobilization has influenced policy by means other than through electoral channels. By mounting opposition to status quo development practices and achieving the ability to hinder mainstream policy, community-based interests have acquired access to policymaking. In San Francisco, for example, community-based advocates were able to mount significant legal challenges to many downtown development projects. As a result of these legal successes they gained access to the policy process and participated in the design of the linkage program and the creation of a number of concessions by the city to the downtown development process.[39]

In a larger sense then, the success of the movement provides support for the contention that politics matters in the formation of urban and state policy. Set against a theoretical backdrop arguing that the important determinants of urban policy are external and economic, the central role of the community-based housing movement in shaping housing policy in the postfederal era is significant. In fact, both community-based activism and political culture are important statistical correlates of progressive policy activity at the city level.

The importance of the political culture variable in the statistical analysis indicates that a historical heritage of inclusive politics is important in providing a political environment conducive to alternative policy strategies. The political culture of cities provides the setting for progressive politics by expanding the vocabulary of local politics to include nontraditional policy objectives. In addition, political culture can provide for the nourishment of community-based movements which, in turn, expand the boundaries of political interchange. As Walton argues, "Where a tradition of popular action perseveres in broadly mobilized community organizations, countermovements may restrain the maldistributive effects of unfettered growth."[40] In the cities studied here, political tradition has been shown to be an important condition for the emergence of progressive housing policy.

Economic Restructuring and Progressive Housing

What also emerges from the statistical analysis is a picture of cities and states in which the existence of both wealth and poverty influence the form of housing policy. The economic-constraints model only partially explains the impact of external economic factors. This analysis suggests that economic polarization is one key to redistributive policy responses. Cities that experience greater maldistribution of income pursue more innovative housing policy. The postindustrial restructuring of urban economies has produced a growing disparity of incomes. The fastest-growing sector of the economy, the service sector, produces more technologically oriented and higher-paying jobs on the one hand and low-paying, low-status jobs on the other. At the same time, the economy is losing well-paid blue-collar manufacturing jobs. The result is a vanishing middle class and an "hour glass" income distribution, relatively heavier at both the top and the bottom.

Cities that "successfully" restructure their economies and bring them in line with post-industrial realities are often faced with this type of maldistribution in wealth.[41] The spatial manifestation of this inequality is often the juxtaposition of thriving downtowns with neglected communities of poverty. The achievement of wealth and prosperity for one segment of society is set against the increased poverty and emiseration of another segment. In this environment, status quo policy strategies become suspect, and pro-growth coalitions have trouble staying the course. The growing disparity in wealth and incomes produced by economic restructuring contributes to the creation of a political environment conducive to more progressive policy. Extreme income polarization leads to organizing around a low-income equity issue such as affordable housing by making the issue itself more salient. In addition, deteriorating conditions in neighborhoods can produce resentment and backlash against the heavy public subsidies channeled into downtown development. As a result, cities with these conditions are being forced to pursue progressive and more redistributive development policies in an effort to bring greater equity to the development process. In this respect, the economic-constraints argument, which contends that economic conditions supersede local political factors in determining policy, is in fact wrong. Instead of neutering local politics, economic conditions in urban areas during the 1980s created conditions around which a community-based political response to status quo growth politics has emerged.

8
Social Action, Economic Restructuring, and Progressive Housing Policy

> *More democratic control over home and neighborhood spaces. More control over the quality of life in communities. More direct democratic input into housing development. More popular control over local developers and lenders. . . . People are demanding control over investors and corporate executives who too callously abandon communities, and thereby create severe social costs for workers with deep-rooted ties to particular places.*
> —Joe Feagin and Robert Parker, Building American Cities

THIS BOOK has attempted to show that contemporary housing policy in the United States as practiced by state and local governments has dramatically departed from previous federal approaches and has been significantly influenced by the political activism of a community-based and locally oriented housing movement. It has identified a new paradigm for housing policy in the United States and has documented the assumption of leadership for housing innovation by local governments. In so doing, the book has touched on the nature and importance of local politics, the impact of urban restructuring on local policy, and the politics of community-based social movements.

What has been occurring in housing politics since 1980 might be interpreted as the reorientation of housing advocacy from the federal to the local level. As the Reagan administration put the clamps on domestic social spending, housing advocates moved their efforts to the local level in search of a more sympathetic government response.[1] Yet the local housing movement in the United States is much more than a reorientation of advocacy from national to local levels. For one thing, the content of the housing solutions offered by the local housing movement ran counter to the prevailing trends in domestic policy during the 1980s. While "deregulation" was successfully pursued in a number of economic sectors during the 1980s, governments at the local level were introducing new and different forms of regulation to enhance support of low-income housing. Additionally, whereas the private sector was championed at the national level as being capable of solving social problems, at the local level, with respect to housing, there was a self-conscious move away from using the private sector and toward reliance on a community-based nonprofit sector.

In addition to having countered strong trends in national politics, the local housing movement shares important characteristics with a more broadly based community response to the problems of urban areas during a period of global economic restructuring. The concerns of housing advocates, as described in Chapter 3, go beyond narrowly defined housing issues. The advocates themselves are likely to be involved in a range of social and community-based issues. The local housing movement itself is part of a larger effort by urban communities to reinvent themselves as economic entities and to reclaim a measure of control over the use and development of urban space.

The local housing movement of the 1980s and 1990s can, in fact, be placed within a more broadly based political tradition, one emphasizing local control and democratic accountability in both political and economic matters. In the 1960s, for example, "community control" was one of the organizing themes of the urban movement. The phrase was generally used by organizers in African American neighborhoods and referred primarily to demands for local, decentralized authority over political and social institutions.[2] In the context of the Great Society programs of the 1960s, community control meant local influence over government and the quasi-governmental agencies that were delivering social services to urban neighborhoods.[3] According to Fainstein and Fainstein, the movement had strong roots in a Jeffersonian concept of local governance, uniting 1960s urban radicalism with the most basic of American political ideologies.[4] As Chapter 3 recounts, this same political orientation motivated the "neighborhood movement" of the 1970s.

In the 1980s and 1990s the objectives of community control took on a different aspect. In the face of growing globalization of the economy, the increasing mobility of private capital, the withdrawal of manufacturing to other shores, and the introduction of nonlocal investment in many city centers, community control today refers to the ability of a community to define itself economically. Can local actors shape an economy that is not dependent on the profit-based decisions of corporate leaders who increasingly orient themselves toward global markets and decreasingly identify themselves or their product with any given locality? Community activism in the United States is attempting to answer that question in the affirmative. The contemporary progressive movement in urban America is concerned with returning a sense of political and economic efficacy to local communities. Housing is but one element in a larger agenda aimed at both taming and modifying the impacts of unfettered, market-driven development.

PROGRESSIVE DEVELOPMENT

The larger progressive agenda is seen notably in community-based responses to economic development and in alternatives to growth initiated by community-based interests. In the area of economic development, for example, community activists have begun to advocate policies that channel the benefits of development to non-downtown areas and non-elite groups. First-source hiring agreements, in which jobs are reserved for local residents, and requirements for the participation of minority-owned and women-owned business enterprises, (MBE and WBE) are two examples. Other techniques such as shared equity arrangements are designed to capture some of the fiscal benefits of development for local governments or community groups. In an earlier study I labeled these kinds of policies "Type II" economic development because they challenge the conventional wisdom of development subsidies and incentives.

Under conventional (Type I) development policy, subsidies and incentives are provided to the private sector in return for investment in the form of land development. The benefits, in theory, reach all sectors of the community as a result of jobs created by development, increased property tax revenues, and the multiplier effect through which new developments are assumed to create "ripple" or "trickle-down" economic activity. The reality of late urban development in the United States has not been so benign, however. Communities of color, low-income households, and peripheral neighborhoods have paid a large price for the downtown renaissance of many cities. The destruction of low-cost housing, gentrification, and targeted public subsidies in downtown areas have all contributed to a very uneven incidence of costs and benefits. Type II development policies attempt to correct such uneven distribution by directing benefits to specific recipient groups, such as minority business enterprises or local unemployed workers. In addition, Type II policies emphasize community-based ownership of housing, land, and capital and often impose obligations upon private developers to provide social benefits such as housing and child care.[5] There is some evidence that these more broadly defined progressive policies are being undertaken at the state level as well. Osborne describes a number of state policy initiatives that incorporate the objectives of greater public intervention in the marketplace, growth with equity, and the development of a third sector to control many development and land assets.[6]

The progressive policy paradigm is generally characterized by three attributes: a concern for equity as well as growth, a focus on economic democracy, and the advocacy of a distinctive set of policy techniques for achieving economic democracy and equity.[7]

Growth with Equity

Progressive analysis focuses on the role of private development in creating adverse conditions for low-income households. Specifically, the analysis emphasizes the uneven distribution of benefits from urban development. Particularly destructive in this respect has been the impact of downtown development, both private and publicly subsidized. The removal of affordable, low-cost housing in favor of commercial office buildings that house corporate headquarters and management facilities, and the elimination of SRO housing and sometimes entire neighborhoods of low-cost housing through public "redevelopment" have contributed significantly to the shortage of affordable housing.

Second, the tendency toward neighborhood decline even as

local officials cater to downtown revitalization is another aspect of the increasing difficulty for low-income households. The financial and symbolic importance of downtowns has led many cities to ignore declining neighborhoods and decaying infrastructure in order to put all their fiscal eggs in the basket of a rejuvenated downtown commercial core. Though community-based groups have voiced the downtown-versus-neighborhoods theme since the 1960s, the discontent on this particular issue continues to grow.

Third, the neighborhood "revitalization" that has occurred has generally been characterized by a high degree of gentrification. Speculation in real estate and rapidly escalating land values have led to the indirect displacement of low-income households in most of the neighborhoods that have received attention from public and private investors. The progressive analysis of urban problems attempts to identify more sensitive ways of revitalizing neighborhoods so that lower-income households can maintain their residences. An important element among the problems identified by the progressive analysis is the lack of community-based investment in neighborhoods by local lending institutions. The neighborhood movement of the 1970s made this issue its highest priority and succeeded in generating federal legislation such as the Home Mortgage Disclosure Act and the Community Reinvestment Act, which have made lending institutions more accountable. The community-based movement of the 1980s and 1990s has successfully used those legislative achievements as a foundation for continued monitoring of private-sector investment in low-income neighborhoods.

Fourth, the corporate strategies of disinvestment in the manufacturing sector have robbed many urban areas of the employment base necessary to maintain viability. The replacement of manufacturing jobs with inferior service-sector alternatives and the replacement of investment in productive capital with speculative investment in urban real estate have produced severe conditions for working-class and low-income inner-city neighborhoods.

The progressive movement thus begins with an acknowledgment of the inequalities produced by the private development process and works to accomplish a greater equity in the distribution of growth benefits.

Economic Democracy

A related element of the progressive agenda is the achievement of greater economic democracy. Bruyn and Meehan argue that efforts at community-based economic development derive from a sense that the power of self-determination has eroded at the community level.[8] In this context, economic democracy means self-determination, or the ability of communities to define themselves and shape their own economic realities. In another sense, the thrust of economic democracy is a reaction to what is perceived as the very undemocratic nature of recent urban development. The channeling of billions of subsidy dollars and tax incentives to multinational development firms in order to create highrise office buildings, plus the fact that the social costs of these developments are concentrated among lower-income groups, has created a political response. As Feagin and Parker argue, "The social costs of private development are the underlying reasons for much urban protest."[9]

The specific policy responses offered by communities have been direct reactions to the overuse and abuse of corporate subsidies and giveaways.[10] Community-based responses to plant closings, for example, focus on the nondemocratic nature of the economic decisionmaking that affects urban communities.[11] Portz describes the "populist" response to plant closings as an attempt to "democratically transform the American political economy" by inserting new actors and new demands into the economic process.[12]

Policy Techniques

The new progressive paradigm is based on an active citizen role and on active government. The creation of a viable nonprofit sector devoted to housing and community development is a method of both democratizing development and replacing the market-driven model of growth. A viable third sector is critical in developing an alternative to private-sector urban development. Community groups are attempting to expand the scope and role of the (community-based) nonprofit sector in both housing and business development. This constitutes a fundamental requirement of economic democracy and local self-determination, according to the progressive model.

The importance of a third sector has implications for other policy techniques as well. As Gunn and Gunn argue: "Development of an alternative sector also necessitates constraining the prerogatives that mainstream institutions now enjoy. For development of community-based, more democratic economic activity, that means constraining capital."[13] Thus, a third-sector approach to housing and community development requires greater regulation of the private development process. This has been achieved through various land-use regulations such as linkage, development moratoria, and inclusionary zoning. Other legislative and regulatory activities that help constrain the options of the private sector include, for example, plant closing legislation, first-source hiring, MBE and WBE requirements, and prepayment regulations. Together, these techniques constitute the second major method utilized in the new policy paradigm.

Finally, community-based planning and political mobilization are looked to as ways of institutionalizing a community orientation to urban policy and permanently incorporating community interests in policymaking. This has been especially true in housing. In a large number of U.S. cities, housing advocates have been able to insinuate themselves into the policymaking process. The vitality of the housing movement is related to its ability to tap into a widespread discontent regarding the life and death of urban communities. The objectives of sound and affordable housing have resonated with people uncertain about their own economic futures and living in communities with uncertain economic futures. The movement undoubtedly benefited from the more widespread crisis in U.S. housing: the fact that, for example, only 17 percent of Los Angeles residents could afford a median-priced home in 1987 (see Chapter 6); or the fact that the increase in rents in the state of Ohio during the 1980s was 33 percent higher than the increase in renter income (see Chapter 4); or the fact that homeownership among younger households fell 17 percent between 1980 and 1987.[14] The extent to which the movement has succeeded confounds conventional wisdom in the study of urban politics.

LOCAL POLITICS AND EXTERNAL CONSTRAINTS

Despite theoretical arguments that would lead us to expect local governments *not* to engage in progressive housing policy that redistributes resources from private developers to low-income households, or policy that usurps the role of the private development sector in housing production, local governments have indeed done just those things. Political scientists have argued for a long time that local governments have the tendency to be more conservative than their federal counterpart.[15] The capture of public life by dominant social and business interests is an inherent tendency of small governmental units.[16] Add to that tendency the strong economic constraints imposed by federalism (limited local authority and reliance on property tax revenues) and capitalism (mobile capital), and the theoretical argument against active pursuit of progressive or redistributive policies by local governments is very strong. Further, the logic implies that local governments will do little to encumber the private investment and development process. Yet, the experience of local governments in postfederal housing policy belies these theoretical expectations.

The constraints model, as its critics argue, devalues the role of local political factors in determining policy outputs. Local political debate is, according to the model, strongly limited by economic realities. These exogenous determinants are mediated by internal concerns related to maintaining high bond ratings and sufficient property tax revenue. Urban policy decisions in support of private capital investment are fairly uniformly made on the basis of these considerations. This argument ignores, however, the empirical reality of widespread variation in development and redistributive policy in U.S. cities. Clearly, in some cities the "constraints" of exogenous economic factors are overcome. The constraints model errs in its neglect of local political actors and their role in interpreting the strength or relevance of external policy constraints.

The "growth politics"[17] model became the dominant policy paradigm for cities during the postwar era not because of the automatic importance of external economic realities but because of the ascendancy of a particularly constituted "growth coalition" regime in most U.S. cities.[18] The policies of downtown renewal were not delivered on scrolls; they were formulated by the growth coalitions that controlled city governments. In Denver, for example, growth politics were championed by "a postwar generation of bankers, real estate brokers, merchants and small industrialists who, in concert with the Chamber of Commerce, sought growth at any price."[19] This description holds for a number of U.S. cities during the postwar years. In New Orleans, on the other hand, pro-growth policies were much more limited as a result of divisions among economic elites and the influence of a more traditional governing coalition.[20] The difference between just these two cities suggests that the nature of the governing coalition is important in determining local policy outcomes. As Judd and Parkinson argue, "Leadership may make a considerable difference in whether, and how, a city regenerates its economy."[21] Political fragmentation or a weakly constituted or unstable governing coalition can create conditions in which the articulation of a proactive growth agenda is problematic.

The constraints of exogenous economic factors are interpreted and made meaningful by local governing elites and by the distribution of political power within a locality. The Fainsteins and others, while arguing that economic factors are the "strongest" influence on local policy, nevertheless identify three important endogenous influences: the organization of local economic elites (echoed by the analysis of Judd and Parkinson, cited above),[22] racial and ethnic cleavages, and "the political situation" of localities.[23] This political situation is in part defined by the organizational capacity of lower- and working-class communities and their ability to articulate an alternative development agenda. In the Petersonian world of economic constraints, growth is universally acknowledged to be in the "interest of the city."[24] In the real world, such consensus is a good deal more problematic. As Logan and Molotch, as well as Davis, argue, one's interest in development and growth depends upon one's land-based interests.[25] To the extent that these interests vary and compete, development and growth will produce political conflict. How that conflict is resolved depends upon the differential ability of competing interests to coalesce, organize, and control the political agenda. It is the resolution of these political questions that determines which interests are able to interpret external factors. To ask, then, whether San Francisco, by virtue of its economic position, has more latitude than, say, Buffalo on development and redistributive matters is not really the primary question. One needs to examine the political capacities of competing land-based interests within the two cities, the distribution of political power locally, and the composition of the local governing elite (or regime) in order to understand the political lens through which external economic factors are defined and interpreted.

Indeed, the evidence presented in this book suggests that the economic-constraints model misspecifies the impact of the economy on local policy. Economic restructuring in the 1970s and 1980s created both benefits and costs to urban areas. In places where the dichotomy between these results is the greatest (that is, in places where the distribution of income is most unequal), there has been less adherence to the growth politics model, at least with respect to housing issues. This suggests, as I have already argued, that to some extent exogenous conditions influence the configuration of political interests within cities. The polarization of income and wealth in U.S. cities during the 1980s created the impetus for political mobilization in lower- and working-class neighborhoods. As Davis argues, the potential for collective action based on community interests hinges on the degree to which "a locality's material base" is linked with "the differentiation and political action of its indigenous groups"—a linkage of the spatial and the social.[26] Late urban economic restructuring has emphasized that link by radically transforming spatial relationships in ways that reinforce social inequalities. This has created the base for an urban social movement focused on the declining housing conditions and life chances experienced by a growing sector of lower- and working-class residents.

Housing policy is especially useful to examine in this respect because it bridges the gap between developmental policies related to land use and social service policies with more redistributive objectives. In Davis's terms, it bridges the spatial and the social. The fact that housing is part of the built environment, and therefore plays a key role in the accumulation of land value and the spatial configuration of restructured urban areas, means that it is vulnerable to manipulation by the investment and development objectives of private capital. Urban restructuring is in part about the reorganization of the built environment in a way that better facilitates capital accumulation in an era of flexible production. Housing, as part of the built environment, is thus a central element of restructuring.[27] Typically, low-cost urban housing suffers in competition with "higher uses" that provide greater return on investment. The elimination or decline of low-income neighborhoods is the frequent result. Because housing is a social issue as well—that is, because the provision of affordable housing is a social service—it has mobilized the political participation of community-based, low-income interests. The housing issue provides a unique opportunity to observe the social implications of urban development and economic restructuring. Given this reading, it is, at last, not surprising that the local, neighborhood-based response to housing in the 1980s was so strong.

This study reinforces the importance of urban social movements engendered by economic restructuring and mobilizing in response to the income disparities produced by development and redevelopment.[28] In fact, this analysis largely describes a process anticipated by Walton. As he argues, an "enriched theory" of local policy "would suggest that varied collective actions are explained by an interaction of the scope and timing of market reorganization and the history and organizational resources of local communities."[29] Indeed, these findings show that each of these factors—income polarization or the specific local impacts of "market reorganization," political culture, and community mobilization—has significantly contributed to an expansion of traditional policy alternatives and the realization of greater latitude for public policy at the local level.

THE FUTURE OF HOUSING POLICY

As some analysts begin to fear that low productivity, higher unemployment, and sagging performance will be the norm for the U.S. economy, the chances for prolonged fiscal problems at the local level are hardly remote. In such an environment, can we expect a continued vitality in local housing policy? Are the gains that have been made by housing advocates at the local level likely to evaporate as fiscal conditions worsen and priorities change? Such questions overlook the fact that the postfederal era in housing began in an era of fiscal retrenchment, recession, and budgetary cutbacks. The methods of the new policy paradigm were developed in response to scarcity; there is little reason to think that continuing scarcity will stall the movement. The increased regulation of the private sector, the use of a nonprofit third sector, nonbudgetary sources of support for trust funds and the like make the progressive paradigm unlike those social service agendas which are more heavily reliant on budgetary allocations.

At the state level, budgetary considerations are more relevant. The 1980s saw a vast expansion in state-funded programs and a threefold increase in state expenditures for housing. Despite these dramatic changes, it is unlikely that state legislators will ever consider the state the primary source of housing assistance. Even given the funding increases and the increased awareness of housing issues at the state level since 1980, the continued expansion of housing programs by the states is uncertain. At the same time, however, their commitment to a basic level of housing assistance appears permanent. The reaction of state governments to the 1991 recession has been mixed; though some states have backed off the expenditure levels that were reached during the peak (1987–89) years, none has abandoned the issue and returned to federal-era levels of expenditure. In fact, in states such as Minnesota, the commitment to affordable housing continues despite budget problems. In 1991, facing a multibillion-dollar deficit, the Minnesota legislature nevertheless passed a $29 million package for housing.[30] The severe budget cuts enacted by a number of state governments in 1991 may limit the expansion of the postfederal commitment of state funds for housing, but they are unlikely to reduce significantly or eliminate that commitment.

The progressive housing agenda has not, of course, been universally adopted by localities. There remain local governments unresponsive to affordable housing needs, governments that have adopted none of the innovations of the postfederal era. In those cities and states the housing movement is either nonexistent or has been unsuccessful in advocating for increased responsiveness to low-income housing needs. Even in the places that *have* created a postfederal housing policy, political reversals are possible. The new policy paradigm emerged in these localities because of dramatic need and the effective political work of the local housing movement. But as political battles can be won, they can also be lost. As the discussion in Chapter 4 indicated, elements of the progressive agenda, such as rent control, may face continual challenge from the private-sector development community even after they have been initiated. The political battle over housing policy at the local level is likely to be a continuing one.

At the federal level, continuing advocacy during the 1980s and 1990s has resulted in a modest expansion of federal commitment since its low point in 1987. In 1987 Congress passed the Stewart B. McKinney Homeless Assistance Act, which allocated federal funds to provide housing and social services for homeless persons. In 1988 and 1990 Congress passed other important housing legislation. In addition, some elements of the progressive paradigm have been introduced into federal legislation. The 1990 National Affordable Housing Act incorporated capacity building for nonprofits. A 15 percent set-aside for community-based housing development organizations was included as part of the HOME program. In 1987, one-for-one replacement was required for CDBG-funded projects that eliminated existing residential units.

A presidential administration of the future may make housing assistance a more central part of domestic priorities. Even so, given the great rupture with the past that occurred in 1981, future increases in housing assistance are likely to be incremental in nature and are therefore unlikely to restore funding to pre-1980 levels. The postfederal era in housing seems likely to endure for some time, even with renewed federal involvement.

In the end, of course, local governments cannot match the resources that the federal government can devote to housing. There are analysts who have written that for all their merits, policies such as housing linkage will never constitute a sufficient housing policy, that the federal government must reassume its leadership position in housing assistance.[31] It is true enough that linkage and other programs by themselves are inadequate to meet housing needs in most cities and states. Most observers agree that the federal government must increase its commitment to housing assistance. At its peak, federal housing assistance through HUD was at a budgetary level of over $32 billion a year. In 1989, after nine years of unprecedented growth in state expenditures for housing, the combined effort of the fifty states was slightly over $3 billion. Even the aggregate efforts of city governments do not bring the total local effort to a level near the current, reduced federal expenditure level. It is clear that a complete and adequate national approach to housing needs must incorporate a strong federal presence, even if innovation and leadership remain local.

This recognition does not, however, diminish the importance of postfederal policy innovations. The lessons of the new housing paradigm should be instructive. For example, awareness of the ways in which unfettered urban development contributes to housing problems should continue to inform housing policy. The current call for greater federal resources in housing should not be a call for the return to the policies of the federal era.

Notes

CHAPTER 1

1. See, e.g., David C. Schwartz, Richard C. Ferlauto, and Daniel N. Hoffman, *A New Housing Policy for America* (Philadelphia: Temple University Press, 1988); and Paul A. Leonard, Cushing N. Dolbeare, and Edward B. Lazere, *A Place to Call Home: The Crisis in Housing for the Poor* (Washington, D.C.: Center on Budget and Policy Priorities and Low Income Housing Information Service, 1989).

2. Schwartz, Ferlauto, and Hoffman *New Housing Policy*. See also Raymond J. Struyk, Neil Mayer, and John A. Tuccillo, *Federal Housing Policy at President Reagan's Midterm* (Washington, D.C.: Urban Institute Press, 1983).

3. Richard P. Nathan, Fred C. Doolittle, and Associates, *Reagan and the States* (Princeton, N.J.: Princeton University Press, 1987).

4. Ibid.

5. Eileen Brettler Berenyi, *Locally Funded Housing Programs in the United States: A Survey of the 51 Most Populated Cities* (New York: New School for Social Research, 1989).

6. See Peter R. Morris, *State Housing Finance Agencies* (Lexington, Mass.: Lexington Books, 1974).

7. Schwartz, Ferlauto, and Hoffman, *New Housing Policy*.

8. Paul E. Peterson, *City Limits* (Chicago: University of Chicago Press, 1981); Paul Kantor with Stephen David, *The Dependent City* (Glenview, Ill.: Scott, Foresman, 1988); Todd Swanstrom, "Semi-Sovereign Cities: The Politics of Urban Development," *Polity* 21 (Winter 1988): 83; Mark Gottdeiner, *The Decline of Urban Politics: Political Theory and the Crisis of the Local State* (Newbury Park, Calif.: Sage, 1987). See also David Harvey, *The Urbanization of Capital* (Baltimore, Md.: Johns Hopkins University Press, 1985).

9. Peterson, *City Limits*.

10. See Charles M. Tiebout, "A Pure Theory of Local Expenditures," *Journal of Political Economy* 64 (1956): 416. See also, Todd Swanstrom,

The Crisis of Growth Politics (Philadelphia: Temple University Press, 1985), for a description of the economic logic in Peterson's argument.

11. Clarence N. Stone and Heywood T. Sanders, *The Politics of Urban Development* (Lawrence: Kansas University Press, 1987). The particular element of this argument that has been challenged is the implication that politics doesn't matter in urban policy. Insofar as development is the defining issue in urban politics, the argument that development is consensual because of the larger economic constraints placed upon urban areas implies that local politics is largely devoid of important struggle or conflict. A host of analysts have taken on this proposition and shown it to be incorrect for a range of issues in a range of cities. Besides the Stone and Sanders collection, see also Susan S. Fainstein, Norman I. Fainstein, Richard Child Hill, Dennis Judd, and Michael Peter Smith, *Restructuring the City: The Political Economy of Urban Redevelopment* (New York: Longman, 1983); and Kenneth K. Wong, *City Choices: Education and Housing* (Albany, N.Y.: State University of New York Press, 1990).

12. See the collection of essays in Gregory D. Squires, ed., *Unequal Partnerships* (New Brunswick, N.J.: Rutgers University Press, 1989), for discussion of the "universal" benefits of development.

13. The classic statement is Harvey Molotch, "The City as a Growth Machine: Toward a Political Economy of Place," *American Journal of Sociology* 82 (1976): 309. The concept has been expanded by, among others, John H. Mollenkopf, *The Contested City* (Princeton, N.J.: Princeton University Press, 1983); and Swanstrom, *Growth Politics*. The analysis of privatistic urban policy is described by Timothy Barnekov and Daniel Rich, "Privatism and Urban Development: An Analysis of the Organized Influence of Local Business Elites," *Urban Affairs Quarterly* 23 (June 1977): 431. See also Timothy K. Barnekov, Robin Boyle, and Daniel Rich, *Privatism and Urban Policy in Britain and the United States* (London: Oxford University Press, 1989).

14. Ann O'M. Bowman, "Competition for Economic Development among Southeastern Cities," *Urban Affairs Quarterly* 23 (June 1987): 511.

15. Squires, *Unequal Partnerships*.

16. Peterson, *City Limits*, p. 41.

17. See Paul E. Peterson and Mark C. Rom, *Welfare Magnets: A New Case for a National Standard* (Washington, D.C.: Brookings Institution, 1990). See John D. Kasarda, "Transforming Cities and Employment Policy for Displaced Workers," in *Local Economies in Transition,* ed. Edward M. Bergman (Durham, N.C.: Duke University Press, 1986), for the argument that welfare is not only a magnet that attracts a dependent population but also an anchor that keeps a dependent population from pursuing opportunities elsewhere.

18. Swanstrom, *Growth Politics*.
19. See Kantor with David, *Dependent City*.
20. Bernard J. Frieden and Lynn B. Sagalyn, *Downtown, Inc.* (Cambridge, Mass.: MIT Press, 1989).
21. Kantor with David, *Dependent City*.
22. Ibid., p. 21.
23. Peterson, *City Limits*, p. 69.
24. See, e.g., Eugene J. Meehan, "The Evolution of Public Housing Policy," in *Federal Housing Policy and Programs*, ed. J. Paul Mitchell (New Brunswick, N.J.: Center for Urban Policy Research, 1985).
25. R. Allen Hays, *The Federal Government and Urban Housing* (Albany: State University of New York Press, 1985). See also A. James Reichley, *Conservatives in an Age of Change* (Washington, D.C.: Brookings Institution, 1981), chap. 8, on the conservative Republican view of federal local relations.
26. See Mollenkopf, *Contested City*, for an analysis of the national electoral considerations in Democratic urban policy.
27. Nathan et al., *Reagan and the States*.
28. Charles R. Warren, ed., *Urban Policy in a Changing Federal System* (Washington, D.C.: National Academy Press, 1985), p. 8.
29. Nathan et al., *Reagan and the States*.
30. Peterson, *City Limits*.
31. Stone and Sanders, *Urban Development;* and John R. Logan and Todd Swanstrom, eds., *Beyond the City Limits: Urban Policy and Economic Restructuring in Comparative Perspective* (Philadelphia: Temple University Press, 1990).
32. It should be noted that Peterson, *City Limits*, does not attribute any significance to economic restructuring; he argues that the economic imperative is always there for local officials to pursue developmental policies. Gottdeiner, (*Urban Politics*) and Kantor with David (*Dependent City*), however, use the postrecession restructuring to emphasize their point about the futility of local politics. In each case, recent economic trends are posited to have increased the dependency of local officials on nonlocal factors.
33. Richard V. Knight, "Preface," in *Cities in a Global Society*, ed. Richard V. Knight and Gary Gappert (Newbury Park, Calif.: Sage, 1989).
34. In *Urbanization of Capital*, Harvey argues that during economic restructuring capital investment moved away from production and into land and the built environment. The result, abetted by the 1981 Tax Act that provided tax credits for office development, was an unprecedented amount of land speculation and a significant remaking of the built environment in downtown areas of U.S. cities.

35. See, e.g., Bennett Harrison and Barry Bluestone, *The Great U-Turn* (New York: Basic Books, 1988); and Saskia Sassen, *The Mobility of Labor and Capital: A Study in International Investment and Labor Flow* (Cambridge: Cambridge University Press, 1988).

36. See Edward G. Goetz, " 'Type II Policy' and Mandated Benefits in Economic Development," *Urban Afffairs Quarterly* 26 (December 1990): 170.

37. See, e.g., Stone and Sanders, *Urban Development;* Clarence N. Stone, *Regime Politics: Governing Atlanta, 1946–1988* (Lawrence: Kansas University Press, 1989); and Stephen L. Elkin, *City and Regime in the American Republic* (Chicago: University of Chicago Press, 1987).

38. Susan E. Clarke, "More Autonomous Policy Orientations: An Analytic Framework," in Stone and Sanders, *Urban Development.*

39. Cynthia Horan, "Beyond Governing Coalitions: Analyzing Urban Regimes in the 1990s," *Journal of Urban Affairs* 13. 2(1991): 130, improves upon the original regime paradigm by broadening its scope to include institutional analysis and the ways in which institutions serve or constrain the pursuit of coalitional objectives. Horan also improves the treatment of the intersection of local governing coalitions and nonlocal capital by emphasizing both the mediating influences of institutions and the reciprocal impacts of economic restructuring and local institutional reforms: "Economic restructuring in cities presents the sort of situation which . . . could inaugurate a new round of urban institutional reform"; at the same time, "the effectiveness of local coalitions [in controlling the restructuring process] is in part determined by the bureaucratic and financial resources they control."

40. Peterson, *City Limits.*

41. Alan DiGaetano, "Urban Political Regime Formation: A Study in Contrast," *Journal of Urban Affairs* 11. 3(1990): 261.

42. Frances Fox Piven and Richard A. Cloward, *Poor People's Movements: Why They Succeed, How They Fail* (New York: Vintage Books, 1977).

43. Marilyn Gittell, *Limits to Citizen Participation: The Decline of Community Organizations* (Beverly Hills: Sage, 1980).

44. Christopher Gunn and Hazel Dayton Gunn, *Reclaiming Capital: Democratic Initiatives and Community Development* (Ithaca, N.Y.: Cornell University Press, 1991); and Thomas J. Lenz, "Neighborhood Development: Issues and Models," *Social Policy* 18 (Spring 1988): 24.

45. See Institute for Policy Studies, *A Progressive Housing Program for America* (Washington, D.C., 1987). The term "social sector" as used by the IPS encompasses nonprofits, public agencies, tenant organizations, community groups, and labor unions. I focus here specifically on the nonprofit sector.

46. The first survey used the mailing list of the National Association of Housing and Redevelopment Officials (NAHRO) to identify the relevant housing officials in these cities. For those cities with no representative on the NAHRO mailing list, letters were sent to the "Department of Housing and Community Development." For some cities on the NAHRO mailing list, multiple names and agencies appeared, usually a redevelopment agency and a community development department; in all such cases the questionnaire went to the community development department, which was thought more likely to supervise the entire range of housing-related policy in the city.

The same procedure was followed for state agencies. Each state that did not respond was contacted by phone; twelve questionnaires were administered in this manner. In addition, follow-up phone calls were made to some state officials who had responded, in order to clarify answers and fill in blanks.

Statewide housing coalitions were identified in two ways. First, the survey of state housing officials requested information on the statewide housing coalition, if one existed. Second, the National Coalition for the Homeless (NCH) provides "A National Directory of Statewide Homeless, Housing, and Rural Housing Coalitions and State Government Contacts." This directory was used to verify and, in some cases, complete the information received from the survey of state officials. The interviews with coalition leaders were semistructured conversations conducted over the phone.

CHAPTER 2

1. See, e.g., J. Paul Mitchell, ed., *Federal Housing Policy and Programs* (New Brunswick, N.J.: Center for Urban Policy Research, 1985); Hays, *Federal Government;* John C. Weicher, *Housing: Federal Policies and Programs* (Washington, D.C.: American Enterprise Institute for Public Policy Research, 1980); and Jon Pynoos, Robert Schafer, and Chester W. Hartman, eds., *Housing Urban America*, 2d ed. (New York: Aldine, 1980).

2. Milton P. Semer, Julian H. Zimmerman, Ashley Foard, and John M. Frantz. "Evolution of Federal Legislative Policy in Housing: Housing Credits," in Mitchell, *Federal Housing Policy.*

3. Ibid.

4. Ibid. See also Ann Meyerson, "Deregulation and the Restructuring of the Housing Finance System," in *Critical Perspectives on Housing*, ed. Rachel G. Bratt, Chester Hartman, and Ann Meyerson (Philadelphia: Temple University Press, 1986).

5. Patric H. Hendershott and Keven E. Villani, "Direct Intervention in the Mortgage Market," in Mitchell, *Federal Housing Policy;* and Hays, *Federal Government.*

6. Hays, *Federal Government.*

7. Barry Checkoway, "Large Builders, Federal Housing Programs, and Postwar Suburbanization," in Bratt, Hartman, and Meyerson, *Critical Perspectives.*

8. See Lawrence M. Friedman, "Housing Reform: Negative Style," in Mitchell, *Federal Housing Policy.* Friedman argues that housing reformers actually had a greater concern for minimizing the "social costs" of slum housing, such as the spread of disease and crime, which could represent a problem to greater society.

9. See Meehan, "Evolution of Public Housing," p. 289. See also Robert M. Fisher, *Twenty Years of Public Housing: Economic Aspects of the Federal Program* (New York: Harper, 1959); and Robert Taggert, *Low Income Housing: A Critique of Federal Aid* (Baltimore, Md.: Johns Hopkins University Press, 1970).

10. Meehan, "Evolution of Public Housing"; and Rachel G. Bratt, "Public Housing: The Controversy and Contribution," in Bratt, Hartman, and Meyerson, *Critical Perspectives.*

11. See the analyses of the state's role in housing production in Western Europe, Scandinavia, and parts of Asia in Willem van Vliet, Elizabeth Huttman, and Sylvia F. Fava, eds., *Housing Needs and Policy Approaches: Trends in Thirteen Countries* (Durham, N.C.: Duke University Press, 1985). See also John I. Gilderbloom and Richard P. Appelbaum, *Rethinking Rental Housing* (Philadelphia: Temple University Press, 1988), chap. 8.

12. Meehan, "Evolution of Public Housing," describes a series of fiscal policies and subsidy decisions in the public housing program that practically ensured the program's failure. Public housing legislation limited local housing authority (LHA) income to only what was collected in rents (at least until 1961). In addition, a payment to local governments from LHAs in the amount of 10 percent of gross rents was required in lieu of taxes, cash reserves were limited, and excess income (such "profits" actually did occur early on in the program) was applied to the retirement of capital debt. In 1969 the Brooke Amendment to the 1968 Housing Act limited rents to 25 percent of tenants' income. At the same time that Congress dramatically reduced the income of LHAs, it also imposed significant social obligations in the form of tenant services, educational counseling, security, and recreational services. These administrative aspects, according to Meehan, crippled the program.

13. Recent analyses of life in public housing describe the bleak outlook for families in an environment of hopelessness, fear, and poverty. See Alex Kotlowitz, *There Are No Children Here* (New York: Doubleday, 1991) and Nicholas Lemann, *The Promised Land* (New York: 1991), for two examples that reveal the discrepancy between the potential of public

housing and its realities. In most Western European countries the experience of public housing is dramatically different because it serves a much broader socioeconomic range, not the intense concentration of poverty represented by U.S. public housing; consequently, there are fewer management and financial problems.

14. Marc A. Weiss, "The Origins and Legacy of Urban Renewal," in Mitchell *Federal Housing Policy*.

15. Ibid. See also Mark I. Gelfand, *A Nation of Cities: The Federal Government and Urban America, 1933–1965* (New York: Oxford University Press, 1975).

16. Initially, urban renewal project areas had to be "predominantly residential" in their re-use. Technically, this meant that at least 50 percent of the total square footage was to be residential. After only five years (in 1954) Congress allowed a 10 percent exemption. In 1959 "the exemption was extended to 20 percent plus colleges and universities, and in the New Frontier–Great Society years it was further extended to 35 percent, plus hospitals, medical schools, nursing schools, and several other special exemptions" (Weiss, "Origins and Legacy," p. 267).

17. Senate Committee on Banking, Subcommittee on Housing and Urban Affairs, *Report on the Central City Problems and Urban Renewal Policy*, 93d Cong., 1st sess., 1973, p. 56.

18. See, e.g., Jewell Bellush and Murray Hausknecht, eds., *Urban Renewal: People, Politics, and Planning* (Garden City, N.Y.: Anchor Books, 1967); and James Q. Wilson, ed., *Urban Renewal: The Record and the Controversy* (Cambridge, Mass.: MIT Press, 1966).

19. Roger Friedland, "Corporate Power and Urban Growth: The Case of Urban Renewal," *Politics and Society* 10.2 (1980): 203.

20. Hays, *Federal Government*; Roger W. Caves, "An Historical Analysis of Federal Housing Policy from the Presidential Perspective: An Intergovernmental Focus," *Urban Studies* 26 (1989): 59; and Mollenkopf, *Contested City*.

21. William Lilley III, "The Homebuilders' Lobby," in Pynoos, Schafer, and Hartman, *Housing Urban America*, p. 33.

22. Chester W. Hartman, *Housing and Social Policy* (Englewood Cliffs, N.J.: Prentice-Hall, 1975), p. 137.

23. Hays, *Federal Government*.

24. Paul R. Dommel and Associates, *Decentralizing Urban Policy: Case Studies in Community Development* (Washington, D.C.: Brookings Institution, 1982).

25. Cushing Dolbeare, "How the Income Tax System Subsidizes Housing for the Affluent," in Bratt, Hartman, and Meyerson, *Critical Perspectives*.

26. Ibid.

27. In addition to the Federal National Mortgage Association (FNMA), formed in 1934 to increase investment in housing, the Government National Mortgage Association (GNMA) was established in 1968 and the Federal Home Loan Mortgage Corporation (FHLMC) in 1970. Each of these agencies played specialized roles in the secondary mortgage market to increase the flow of investment capital into housing.

28. J. Paul Mitchell, "The Historical Context for Housing Policy," in Mitchell, *Federal Housing Policy;* and Peter D. Salins, "America's Permanent Housing Problem," in *Housing America's Poor,* ed. Peter D. Salins (Chapel Hill: University of North Carolina Press, 1987).

29. Mitchell, "Historical Context."

30. Ibid.

31. Todd Swanstrom, "No Room at the Inn: Housing Policy and the Homeless," *Journal of Urban and Contemporary Law* 35 (1990): 81.

32. Swanstrom (ibid.) argues that the FHA and especially the tax deduction program have utilized the filtering theory to justify government subsidy of high-end housing production; any increase in the stock of housing is seen as benefiting low-income people because units will eventually filter down to them. See Anthony Downs, *Neighborhoods and Urban Development* (Washington, D.C.: Brookings Institution, 1981), on the filtering theory.

33. Lilley, "Homebuilders' Lobby."

34. Salins, in "America's Permanent Housing," argues that housing has fallen victim to the "moving target" syndrome in which advocates continually redefine the objectives as each old target is met. In his way of thinking, there is no housing crisis in the United States, only a crisis of analysis that continually finds problems for the public sector to address. Salins does provide a useful description of the changing, ever more refined objectives of housing policy. His contention that there is no objective crisis in housing is, however, untenable.

35. See Caves, "Historical Analysis."

36. Mitchell, "Historical Context," p. 3.

37. Nathan et al., *Reagan and the States.*

38. Morris, *State Housing Finance;* and Frank Keefe and Michael Barker, "Housing and the States," in *Housing and Local Government,* ed. Mary K. Nenno and Paul C. Brophy (Washington, D.C.: International City Management Association, 1982).

39. Seventy-two percent of HFA-assisted housing through 1973 was assisted through the Section 236 program (Morris, *State Housing Finance).*

40. General Accounting Office, Report to the Chairman, Joint Committee on Taxation, *Home Ownership: Mortgage Bonds Are Costly*

and Provide Little Assistance to Those in Need, 100th Cong., 2d sess., 1988.

41. Keefe and Barker, "Housing and the States."
42. General Accounting Office, *Home Ownership*.
43. Keefe and Barker, "Housing and the States," p. 169.
44. Morris, *State Housing Finance*, p. 21.
45. Ibid.
46. Michael A. Stegman and J. David Holden, *Nonfederal Housing Programs* (Washington, D.C.: Urban Land Institute, 1987).
47. Program Evaluation Division, Office of the Legislative Auditor, State of Minnesota, *Minnesota Housing Finance Agency* (St. Paul, Minn., 1989).
48. Council of State Community Affairs Agencies (COSCAA), *State Housing Initiatives: The 1988 Compendium* (Washington, D.C., 1988).
49. See Michael N. Danielson and Jameson W. Doig, *New York: The Politics of Urban Regional Development* (Berkeley: University of California Press, 1982), esp. chap. 3, on the dynamics of exclusionary zoning in suburbs. See also Alan Mallach, *Inclusionary Housing Programs: Policies and Practices* (New Brunswick, N.J.: Center for Urban Policy Research, 1984).
50. See, e.g., George E. Peterson, "Urban Policy and the Cyclical Behavior of Cities," in *Reagan and the Cities*, ed. George E. Peterson and Carol Lewis (Washington, D.C.: Urban Institute Press, 1986); and Everett Carll Ladd, "The Reagan Phenomenon and Public Attitudes toward Government," in *The Reagan Presidency and the Governing of America*, ed. Lester Salamon and Michael S. Lund (Washington, D.C.: Urban Institute Press, 1984).
51. Nathan et al., *Reagan and the States*.
52. E. Blaine Liner, "Sorting Out State-Local Relations," in *A Decade of Devolution: Perspectives on State-Local Relations*, ed. E. Blaine Liner (Washington, D.C.: Urban Institute Press, 1989), p. 5.
53. Jack A. Brizius, "An Overview of the State-Local Fiscal Landscape," in Liner, *Decade of Devolution*.
54. Nathan et al., *Reagan and the States*.
55. Hays, *Federal Government*, argues that the gradual reduction in federal involvement dating to the Nixon years was simply accelerated under Reagan. This construction ignores the fact that it was Reagan's intent to abolish the federal housing presence, not merely reduce it.
56. See, e.g., Paul R. Dommel, Michael J. Rich, Leonard S. Rubinowitz, and Associates, *Deregulating Community Development* (Washington, D.C.: Department of Housing and Urban Development, 1983).
57. Paul R. Dommel, Richard P. Nathan, Sarah F. Liebschutz, Margaret

T. Wrightson, and Associates, *Decentralizing Community Development* (Washington, D.C.: Department of Housing and Urban Development, 1978).

58. David R. Beam, "New Federalism, Old Realities: The Reagan Administration and Intergovernmental Reform," in Salamon and Lund, *Reagan Presidency*.

59. Nathan et al., *Reagan and the States*, pp. 61–64.

60. See, e.g., ibid., pp. 5–10; Struyk, Mayor, and Tuccillo, *Federal Housing Policy*; and Warren, *Urban Policy*.

61. Charles R. Warren, "Trends and Developments in Federalism: The Meaning for Urban Policy," in Warren, *Urban Policy*.

62. Hale Champion, "Comment," Theodore J. Lowi, "Ronald Reagan—Revolutionary?" both in Salamon and Lund, in *Reagan Presidency*.

63. Quoted in Lowi, "Reagan—Revolutionary?" p. 40.

64. Nathan et al., *Reagan and the States*.

65. Liner, "Sorting Out," p. 12.

66. Lowi, "Reagan—Revolutionary?"

67. Harrison and Bluestone, in *Great U-Turn*, present the most fully developed articulation of the thesis that intentional government action resulted in maximizing corporate benefits during restructuring at the direct expense of labor and low-income people.

68. Richard P. Nathan, Fred C. Doolittle, and Associates, *The Consequences of Cuts: The Effects of the Reagan Domestic Programs on State and Local Governments* (Princeton, N.J.: Princeton Urban and Regional Research Center, 1983).

69. Nathan et al., *Reagan and the States*.

70. John William Ellwood, ed., *Reductions in U.S. Domestic Spending* (New Brunswick, N.J.: Transaction Books, 1982), p. 18.

71. Schwartz, Ferlauto, and Hoffman, *New Housing Policy*, p. 48.

72. Ibid.

73. National Council of State Housing Agencies, *The Low-Income Housing Tax Credit in the 1990s* (Washington, D.C., 1989).

74. Schwartz, Ferlauto, and Hoffman, *New Housing Policy*, pp. 56–58.

75. Richard P. Nathan, "Institutional Change under Reagan," in *Perspectives on The Reagan Years*, ed. John L. Palmer (Washington, D.C.: Urban Institute Press, 1986). See also Stephen B. Farber, "Federalism and State-Local Relations," in Liner, *Decade of Devolution*.

76. Nathan et al., *Reagan and the States*, p. 357.

77. Warren, "Trends and Developments," p. 19. See also Allen Schick, "The Budget as an Instrument of Presidential Policy," in Salamon and Lund, *Reagan Presidency*.

78. Nathan et al., *Consequences of Cuts*.

79. Nathan et al., *Reagan and the States*, p. 15.
80. Jerry Hagstrom, "Liberal and Minority Coalitions Pleading Their Cases in State Capitals," *National Journal* 17.8 (1985): 426.
81. Hagstrom, "Liberal and Minority Coalitions"; and Nathan et al., *Reagan and the States*. See also Robert C. Wood and Beverly Klimkowsky, "Cities in the New Federalism," in Warren, *Urban Policy*.
82. Hagstrom, "Liberal and Minority Coalitions," p. 246.
83. Nathan et al., *Reagan and the States*, p. 14.
84. See, e.g., Karen S. Christensen, Michael Smith-Heimer, and Ayse Pamuk, *Local Government Response to Severe Reductions in Federal Funding for Low-Income Housing*, Working Paper No. 490 (Berkeley: Institute of Urban and Regional Development, 1988).
85. Nathan et al., *Reagan and the States*, p. 95.
86. See, e.g., James Pickman, Benson F. Roberts, Mindy Leiterman, and Robert N. Mittle, eds., *Producing Lower Income Housing: Local Initiatives* (Washington, D.C.: Bureau of National Affairs, 1986); Stegman and Holden, *Nonfederal Housing*; Mary K. Nenno and George Colyer, *New Money and New Methods* (Washington, D.C.: National Association of Housing and Redevelopment Officials, 1988); and Community Information Exchange, *Raising the Roof: A Sampler of Community Partnerships for Affordable Housing* (Alexandria, Va., 1988).
87. Christensen, Smith-Heimer, and Pamuk, *Local Government Response*.
88. Nathan et al., *Reagan and the States*.
89. Berenyi, *Locally Funded Housing*.
90. Stegman and Holden, *Nonfederal Housing*.
91. Dommel et al., *Deregulating Community Development*; and, Christensen, Smith-Heimer, and Pamuk, *Local Government Response*.
92. Michael J. Rich, *National Goals and Local Choices: Distributing Federal Aid to the Poor* (Princeton, N.J.: Princeton University Press, 1993), chap. 4. According to Rich, housing remains the focus of state CDBG programs in California, Connecticut, Maine, Massachusetts, Minnesota, New Hampshire, North Carolina, Pennsylvania, and Vermont. Rich's is the most comprehensive study on state implementation of the small cities CDBG program.
93. Schwartz, Ferlauto, and Hoffman, *New Housing Policy*, p. 63.
94. Pickman et al., *Producing Lower Income Housing*, p. 14.
95. Dommel et al., *Deregulating Community Development*; and, Christensen, Smith-Heimer, and Pamuk, *Local Government Response*.
96. Avis C. Vidal, *Rebuilding Communities: A National Study of Urban Community Development Corporations* (New York: New School for Social Research, 1992).

97. Pickman et al., *Producing Lower Income Housing*, p. 11.

98. See Philip L. Clay, *At Risk of Loss: The Endangered Future of Low-Income Rental Housing Resources* (Washington, D.C.: Neighborhood Reinvestment Corporation, 1987); National Low Income Housing Preservation Commission, *Preventing the Disappearance of Low Income Housing* (Washington, D.C., 1988); and General Accounting Office, *Rental Housing: Potential Reduction in the Privately Owned and Federally Assisted Inventory* (Washington, D.C., 1986).

99. Peter Dreier, "Community-Based Housing: A Progressive Approach to a New Federal Policy," *Social Policy* 18.2 (1988): 18.

100. Rachel G. Bratt, "Dilemmas of Community-Based Housing," *Policy Studies Journal* 16.2 (1987): 324.

101. Edward G. Goetz, "Local Government Support for Nonprofit Housing: A Survey of U.S. Cities," *Urban Affairs Quarterly* 27 (March 1992): 420.

102. Christensen, Smith-Heimer, and Pamuk, *Local Government Response*.

103. Neal R. Peirce, "Reagan's Surprise Legacy to States and Cities," *National Journal* 21 (January 21, 1989): 145.

104. See, e.g., Edward G. Goetz, "Office-Housing Linkage in San Francisco," *Journal of the American Planning Association* 55 (Winter 1989): 66, on the origins of the housing linkage program.

105. Wong, *City Choices*, pp. 15–18.

106. The research on the small cities CDBG program and its state implementation provides support for the contention that state and local governments have used federal funds for nonredistributive purposes. See, e.g., Rich, *National Goals:* and David R. Morgan and Robert E. England, "The Small Cities Community Development Block Grant Program: An Assessment of Programmatic Change under State Control," *Public Administration Review* 44 (1984): 477.

CHAPTER 3

1. "Organizing in the South: Housing Issues Take Hold," *Shelterforce* 7 (July, 1982).

2. Baseline information on the presence of coalitions in U.S. cities and states was collected through the questionnaire surveys of housing officials. Telephone interviews were conducted at the University of Minnesota between November 1989 and November 1990. Repeated attempts to contact organization representatives in Texas were unsuccessful, and the Idaho and Wisconsin groups were formed too late to be

included in the sample. The information provided in this chapter is therefore based on interviews with thirty-two advocacy coalitions and follow-up interviews with their directors, supplemented by journalistic accounts of the activities of groups in the local housing movement.

3. See the history presented by Allan David Heskin in *Tenants and the American Dream: Ideology and the Tenant Movement* (New York: Praeger, 1983), chap. 2. See also Ronald Lawson, ed., *The Tenant Movement in New York City, 1904–1984* (New Brunswick, N.J.: Rutgers University Press, 1986).

4. Peter Marcuse, "The Rise of Tenant Organizations," *The Nation* 213 (July 19, 1971). For history and analysis of the Harlem rent strikes, see Michael J. Lipsky, *Protest in City Politics: Rent Strikes, Housing, and the Power of the Poor* (Chicago: Rand McNally, 1970).

5. Marcuse, "Tenant Organizations."

6. John Atlas and Peter Dreier, "Mobilize or Compromise? The Tenants' Movement and American Politics" in *America's Housing Crisis: What Is to Be Done?* ed. Chester Hartman (Boston: Routledge & Kegan Paul, 1983).

7. Marcuse, "Tenant Organizations."

8. Ronald Lawson with Reuben B. Johnson III, "Tenant Responses to the Urban Housing Crisis, 1970–1980," in Lawson, *Tenant Movement*.

9. Heskin, *American Dream*.

10. Atlas and Dreier, "Mobilize or Compromise?"

11. Heskin, *American Dream;* and Gilderbloom and Appelbaum, *Rethinking Rental Housing*.

12. Joe R. Feagin and Robert Parker, *Building American Cities: The Urban Real Estate Game*, 2d ed. (Englewood Cliffs, N.J.: Prentice-Hall, 1990).

13. Quoted in Atlas and Dreier, "Mobilize or Compromise?" p. 172. Atlas and Dreier's optimistic viewpoint on the health of the tenant movement is not shared by all. See, e.g., Kathy McAfee, "Socialism and the Housing Movement: Lessons from Boston," and John Cowley, "The Limitations and Potential of Housing Organizing," both in Bratt, Hartman, and Meyerson, *Critical Perspectives*.

14. Renters in Berkeley, Santa Monica, and West Hollywood, California, and in Burlington, Vermont, have been extremely successful in leading movements to elect progressive coalitions to local councils and in redirecting city policies to support tenant interests.

15. Norman I. Fainstein and Susan S. Fainstein, *Urban Political Movements* (Englewood Cliffs, N.J.: Prentice-Hall, 1974), identify tenants' organizations among the class- and race-based movements developed in urban areas during the 1960s and 1970s.

16. Joe R. Feagin and Harlan Hahn, *Ghetto Revolts: The Politics of Violence in American Cities* (New York: Macmillan, 1973).

17. Marcuse, "Tenant Organizations."

18. The literature on community resistance to urban renewal is a rich one. Perhaps the best detailed account of tenant-based resistance is Chester Hartman, *Yerba Buena: Land Grab and Community Resistance* (San Francisco: Glide, 1974). For other examples, see Mollenkopf, *Contested City;* Richard A. Cloward and Frances Fox Piven, *The Politics of Turmoil: Poverty, Race, and the Urban Crisis* (New York: Vintage Books, 1975); and Peter H. Rossi and Robert A. Dentler, *The Politics of Urban Renewal* (Glencoe, Ill.: Free Press, 1961).

19. Chester Hartman, *The Transformation of San Francisco* (Totowa, N.J.: Rowman & Allanheld, 1984), chap. 10.

20. See Joel Schwartz, "Tenant Power in the Liberal City, 1943–1971," in Lawson, *Tenant Movement,* for a comprehensive description of the context for action by New York tenants and housing activists.

21. National Commission on Neighborhoods, *People Building Neighborhoods: Final Report to the President and the Congress of the United States* (Washington, D.C.: Government Printing Office, 1979).

22. Harry Boyte, *The Backyard Revolution: Understanding the New Citizen Movement* (Philadelphia: Temple University Press, 1980). Robert Fisher, *Let the People Decide: Neighborhood Organizing in America* (Boston: Twayne, 1984), notes that in 1970 there were over 400 ongoing community struggles against highway construction projects alone.

23. Quoted in Fisher, *Let the People Decide,* p. 126.

24. Fisher, *Let the People Decide.* See also National Commission on Neighborhoods *People Building Neighborhoods;* and Gary Delgado, *Organizing the Movement: The Roots and Growth of ACORN* (Philadelphia: Temple University Press, 1986), on the connection between the civil rights struggle and the neighborhood movement.

25. These groups are often referred to as neo-Alinsky groups (see, e.g., Fisher, *Let the People Decide*) because they follow the model of local control and political action created by Saul Alinsky in Chicago during the 1930s. Alinsky is, of course, probably the most famous of American community organizers, and his model has served subsequent generations of neighborhood organizations and organizers. The emphasis in the Alinsky model is on political confrontation orchestrated by an indigenous leadership that is assisted but never replaced by professional organizers. See Saul D. Alinsky, *Rules for Radicals* (New York: Vintage Books, 1972).

26. See *CDCs: New Hope for the Inner City,* Report of the Twentieth

Century Fund Task Force on Community Development Corporations (New York: Twentieth Century Fund, 1971).

27. Jeffrey L. Katz, "Neighborhood Politics: A Changing World," *Government,* November 1990, p. 48.

28. Douglas Frantz and Jon Van, "Unlikely Allies Fight Budget Cuts," *Chicago Tribune,* May 7, 1981 p. 1–11. See also Delgado, *Organizing the Movement.*

29. Harrison and Bluestone (*Great U-Turn*) argue that the Reagan recovery was unlike other recoveries because it was not based on an increase in industrial productivity but fueled largely through the accumulation of debt. Government, corporate, and household debt increased dramatically during the 1980s and the increased willingness to accumulate debt fed the increase in consumption. In addition, the recovery was quite selective in its benefits: the top quintile in wealth benefited greatly while the remaining 80 percent in the distribution lost ground because of reduced wage and benefit levels.

30. Squires, *Unequal Partnerships.*

31. See Goetz, "Type II Policy."

32. "State Homeless Assistance Act Developed: Campaign Begins in State Capitols," *Safety Network* (newsletter of the National Coalition for the Homeless, Washington, D.C.) 8 (February 1989).

33. Hartman, *Transformation of San Francisco;* interview with Renae Vowels, Michigan Housing Coalition, April 3, 1990; and interview with Linda Panori, Affordable Housing Advocates of New Hampshire, December 5, 1989.

34. Interview with Hillary Frank, Massachusetts Affordable Housing Alliance, May 8, 1990.

35. "From the Grassroots," *Shelterforce* 10 (November–December 1987): 20.

36. Eva Gladstein, "The Philadelphia Story: Building the Tenant Action Group" *Shelterforce* 11 (October–November 1988): 8–9.

37. "Housing Programs and Organizations Try to Keep City Affordable," *Shelterforce* 9 (July 1985): 12–13.

38. Interview with Peter DiSimone, Missouri Association for Social Welfare, August 14, 1990.

39. Interview with Mark Lundgren, Utah Housing Coalition, August 14, 1990. The LIHAC leaders in Massachusetts, South Carolina, California, and Minnesota reported cooperative relationships with homeless advocates. In Iowa, Kentucky, New Jersey, Washington, and Missouri the coalition was playing both roles: housing advocate and homeless advocate.

40. 26 U.S.C. 501(c)(3) and 501(c)(4) describe the tax status of nonprofit and charitable nonprofit organizations respectively.

41. "Pennsylvania Housing Coalition: Watchdog and Advocate," *Low Income Housing Roundup* (newsletter of the Low Income Housing Information Service), No. 121 (April 1989): 6–7.

42. Interview with Kathy Davis, Georgia Housing Coalition, May 17, 1990.

43. "Pennsylvania Housing Coalition," *Low Income Roundup*.

44. Samuel K. Gove, "State Impact: The Daley Legacy," in *After Daley: Chicago Politics in Transition*, ed Samuel K. Gove and Louis H. Masotti (Urbana: University of Illinois Press, 1982).

45. Interview with Fran Tobin, State Housing Action Coalition of Illinois, January 26, 1990.

46. Interview with Chip Halbach, Minnesota Housing Partnership, November 13, 1989.

47. Interview with Marc Brown, California Coalition for Rural Housing, May 10, 1990.

48. *CHAS Monitor* (newsletter of the National Support Center, Low Income Housing Information Service, Washington, D.C.), No. 1 (July 1991).

49. "Idaho Coalition Is Born," *Roundup*, No. 142 (June 1991): 8–9.

50. *CHAS Monitor*, No. 1 (July 1991).

51. *Roundup*, No. 129 (February 1990): 7.

52. *Shelterforce* 9 (December 1985).

53. See, e.g., Alan Rosenthal, *Governors and Legislatures: Contending Powers* (Washington D.C.: Congressional Quarterly Press, 1990); Michael J. Ross, *State and Local Politics and Policy: Change and Reform* (Englewood Cliffs, N.J.: Prentice-Hall, 1987); and Samuel C. Patterson, "State Legislators and the Legislatures," in *Politics in the American States*, 5th ed. ed., Virginia Gray, Herbert Jacob, and Robert B. Albritton (Glenview, Ill.: Scott-Foresman, 1990).

54. Interview with Charlie Blair, Tennessee Network for Community Economic Development, May 21, 1990.

55. Nathan et al., *Reagan and the States*.

56. Michael Decourcey Hinds, "Half of States Strive to Avert Perilous Deficits," *New York Times*, March 4, 1990, p. 1-1.

57. Matthew Hickerson, "From Albany, Bad News for Community Groups," *New York Times*, June 30, 1991, p. LI-6.

58. Interview with Mary Beth Gregg, Kentucky Coalition for the Homeless, May 22, 1990.

59. Charlie Blair (Tennessee) interview.

60. "Texas LIHIS: Shaking Up the Lone Star State," *Roundup*, No. 143 (July–August, 1991): 7.

61. Kenneth Grimes, "A Successful Affordable Housing Campaign," *Shelterforce* 13 (May–June 1991).
62. W. Dennis Keating, "From the Neighborhood to City Hall," *Shelterforce* 12 (May–June 1990): 8–9.
63. Peter Dreier, "Housing Activist Elected to Massachusetts Legislature," *Shelterforce* 13 (January–February 1991): 17, 22.
64. Peter Dreier and W. Dennis Keating, "The Limits of Localism: Progressive Housing Policies in Boston, 1984–1989," *Urban Affairs Quarterly* 26 (December 1990): 191.
65. "Burlington: Running a Progressive Streak," *Shelterforce* 11 (May–June, 1989): 20.
66. Interview with Mary Ann Holloway, Pennsylvania Low Income Housing Coalition, May 31, 1990.
67. "Miami Advocates Challenge Anti-Homeless Policies," *Safety Network* 8 (May 1989).
68. "Tapped Out," *Shelterforce* 11 (May–June 1989): 5.
69. *Roundup*, No. 142 (June, 1991), p. 9.
70. "Protesters Take Over Repossessed Homes in Minneapolis," *St. Paul Pioneer Press*, May 2, 1990, p. B–1. Subsequent reports appeared on May 9, August 21, September 7, December 2, 3, and 14. The December takeovers took place in St. Paul; the group expanded to suburban sites in 1991. Similar takeovers occurred in New York, Philadelphia, and Tucson, Arizona, where activists were arrested for trespassing (and ultimately acquitted of charges) after occupying vacant HUD-foreclosed properties. Two months after their acquittal, HUD made available 240 federally subsidized single-family houses for use by the homeless; *Safety Network* 8 (January and March 1989).
71. Marc Brown (California) interview.
72. This paragraph is based on "Profile of California's Housing Movement," *Shelterforce* 13 (March–April 1991).
73. This section is based on an interview with Bruce Abernathy of the Maryland Low Income Housing Coalition, March 28, 1990.
74. "Housing Advocates Bite Hand That Feeds Them over Md. Budget," *Washington Post*, February 20, 1990.
75. R. Allen Hays, "Voices for Urban Housing: Interest Group Action and Advocacy Before Congress," paper presented at Twentieth Annual Meeting of the Urban Affairs Association, Charlotte, N.C., April 1990.
76. *Roundup*, No. 134 (July–August 1990): 5–6.
77. The exception is the Idaho Housing Coalition, formed in 1991 at a conference facilitated by the National Support Center; see *Roundup*, No. 142 (June 1991). Generally, NLIHC provides local coalitions

the opportunity to meet one another at least once a year at its national conference, which generally includes sessions on the issues related to local organizing and networking.

78. National Low Income Housing Coalition, Memo to Members, September 1990.

79. *Safety Network* 9 (November 1990).

CHAPTER 4

1. See COSCAA, *State Housing Initiatives*.

2. Michael J. Wolkoff, *Housing New York: Policy Challenges and Opportunities* (Albany: State University of New York Press, 1990).

3. See COSCAA, *State Housing Initiatives*.

4. Ibid.

5. These figures are from the annual Bureau of the Census publication *State Government Finances* (Washington, D.C.: Government Printing Office).

6. From 1972 to 1973 aggregate expenditures jumped from $149.2 million to $429.9 million. Most of the increase was due to New York's injection of $178 million to bail out the State Urban Development Corporation.

7. Berenyi, "Locally Funded Housing."

8. Among the cities that responded to the survey (New York did not respond), Honolulu had the highest level of local-source expenditures on housing—$45.5 million for 1989—followed closely by Los Angeles with $43 million. The highest per capita expenditure was made by Durham, North Carolina, at $58.92; Honolulu was second at $56.50.

9. Redevelopment agency funds are generally in the form of "set-asides" for low-income housing on the earnings from tax increment districts.

10. This "progressive" agenda has been only recently articulated, primarily by planners and academicians in the service of providing an alternative to traditional U.S. policy approaches. See Nancy Pick, "Progressive Housing 101," *Shelterforce* 13 (March–April 1991): 18. Most academicians in this tradition have focused their attention on changing federal policy; assuming perhaps that this kind of paradigm change is less likely to occur at the state and local levels.

11. See Marc V. Levine, "Downtown Redevelopment as an Urban Growth Strategy: A Critical Appraisal of the Baltimore Renaissance," *Journal of Urban Affairs* 9.2 (1987): 133; Timothy Barnekov and Daniel Rich, "Privatism and the Limits of Local Economic Development Policy," *Urban Affairs Quarterly* 25 (December 1989): 212; and Dennis R. Judd,

"From Cowtown to Sunbelt City: Boosterism and Economic Growth in Denver," in Fainstein et al., *Restructuring the City*.

12. See Pierre Clavel, *The Progressive City* (New Brunswick, N.J.: Rutgers University Press, 1986); Goetz, "Type II Policy"; Dreier and Keating, "Limits of Localism"; Peter Dreier and Bruce Ehrlich, "Downtown Development and Urban Reform: The Politics of Boston's Linkage Policy," *Urban Affairs Quarterly* 26 (March 1991); and David Osborne, *Laboratories of Democracy* (Boston: Harvard Business School Press, 1990).

13. Osborne (*Laboratories of Democracy*) would disagree with this formulation of progressive policy. In his schema, progressive policy unites growth and equity considerations. Yet in his formulation these are not exactly equal partners; economic growth is the "first agenda," and only after it has been achieved can equity issues be addressed. While much of the rest of Osborne's argument is consistent with the notion of progressive policy presented here, he is less likely to acknowledge that growth *creates* the social and economic inequities addressed by progressive policy.

14. See, Goetz, "Type II Policy."

15. Dennis Judd and Michael Parkinson, "Patterns of Leadership," in *Leadership and Urban Regeneration*, ed. Dennis Judd and Michael Parkinson (Newbury Park, Calif.: Sage, 1989).

16. Clavel, *Progressive City*.

17. Clarke, "More Autonomous Policy Orientations."

18. Ibid., p. 107.

19. Susan E. Clarke and Michael J. Rich, "Making Money Work: The New Urban Policy Arena," *Research in Urban Policy* 1 (1985): 101.

20. Pierre Clavel and Nancy Kleniewski, "Space for Progressive Local Policy: Examples from the United States and the United Kingdom," in Logan and Swanstrom, *Beyond the City Limits*.

21. Severyn T. Bruyn and James Meehan, eds., *Beyond the Market and the State: New Directions in Community Development* (Philadelphia: Temple University Press, 1987).

22. Gunn and Gunn, *Reclaiming Capital*.

23. Dreier, "Community-Based Housing," p. 18.

24. Severyn T. Bruyn, "Beyond the Market and the State," in Bruyn and Meehan, *Beyond the Market*.

25. Steven D. Soifer, "The Burlington Community Land Trust: A Socialist Approach to Affordable Housing?" *Journal of Urban Affairs* 12.3 (1990); and Kirby White and Charles Matthei, "Community Land Trusts," in Bruyn and Meehan, *Beyond the Market*.

26. Charles Turner, "Worker Cooperatives and Community Development," in Bruyn and Meehan, *Beyond the Market*.

27. Ann Markusen, "Planning for Industrial Decline: Lessons from Steel Communities," *Journal of Planning Education and Research* 7 (1988): 173.
28. Clavel and Kleniewski, "Progressive Local Policy."
29. Ibid.
30. Alan Altshuler, *Community Control* (Indianapolis, Ind.: Pegasus, 1970).
31. Soifer, "Burlington Community Land Trust."
32. *Roundup*, No. 120 (February 1989).
33. Gilderbloom and Appelbaum, *Rethinking Rental Housing*.
34. Scott B. Franklin, "Housing Cooperatives: A Viable Means of Home Ownership for Low Income Families?" *Journal of Housing*, July 1981.
35. Nenno and Brophy, *Housing and Local Government*.
36. Michael N. Danielson, *The Politics of Exclusion* (New York: Columbia University Press, 1976); and Danielson and Doig, *New York*.
37. Mallach, *Inclusionary Housing;* Danielson, *Politics of Exclusion;* and Danielson and Doig, *New York*.
38. Danielson and Doig, *New York;* and Danielson, *Politics of Exclusion*.
39. Patricia Burgess Stach, "Regulation and Reform in Controlling Urban Land Use: The Future is Past." Paper presented at twentieth Annual Meeting of the Urban Affairs Association, Charlotte, N.C., April 1990.
40. Historical preservation policies are not analyzed here because they are not necessarily linked with affordable housing objectives.
41. Alan Finder, "S.R.O. Hotels: Trying to Revive on Old Idea," *New York Times,* February 9, 1990, p. C–15.
42. Ibid.
43. *Roundup*, No. 130 (March 1990).
44. Housing preservation ordinances can be successfully defended if appropriately fashioned. See Edith M. Netter, "An Uncertain Future for Housing Preservation Ordinances," *Urban Land*, July 1987, p. 34.
45. *Shelterforce* 10 (July–August 1987).
46. W. Dennis Keating, "Linking Downtown Development to Broader Community Goals," *American Planning Association Journal* 52 (Spring 1986): 134; Edward G. Goetz, "Office-Housing Linkage Programs: A Review of the Issues," *Economic Development Quarterly* 2 (May 1988): 182; and Teresa R. Herrero, "Housing Linkage: Will It Play a Role in the 1990s?" *Journal of Urban Affairs* 13.1 (1991):1.
47. Keating, "Linking Downtown."
48. Douglas R. Porter, "The Linkage Issue: Introduction and Summary of Discussion," in *Downtown Linkages*, ed. Douglas R. Porter (Washington, D.C.: Urban Land Institute, 1985).

49. Ann O'M. Bowman, *Tools and Targets: The Mechanics of City Economic Development* (Washington, D.C.: National League of Cities, 1987).

50. Goetz, "Type II Policy."

51. Herrero, "Housing Linkage." The discrepancy between the figures presented by Goetz and Bowman on the one hand and Herrero on the other is due to different definitions of linkage. Herrero reports only formal linkage programs; the data reported by Goetz and by Bowman pick up the sporadic use of linkage in negotiated development agreements.

52. Goetz, "Linkage in San Francisco."

53. See Michael Peter Smith, "The Uses of Linked-Development Policies in U.S. Cities," in *Regenerating the Cities: The UK Crisis and the US Experience*, ed. Michael Parkinson, Bernard Foley, and Dennis R. Judd (Glenview, Ill.: Scott-Foresman, 1989), on the Boston and Hartford cases. See also Chapter 6 on Los Angeles.

54. Mallach, *Inclusionary Housing*, p. 2.

55. Mark A. Hughes and Peter M. Vandoren, "Social Policy through Land Reform: New Jersey's Mount Laurel Controversy," *Political Science Quarterly* 105.1 (1991):97.

56. Mallach, *Inclusionary Housing*.

57. Ibid.

58. See Gilderbloom and Appelbaum, *Rethinking Rental Housing*.

59. William Tucker, *The Excluded Americans: Homelessness and Housing Policies* (Washington, D.C.: Regnery, 1990); and Ira Lowry, *Rental Housing in New York City, vol. 1: Confronting the Crisis* (New York: RAND, 1970). For a more detailed discussion of the attacks on rent control, see David Bartelt and Ronald Lawson, "Rent Control and Abandonment: A Second Look at the Evidence," *Journal of Urban Affairs* 14.4 (1982): 50–55; and Richard P. Appelbaum, Michael Dolny, Peter Dreier, and John I. Gilderbloom, "Scapegoating Rent Control: Masking the Causes of Homelessness," *Journal of the American Planning Association* 57 (Spring 1991): 153–157.

60. Bartelt and Lawson, "Rent Control"; and Gilderbloom and Appelbaum, *Rethinking Rental Housing*, chap. 7.

61. Feagin and Parker, *Building American Cities*.

62. Michael Mandel, "A Real Look at Rent Control," *Dollars and Sense*, January 1986, p. 21.

63. Urban Institute, *Rent Control and the Availability of Affordable Housing in the District of Columbia: A Delicate Balance* (Washington, D.C., 1989).

64. "Beating the Odds: Detroit Wins Rent Control," *Shelterforce* 11 (August–September 1988).

65. Marc Brown (California) interview; "Annual Battle over Rent Control," *Shelterforce* 10 (July–August 1987).

66. "Statewide Coalition Defeats Anti-Tenant Legislation," *Shelterforce* 10 (September–October 1987).

67. Clay, *At Risk of Loss;* National Low Income Housing Preservation Commission, *Preventing the Disappearance;* and General Accounting Office, *Rental Housing.*

68. Ultimately, the National Affordable Housing Act of 1990 incorporated an array of incentives and requirements aimed at preserving federally assisted housing units. The act offers private owners fair-market-value incentives to continue ownership of the housing for low- and moderate-income occupancy, or a fair-market sales price if the owner wishes to sell to a purchaser who intends to preserve the low-income use of the housing. Owners also have the right to prepay federal subsidies if they can show that there will be no adverse affect on the low-income housing market.

69. See, e.g., Daniel D. Pearlman, *State and Local Initiatives to Preserve Subsidized Rental Housing* (Berkeley, Calif.: National Housing Law Project, 1988); Janet Larsen, *Sooner or Later . . .* (Minneapolis: Minnesota Housing Project, Center for Urban and Regional Affairs, University of Minnesota, 1988); *Roundup,* No. 121 (April 1988); and Larry Yates, "Anti-Displacement Report," *Roundup,* No. 134 (July–August 1990), for descriptions of prepayment protests occurring across the country.

70. Pearlman, *State and Local Initiatives.*

71. "States Legislate, Act to Preserve Assisted Housing," *Roundup,* No. 121 (April 1989).

72. Pearlman, *State and Local Initiatives,* pp. 16–17.

73. Title VIII of the Housing and Community Development Act of 1977, Public Law 95-128.

74. Calvin Bradshaw, *Partners for Reinvestment: An Evaluation of the Chicago Neighborhood Lending Program* (Chicago: National Training and Information Center, 1990).

75. Ibid.

76. City of Tampa, Sandra W. Freedman, Mayor. *Challenge Fund Program* (Tampa, Fla., n.d.).

77. This section is based on Robert Stumberg, *State Reinvestment Policy* (Washington, D.C.: Center for Policy Alternatives, 1990).

78. Ibid.

79. Ibid., pp. 6–8.

80. Ibid, p. 11.

81. William Fulton, "A Second Wave of Planning," *Governing* 6.2 (1989): 40. See also Robyne S. Turner, "New Rules for the Growth Game:

The Use of Rational State Standards in Land Use Policy," *Journal of Urban Affairs* 12.1 (1990): 35–47.

82. David L. Callies, "A Report from Hawaii," *Urban Land*, July 1989, pp. 32–33.

83. Gilderbloom and Applebaum, *Rethinking Rental Housing*.

84. Advisory Commission on Regulatory Barriers to Affordable Housing, *Not In My Back Yard: Removing Barriers to Affordable Housing*, report to President George Bush and Secretary Jack Kemp (Washington, D.C.: Department of Housing and Urban Development, 1991).

85. Here the housing movement has been greatly aided by academic analyses of the impacts of rent control. Bartelt and Lawson, "Rent Control"; Gilderbloom and Applebaum, *Rethinking Rental Housing*, chap. 7; and Applebaum et al., "Scapegoating Rent Control," are among those showing none of the purported negative side effects suggested by orthodox economists. The arguments of the economists are generally derived from theoretical premises, often without the aid of data; the argument that rent control contributes to homelessness (in Tucker, *Excluded Americans*) is based upon poor methodology.

86. "SRO Housing Rebounds," *Alliance* (publication of the national Alliance to End Homelessness) 5 (October 1989): 1–2; and "SROs: New Respectability for an Old Idea," *Affordable Housing Bulletin* 1 (April 1991): 3, 5.

87. Mary E. Brooks, *A Survey of Housing Trust Funds* (Washington, D.C.: Center for Community Change, 1988).

88. Gunn and Gunn, *Reclaiming Capital*.

89. Fran Tobin (Illinois) interview.

90. Telephone interview with Robert Jodon, San Antonio Housing Trust Foundation, September 4, 1991.

91. *News from the Housing Trust Fund Project* (San Pedro, Calif.: Housing Trust Fund Project, Center for Community Change, 1990).

92. Anne E. Hoskins, Claudia Jadrijevic, Amy Haught, and Sandra Green, *Survey of State and Local Housing Trust Fund Prgrams* (Washington, D.C.: Center for Policy Alternatives, 1991).

93. Weiss, "Origins and Legacy"; Hartman, *Housing and Social Policy;* and, Bernard J. Frieden and Lynne B. Sagalyn, *Downtown, Inc.* (Cambridge, Mass.: MIT Press, 1990).

94. Charles Hoch and Robert A. Slayton, *New Homeless and Old: Community and the Skid Row Hotel* (Philadelphia: Temple University Press, 1989).

95. "Appeals Court to Rule on Law to Help S.R.O.'s," *New York Times,* June 28, 1989.

96. Hoch and Slayton, *New Homeless*.
97. Mary Papenfuss, "War of the SROs," *City Limits*, August–September 1985.
98. Hoch and Slayton, *New Homeless*.
99. Judith A. Martin and Antony Goddard, *Past Choices/Present Landscapes* (Minneapolis, Minn.: Center for Urban and Regional Affairs, 1989).
100. Diane R. Suchman, "Housing the Poor in Central City East, Los Angeles," *Urban Land* 46 (1987): 12.
101. Department of City Planning of the City and County of San Francisco, *Residential Hotel Unit Conversion and Demolition Ordinance Status Report* (San Francisco, 1985).
102. Marsha Ritzdorf and Sumner M. Sharpe, "Portland, Oregon: A Comprehensive Approach," in *The Homeless in Contemporary Society*, ed. Richard D. Bingham, Roy E. Green, and Sammis B. White (Beverly Hills, Calif.: Sage, 1986).
103. Hoch and Slayton, *New Homeless*.
104. Kim Hopper and Jill Hamburg, "The Making of America's Homeless: From Skid Row to New Poor," in Bratt, Hartman, and Meyerson, *Critical Perspectives;* and Hoch and Slayton, *New Homeless*.
105. Housing Blueprint Technical Working Group, *A Blueprint for Housing Production in Cincinnati* (Cincinnati, Ohio, 1989).
106. Suchman, "Housing the Poor."
107. Ibid.
108. Community Redevelopment Agency of the City of Los Angeles, *Inventory of Homeless Housing and Special Needs Programs* (Los Angeles, 1987).
109. Suchman, "Housing the Poor."
110. "In San Diego, the Developers Profit as Homeless Get Low-Cost Housing," *New York Times*, September 6, 1988. See also *Alliance* 6 (January 1990).
111. Stegman and Holden (*Nonfederal Housing*) provide information on this process in a number of jurisdictions.
112. The study was done by the Low Income Housing Committee of Minneapolis, a group of advocates comprising representatives of Legal Aid, community councils in downtown neighborhoods, CDCs, and other service providers.
113. "Record Death Toll among San Francisco Homeless in 1988," *Safety Network* 8 (February 1989): 1.
114. Ed Goetz and Barbara Lukermann, "Putting Housing on the Front Burner in Rochester and Olmsted County," *CURA Reporter* 20 (April 1990): 1.

115. Stegman and Holden, *Nonfederal Housing*, p. 23.
116. Governor's Commission on Housing, *Affordable Homes—Within Our Reach*, report to Richard F. Celeste (Columbus, Ohio, 1989).
117. Ibid.
118. Kathy Rosner, "Housing as a Public Purpose," *Shelterforce* 12 (September–October 1990): 19.
119. "Ohioans Approve Affordable Housing Measure" *Safety Network* 2 (February 1991).
120. "State Housing Initiatives on the Ballot" *Shelterforce* 13 (January–February 1991); and "Ohioans Approve," *Safety Network*.
121. Interview with Julie Kyle, Ohio Housing Coalition, May 23, 1990.
122. David P. Varady and Charlotte T. Birdsell, "Conserving Single Room Occupancy Housing: A Cincinnati Case Study," *Urban Resources* 2.3 (1987): 39.
123. Ann Greiner, *The Housing Affordability Gap and Boston's Economic Growth: Potential for Crisis* (Boston: Boston Redevelopment Agency, 1987).
124. Osborne, *Laboratories of Democracy*.

CHAPTER 5

1. Much of this chapter is taken from Goetz, "Local Government Support."
2. See Institute for Policy Studies, *Progressive Housing*.
3. Social ownership is defined as "housing that is operated solely for resident and community benefit, subject to resident control, and cannot be resold for a profit. No one form of social ownership is to be favored over another, so long as the ownership arrangement is designed to further social housing goals, rather than private profits" (Institute for Policy Studies, *Progressive Housing*, p. 25).
4. Lester B. Salamon and Alan J. Abramson, "The Nonprofit Sector," in *The Reagan Experiment*, ed. John L. Palmer and Isabel V. Sawhill (Washington, D.C.: Urban Institute Press, 1982).
5. Lester B. Salamon, "Government and the Voluntary Sector in an Era of Retrenchment: The American Experience," *Journal of Public Policy* 6.1 (1986):1.
6. Neal R. Peirce and Carol Steinbach, *Corrective Capitalism* (New York: Ford Foundation, 1987); Ronald Shiffman with Susan Motley, *Comprehensive and Integrative Planning for Community Development* (New York: New School for Social Research, 1990); and Robert Zdenek,

"Community Development Corporations," in Bruyn and Meehan, *Beyond the Market*.

7. See Boyte, *Backyard Revolution;* and National Commission on Neighborhoods, *People Building Neighborhoods*.

8. Vidal, *Rebuilding Communities*.

9. Ibid. Ayse Pamuk and Karen Christensen, "Preliminary Findings on San Francisco Bay Area Nonprofit Housing Developers," *Berkeley Planning Journal* 4 (1989), p. 19, show that 60 percent of CDCs in the Bay Area were formed before 1980.

10. Vidal, *Rebuilding Communities*.

11. Ibid., p. 60.

12. Avis C. Vidal, "A Community-Based Approach to Affordable Housing," *Commentator* 2 (November 1990).

13. National Congress for Community Economic Development (NCCED), *Against All Odds: The Achievements of Community-Based Development Organizations* (Washington, D.C., 1989). Vidal, *Rebuilding Communities,* has the same figure. Eighty-seven percent of the CDCs they study do housing, and of those, 89 percent "mainly" do housing.

14. See Pickman et al, *Producing Lower Income Housing;* and Stegman and Holden, *Nonfederal Housing*.

15. Dreier, "Community-Based Housing."

16. See Bratt, "Dilemmas of Community-Based Housing," p. 324, on the advantages of community-based housing approaches with CDCs. See also NCCED, *Against All Odds;* and Vidal, "Community-Based Approach."

17. See NCCED, *Against All Odds*.

18. The one city with the most CDCs was Los Angeles, which reported forty-five nonprofit developers. However, according to New Ventures, *The Activities and Accomplishments of New York City's Community Development Organizations* (New York: New Ventures, 1989), New York City (not among the respondents to this survey) had seventy active housing CDCs.

19. See NCCED, *Against All Odds*, p. 6.

20. See Vidal, *Rebuilding Communities*. Pamuk and Christensen, "Preliminary Findings," estimate that CDCs in the San Francisco Bay Area have accounted for 42 percent of the affordable housing in that region since 1980. A study of New York CDCs estimates close to 5,000 units under development in 1988. New Ventures, *Activities and Accomplishments*.

21. Low Income Housing Information Service, "The Fiscal Year 1990 Budget and Low Income Housing" (Special Memorandum, March 1989), Table 3, "HUD Subsidized Housing Starts and Completions, 1975–1989."

22. Vidal, *Rebuilding Communities*.

23. See Rachel Bratt, *Rebuilding a Low-Income Housing Policy*

(Philadelphia: Temple University Press, 1989), chap. 11 for a similar presentation.

24. The New York survey was conducted by New Ventures, Inc. (*Activities and Accomplishments*); the Twin Cities' survey by Common Space (*Survey of Nonprofit Developers in Minneapolis and St. Paul* [Minneapolis, 1988]); the survey of Los Angeles area CDCs by Fred Kahane, Jack Neff, and Beth Barad (*Survey of Southern California Nonprofit Housing Organizations* [Los Angeles: Corporate Fund for Housing, 1988]); and the Minnesota Housing Partnership did the state survey (*Survey of Low-income Housing Providers in Minnesota* [Minneapolis: Minnesota Housing Partnership, 1989]).

25. Kahane, Neff, and Barad, *Survey of Southern California*. See, also, Minnesota Housing Partnership, *Survey of Low-Income Housing*.

26. New Ventures, *Activities and Accomplishments;* Kahane, Neff, and Barad, *Survey of Southern California;* Pamuk and Christensen, "Preliminary Findings"; and Vidal, *Rebuilding Communities*.

27. Stegman and Holden, *Nonfederal Housing*.

28. Minnesota Housing Partnership, *Survey of Low-Income Housing*.

29. Kahane, Neff, and Barad, "Survey of Southern California"; and Common Space, "Survey of Nonprofit Developers."

30. See Salamon, "Government and the Voluntary Sector," on this mutual dependence between nonprofit and public sectors in the delivery of human services.

31. Bratt, *Rebuilding a Low-Income Housing Policy*.

32. Ibid., p. 281.

33. Michael Lipsky and Steven Rathgeb Smith, "Nonprofit Organizations, Government, and the Welfare State," *Political Science Quarterly* 104.4 (1989): 625.

34. New Ventures, *Activities and Accomplishments*.

35. Vidal, *Rebuilding Communities*.

36. The following percentages are based on the cities that reported providing technical assistance ($n = 70$). With nine missing cases, the denominator for this analysis is 61.

37. Housing Trust Fund Project, San Pedro, Calif., "Capacity Building with Nonprofit Development Organizations through Housing Trust Funds," September 1990.

38. Ibid.

39. *Bullet* (newsletter of the Minnesota Housing Partnership), July 1991.

40. See W. Dennis Keating, "The Emergence of Community Development Corporations—Their Impact on Housing and Neighborhoods,"

Shelterforce 5 (February–April 1989); and see also Lenz, "Neighborhood Development," p. 24.

41. "Of the CDCs in existence five years ago, 64 percent were predominately cooperative in style at that time—clearly a shift from the early years of CDC formation. Currently, 85 percent of sampled CDCs have predominately cooperative operating styles, including all of the groups founded during the last five years" (Vidal, *Community Economic Development*, p. III–7).

42. See Shiffman with Motley, "Comprehensive and Integrative Planning."

43. Gittell, *Limits to Citizen Participation*.

44. Ibid., p. 40.

45. Ibid., p. 43.

46. Piven and Cloward, *Poor People's Movements*, p. xxi.

47. Lenz, "Neighborhood Development," p. 24.

48. Gunn and Gunn look at the increasing tendency of CDCs to rely on for-profit subsidiaries as a source of increasing tension that results in the erosion of democratic accountabilty. They conclude that "the potential of CDCs as agencies of political and social empowerment seems to have diminished in the 1980s" (*Reclaiming Capital*, p. 94).

49. This section is based on a conversation with Carla Okigwe and Ken Katahira of the Seattle–King County Housing Development Consortium, July 25, 1991.

50. Seattle–King County Housing Development Consortium, "Non-Profit Housing for Seattle-King County," April 1991.

51. The provision of governmental support to CDCs resembles a traditional "distributive" policy: that is the allocation of a public good or service to a particular group. This may account for the fact that support for CDCs is the most common of the progressive policies examined in this book. The connection between policy and beneficiary is more indirect for each of the other elements of the progressive agenda. In fact, this notion is further supported by the pattern of use of "progressive" economic development policies. In an earlier study (Goetz, "Type II Policy") I showed that among a range of alternative economic development policies, programs that channel tangible benefits to a distinct group (for example, programs that require local or minority hiring) and the use of women- or minority-owned businesses are those used most often by cities and counties. See also Dennis R. Judd and Randy L. Ready, "Entrepreneurial Cities and the New Policies of Economic Development," in Peterson and Lewis, *Reagan and the Cities*.

52. These figures are from San Francisco's 1989 CDBG program budgets. In fact, if one outlying corporation is taken out of the analysis (one

that relies on the city for only 2 percent of its administrative costs), the average figure rises to over 60 percent.

53. See Bratt, *Rebuilding Low-Income Housing,* chap. 11.

54. Stegman and Holden, *Nonfederal Housing,* p. 103.

55. Vidal, *Rebuilding Communities;* and Diane R. Suchman with D. Scott Middleton and Susan L. Giles, *Public/Private Housing Partnerships* (Washington, D.C.: Urban Land Institute, 1990).

56. Suchman with Middleton and Giles, *Public/Private Housing,* p. 77.

57. Ibid.

58. Union Institute, *Survey of Nonprofit Associations: Review of the Data* (Washington, D.C.: Union Institute, 1989).

59. Ibid.

60. Bratt, *Rebuilding Low-Income Housing,* p. 281.

61. Rachel G. Bratt, "Private Owners of Subsidized Housing vs. Public Goals: Conflicting Interests in Resyndication," *Journal of the American Planning Association* 53 (1987): 328.

62. Dreier, "Community-Based Housing."

CHAPTER 6

1. Stegman and Holden, *Nonfederal Housing,* p. 21; they make this comment about U.S. cities in general.

2. Edward Banfield and James Q. Wilson, *City Politics* (Cambridge, Mass.: Harvard University Press, 1963); and Alan L. Saltzstein, Raphael J. Sonenshein, and Irving Ostrow, "Federal Aid to the City of Los Angeles: Implementing a More Centralized Local Political System," in *Research in Urban Policy,* vol. 2, ed. Terry N. Clark (Greenwich, Conn.: JAI Press, 1986), p. 55.

3. J. David Greenstone and Paul E. Peterson, *Race and Authority in Urban Politics: Community Participation and the War on Poverty* (Chicago: University of Chicago Press, 1973), p. 29.

4. Ibid.

5. Dommel et al., *Deregulating Community Development.*

6. "Housing the Future," Briefing Book, Blue Ribbon Committee for Affordable Housing, Office of Mayor Tom Bradley, Los Angeles, 1988.

7. Ibid., p. 97. The percentage of CDBG funds going on program administration was 25 to 35 percent through most of the 1980s.

8. Ibid., p. 99.

9. Gilda Haas and Allan David Heskin, "Community Struggle in Los Angeles," *International Journal of Urban and Regional Research* 5 (1981): 546.

10. Jill Stewart, "Advocates of Poor Assail Plan to Revamp Downtown," *Los Angeles Times,* November 28, 1988.

11. *Housing Los Angeles: Affordable Housing for the Future* (Los Angeles: Blue Ribbon Committee for Affordable Housing, 1988), p. 18.

12. Jill Stewart, "L.A. Rentals: A Crisis That Is Growing," *Los Angeles Times,* November 27, 1988, p. A–1.

13. Greenstone and Peterson, *Race and Authority,* p. 29.

14. Haas and Heskin, "Community Struggle."

15. See, e.g., Edward W. Soja, "Economic Restructuring and the Internationalization of the Los Angeles Region," in *The Capitalist City,* ed. Michael Peter Smith and Joe R. Feagin (Oxford: Basil Blackwell, 1987); Sassen, *Mobility of Labor and Capital;* and Robert A. Beauregard, "Capital Restructuring and the New Built Environment of Global Cities: New York and Los Angeles," *International Journal of Urban and Regional Research* 15.1 (1991): 90.

16. Soja, "Economic Restructuring."

17. Sassen, *Mobility of Labor and Capital.*

18. Soja, "Economic Restructuring."

19. See Mike Davis, " 'Chinatown,' Part Two? The Internationalization of Downtown Los Angeles," *New Left Review* 165 (July–August 1987), for figures on the increase in foreign investment. See Sassen, *Mobility of Labor and Capital,* for an analysis of immigrant labor in Los Angeles.

20. *Housing Los Angeles,* p. 5.

21. Stewart, "L.A. Rentals."

22. Davis, " 'Chinatown,' Part Two?"

23. Ibid., p. 71.

24. Stephanie Chavez and James Quinn, "Garages: Immigrants In, Cars Out," *Los Angeles Times,* May 24, 1987, pt. 1, p. 1.

25. Both Bradley and his counterpart in San Francisco, Mayor Dianne Feinstein, undertook a series of trips to Japan and Southeast Asia during the 1980s in attempts to attract foreign investment.

26. Davis, " 'Chinatown,' Part Two?" pp. 71–72.

27. Ibid, p. 71.

28. Haas and Heskin, "Community Struggles."

29. Edward G. Goetz, "Land Use and Homeless Policy in Los Angeles," *International Journal of Urban and Regional Research* 16.4 (1992): 540–54.

30. Ibid.

31. Haas and Heskin, "Community Struggles."

32. See Mike Davis, *City of Quartz: Excavating the Future in Los Angeles* (London: Verso, 1991).

33. Goetz, "Land Use."
34. Ibid.
35. Ibid.
36. Davis, *City of Quartz.*
37. This section borrows heavily from the description of events in Heskin, *American Dream,* pp. 45–55.
38. Kahane, Neff, and Barad, *Survey of Southern California.*
39. Interview with Jennifer Bigelow, Southern California Assocation of Non-Profit Developers, March 22, 1991.
40. Jackie Dupont Walker, member of the city's housing commission and executive director of Ward Economic Development Corporation in south central Los Angeles, argued (in an interview, January 31, 1992) that the formation of CDCs in Los Angeles was not late: "Late relative to what? People began to do housing when they felt the need for greater production of truly affordable housing. When we felt the need, we did it. Part of it has to do with the fact that Los Angeles doesn't have the ghettoized look that eastern cities have. People here didn't realize that we have a housing crisis here until it was painfully obvious. Watts is different from south Philadelphia and the Bronx; you take a look at Watts and it doesn't look all that bad."
41. Bigelow interview.
42. Stewart, "L.A. Rentals."
43. Alan L. Saltzstein and Raphael J. Sonenshein, "Los Angeles: Transformation of a Governing Coalition," in *Big City Politics in Transition,* vol. 38: *Urban Affairs Annual Reviews,* ed. H. V. Savitch and John Clayton Thomas (Newbury Park, Calif.: Sage, 1991).
44. San Fernando Valley council member Joel Wachs led the fight for rent control in 1978, and Ernani Bernardi has been a vocal CRALA critic. In addition, Marvin Braude allied with Yaroslavsky and became a leader of the growth control movement. (*Los Angeles Times,* August 11, 1988, p. II-1).
45. Frank Clifford and Jill Stewart, "Redevelopment Agency under Fire by City Council," *Los Angeles Times,* May 16, 1989.
46. Interview with Gilda Haas, March 18, 1991.
47. Interview with Chuck Elsesser, March 21, 1991.
48. A legal nexus that ties the function being assessed (in this case, office development) to the benefit being created (in this case, housing) is necessary for an office-housing linkage program to survive legal challenges. See, e.g., Fred P. Bosselman, "Downtown Linkages: Legal Issues," in Porter, *Downtown Linkages;* and Dwight H. Merriam and Christine I. Andrew, "Defensible Linkage," paper presented at the annual conference of the American Planning Association, New York, April 1987.

49. Inteview with Gary Squier, March 18, 1991.
50. Interview with Michael Bodaken, March 22, 1991.
51. Bodaken interview.
52. Squier interview.
53. Elsesser interview.
54. Ibid.
55. Michael Bodaken, personal correspondence, January 25, 1992.
56. Frank Clifford, "Bradley Retreats from Affordable Housing Plan," *Los Angeles Times*, November 10, 1991. p. I-1.
57. Walker interview.
58. John Walton, "Theoretical Methods in Comparative Urban Politics," in Logan and Swanstrom, *Beyond the City Limits*.

CHAPTER 7

1. $X^2 = 28.54$, significant at p <.001.
2. See e.g., Clavel, *Progressive City;* Clavel and Kleniewski, "Progressive Local Policy"; Clarke and Rich, "Making Money Work"; Goetz, "Type II Policy,"; Goetz, "Promoting Low Income Housing through Innovations in Land Use Regulations," *Journal of Urban Affairs* 13.3 (1991): 337; and Goetz, "Expanding Possibilities in Local Development Policy," *Political Research Quarterly*, forthcoming.
3. DiGaetano, "Urban Political Regime Formation," p. 261; see also Joe R. Feagin and Michael Peter Smith, "Cities and the New International Division of Labor: An Overview," in Smith and Feagin, *Capitalist City*.
4. Clavel, *Progressive City;* Clavel and Kleinewski, "Progressive Local Policy"; Harvey Molotch, "Urban Deals in Comparative Perspective," in Logan and Swanstrom; *Beyond the City Limits;* Goetz, "Type II Policy"; Goetz, "Expanding Possibilities."
5. Dreier and Keating, "Limits of Localism."
6. See, e.g., Goetz, "Linkage in San Francisco"; and Keating, "Linking Downtown."
7. DiGaetano, "Urban Political Regime Formation."
8. See, e.g., Clarke and Rich, "Making Money Work"; Goetz, "Type II Policy"; and Osborne, *Laboratories of Democracy*.
9. Swanstrom, *Growth Politics*.
10. Sassen, *Mobility of Labor and Capital;* Soja, "Economic Restructuring"; and Norman J. Glickman, "Cities and the International Division of Labor," in Smith and Feagin, *Capitalist City*.
11. Sassen, *Mobility of Labor and Capital;* and Soja, "Economic Restructuring."

12. See the review in Jack M. Treadway, *Public Policymaking in the American States* (New York: Praeger, 1985).

13. See, e.g., Andrew T. Cowart, "Anti-Poverty Expenditures in the American States: A Comparative Analysis," in *State and Urban Politics*, ed., Richard I. Hofferbert and Ira Sharkansky (Boston: Little Brown and Company, 1971).

14. Clavel and Kleniewski, "Progressive Local Policy"; and, Walton, "Theoretical Methods."

15. Sidney Verba, "Comparative Political Culture," in *Political Culture and Political Development*, ed. Lucian W. Pye and Sidney Verba (Princeton, N.J.: Princeton University Press, 1965), p. 513.

16. Daniel J. Elazar, *American Federalism: A View from the States* (New York: Thomas Y. Crowell, 1972).

17. John Kincaid, "Introduction," in *Political Culture, Public Policy, and the American States*, ed. John Kincaid (Philadelphia: Institute for the Study of Human Issues, 1982), p. 9.

18. Elazar, *American Federalism*, p. 94.

19. Sam Bass Warner, Jr., *The Private City: Philadelphia in Three Periods of Its Growth* (Philadelphia: University of Pennsylvania Press, 1968), quoted in Kincaid, "Introduction," p. 10.

20. Ira Sharkansky, "The Utility of Elazar's Political Culture: A Research Note," *Polity* 2 (Fall 1969): 66.

21. Kincaid, "Introduction."

22. See Kantor with David, *Dependent City*, for a version of this argument.

23. Clarke and Rich, "Making Money Work."

24. The political mobilization measure is the additive combination of two items on the survey instrument: "Is there a citywide low-income housing advocacy group in your city?" and "Are nonprofit housing developers organized into a coalition?"

The fiscal capacity of local governments has been measured in a number of ways (see Richard D. Bingham and Brett W. Hawkins, "A Test of Political Bias in Scholars' Preference for Measuring Fiscal Strain," *Urban Affairs Quarterly*, March 25, 1990, p. 515). The measures used here are the ratio of outstanding municipal debt to own revenue in 1986, and the city's 1987 bond rating as rated by Moody's Investors' Service, Inc., New York (from the International City Management Association, *Municipal Year Book, 1988* [Washington, D.C.: ICMA, 1988].

The measures of economic performance are per capita income in 1983, population growth 1980–86, and the concentration of corporate functions in urban areas.

Indictors of need include the unemployment rate for the metropolitan area in 1985 averaged over the twelve months (data from Bureau of the Census, *County and City Data Book, 1988* [Washington, D.C.: Government Printing Office, 1988]); the percentage of the population earning below the poverty level in 1980; and direct measures of housing problems in the responding jurisdictions. Survey respondents were asked to rate the severity of a series of potential housing problems in their locality. Factor analysis of survey responses provided two summary measures of housing needs. A high score on the first indicates severe problems related to either the cost or the availability of affordable housing. A high score on the second indicates problems related to abandonment of and disinvestment in the housing stock (see Goetz "Promotion of Low Income Housing").

Political culture is measured in the way outlined by Sharkansky ("Elazar's Political Culture"). Localities are ranked on a range from 1 (a moralistic culture) to 9 (a more traditional culture). Originally (and most often) used as a statewide measure, this has been transposed to the metropolitan level by John Kincaid, "Political Culture and the Quality of Urban Life," in Kincaid, *Political Culture*.

The measure of bureaucratic experience uses data on the involvement of the city in the categorical aid programs of the federal government prior to 1974. The variable incorporates the average annual total of funds received under the seven categorical programs folded into the CDBG program in 1974 and takes a value from 1 to 4, reflecting low to high levels previous experience. These data are from Michael J. Rich, "Congress, Bureaucracy, and the Cities: Distributive Politics and the Allocation of Federal Grants for Community and Economic Development," Ph.D. diss. Northwestern University, 1985. Finally, population in 1984 is used as a control in the analysis.

25. The multiple regression equation explained 48 percent of the variance in the dependent variable. A more detailed description of the statistical methods employed and the results obtained may be acquired from the author. The models are contained in Goetz, "Expanding Possibilities," and Goetz, "The Determinants of Progressive Housing Policy in U.S. Cities and States" (manuscript, University of Minnesota Housing Program, 1992).

26. See Chapter 3 for the Tennessee coalition's work in creating a housing trust fund.

27. Interview with Ben Zachrich, Iowa Coalition for the Homeless, January 25, 1990; and Gregg (Kentucky) interview.

28. Interview with Chuck Hampshire, West Virginia Coalition for the Homeless, May 7, 1990.

29. $X^2 = 5.11$, significant at p $<.05$.

30. This literature was most dynamic between 1966 and 1978, when the political science field debated the relative importance of political versus economic (or environmental) factors in shaping public policy. The current debate in urban politics on the relative importance of nonlocal economic and fiscal constraints as opposed to local political action is an uncomfortable echo of the earlier literature.

31. Treadway, *Public Policymaking,* provides an excellent summary and review of this literature.

32. Thomas R. Dye, *Politics, Economics, and the Public: Policy Outcomes in the American States* (Chicago: Rand McNally, 1966).

33. Treadway, *Public Policymaking,* pp. 94–99.

34. See Bernard H. Booms and James R. Halldorsen, "The Politics of Redistribution: A Reformulation," *American Political Science Review* 64 (June 1970): 508–22; and Richard E. DeLeon, "Politics, Economic Surplus, and Redistribution in the American States: A Test of a Theory," *American Journal of Political Science* 17 (November 1973): 781–96.

35. John H. Fenton, quoted in Treadway, *Public Policymaking,* p. 82.

36. For the state-level multivariate analysis, the independent variables are measured as follows: The mobilization of the housing movement is measured by the existence of a housing advocacy coalition and/or a nonprofit coalition as in the city level analysis. The variable thus takes a value from 0 to 2, reflecting the number of such organizations in each state.

Economic and fiscal variables include the population growth rate 1980–85, per capita income in 1979, and the percentage of the population that is urban. This last variable is included in the model in deference to a number of studies that have shown its importance in determining state policy outputs (see, e.g., Dye, *Politics, Economics, and the Public).* Need indicators are the percentage of the population below the poverty level in 1979, and the percentage of the population receiving public assistance in 1984. Separate models run with poverty data from 1979 and from 1989 found little difference between the two; therefore, the 1979 data were selected because this baseline could realistically have been used by policymakers in the years from 1980 to 1989. The measure of political culture is the same as that used in the city-level analysis except, of course, that it is applied to the entire state.

Party competition was measured in three different ways in an attempt to ferret out some relationship: first, the average percentage of seats controlled by the majority party between 1980 and 1990 in the state senate; second, the same average for the lower house in the state legislature; third, the number of years between 1980 and 1990 that the same party controlled both the state senate and the governor's office. See Treadway, *Public Policymaking*, for a discussion of these measures and their use in the existing literature on state policy outputs.

37. As in the city-level analysis, I used a backward stepwise regression to isolate the model that produces the highest degree of explanatory power (the highest adjusted R^2). Only four variables remain in the equation that explains 58 percent of the variance in the dependent variable.

38. Unlike the city-level analysis, however, the state analysis shows a negative relationship between poverty and the pursuit of progressive policy (though the coefficient for the poverty variable is not statistically significant). The need hypothesis is nevertheless supported by the significant impact of the percentage of residents receiving public assistance.

39. Hartman, *Transformation of San Francisco*.

40. Walton, "Theoretical Methods," p. 253.

41. Judd and Parkinson, "Patterns of Leadership."

CHAPTER 8

1. E. E. Schattschneider, *The Semisovereign People* (Hinsdale, Ill.: Dryden Press, 1975), p. 10, noted long ago that "one of the most remarkable developments in recent American Politics [*sic*] is the extent to which the federal, state and local governments have become involved in *doing the same kinds of things* in large areas of public policy, so that it is possible for contestants to move freely from one level of government to another in an attempt to find the level at which they might try most advantageously to get what they want" (original emphasis). Clearly, the housing policy arena of the 1980s is a vivid example of advocates shifting from one level of government to another in order to find some political advantage.

2. See, e.g., Altschuler, *Community Control;* and Milton Kotler, *Neighborhood Government* (Indianapolis, Ind.: Bobbs-Merril, 1969).

3. Robert L. Lineberry and Ira Sharkansky, *Urban Politics and Public Policy*, 2d ed. (New York: Harper & Row, 1974).

4. See, e.g., Altschuler, *Community Control;* and Fainstein and Fainstein, *Urban Political Movements*, app. 1.

5. See Goetz, "Type II Policies."

6. Osborne, *Laboratories of Democracy*.

7. In addition to the works of Clavel and others on progressive policies, see Mark E. Kann, *Middle Class Radicalism in Santa Monica* (Philadelphia: Temple University Press, 1986); and Harry Boyte, Heather

Booth, and Steve Max, *Citizen Action and the New American Populism* (Philadelphia: Temple University Press, 1986).

8. Bruyn and Meehan, *Beyond the Market;* see also Gunn and Gunn, *Reclaiming Capital.*

9. Feagin and Parker, *Building American Cities*, p. 276.

10. See, e.g., Swanstrom, *Growth Politics;* Feagin and Parker, *Building American Cities;* and Goetz, "Type II Policy."

11. See, e.g., Gilda Haas, *Plant Closures: Myths, Realities, and Responses* (Boston: South End Press, 1985).

12. John Portz, *The Politics of Plant Closings* (Lawrence: Kansas University Press, 1990), p. 118.

13. Gunn and Gunn, *Reclaiming Capital*, p. 109.

14. Williams C. Apgar, Jr., and H. James Brown, *The State of the Nation's Housing 1988* (Cambridge, Mass.: Joint Center for Housing Studies, Harvard University, 1988).

15. Grant McConnell, *Private Power and American Democracy* (New York: Vintage Books, 1966), pp. 101–110.

16. *Federalist Papers*, No. 10.

17. Swanstrom, *Growth Politics.*

18. Harvey Molotch, "The City as a Growth Machine," *American Journal of Sociology* 82.2 (1976):309.

19. Lyle Dorsett, *The Queen City: History of Denver* (Boulder, Colo.: Pruett, 1977), p. 251, quoted in Judd, "Cowtown to Sunbelt City" p. 178.

20. Michael Peter Smith and Marlene Keller, " 'Managed Growth' and the Politics of Uneven Development in New Orleans," in Fainstein et al., *Restructuring the City.*

21. Judd and Parkinson, "Patterns of Leadership," p. 307.

22. Ibid.

23. Norman I. Fainstein and Susan S. Fainstein, "Regime Strategies, Communal Resistance, and Economic Forces," in Fainstein et al., *Restructuring the City*, p. 270.

24. The dissenters, according to Peterson, are parochial interests that "put their separate interests ahead of that of the community" (*City Limits*, p. 149).

25. John Emmaus Davis, *Contested Ground: Collective Action and the Urban Neighborhood* (Ithaca, N.Y.: Cornell University Press, 1991); John R. Logan and Harvey L. Molotch, *Urban Fortunes: The Political Economy of Place* (Berkeley: University of California Press, 1987).

26. Davis, *Contested Ground*, p. 61.

27. See, e.g., Beauregard, "Capital Restructuring."

28. Susan S. Fainstein and Norman I. Fainstein, "Economic Restruc-

turing and the Rise of Urban Social Movements," *Urban Affairs Quarterly* 21 (December 1985); Walton, "Theoretical Methods."

29. Walton, "Theoretical Methods," p. 255.
30. Minnesota Housing Partnership, *Bullet,* July 1991.
31. See, e.g., Dreier and Keating, "Limits of Localism."

Subject Index

Boston: housing movement in, 70; housing problems in, 113
Boston Housing Partnership, 133, 156, 159
Bradley, Tom (Los Angeles mayor): council support for, 155; electoral coalition, 147–48, 162–64; homeless strategy, 144–47; housing policy, 141–42
BRIDGE, 132
Burlington, housing movement in, 70–71
Burlington Community Land Trust, 88

California: fair share housing program, 95; housing coalition, 65–66, 68–69, 72–73, 178; rent control, 96; tenant activism in, 46–47
Capacity building: for nonprofits, 124–25; in Massachusetts, 132–33; in Seattle, 129–30. *See also* Community development corporations
CDBG, 24, 30, 92; and replacement housing, 92, 199; as support for CDCs, 122–23, 132; coalition of recipients, 36; use for housing, 39; in Los Angeles, 141
Chicago: mortgage disclosure law, 98–99; progressive policy in, 83–84
Chicago Housing Partnership, 133–34, 156, 159
Clavelle, Peter (Burlington mayor), 70–71
Cleveland Housing Network, 134
Coalition for Economic Survival, 147, 151–52, 163

Community-based planning, for housing, 5, 87, 109–10, 193
Community development corporations (CDCs), 4, 39–40, 121; and housing movement, 14–15, 45–46, 49, 59, 62, 87; as part of progressive policy paradigm, 43, 83–84; capacity building for, 124–25; emergence of, 115; in Los Angeles, 152–54; in New York, 121–22; in San Francisco, 131–32; in Seattle, 128–29; needs of, 119–21; politics of, 125–28; profile of, 115–17; production levels, 117–18; support from local governments, 122–25, 131–37, 174–75 (Table 7.1), 181–82 (Table 7.2); support from Los Angeles city government, 160–61. *See also* Nonprofit housing
Community for Creative Non-Violence, 75
Community land trusts, 83, 86, 88
Community Redevelopment Agency of Los Angeles, 108, 142–43, 156–57; budget, 158–59; downtown developments of, 145–46; homeless programs of, 146–47; opposition to, 154–57, 166; $2.5 million housing proposal, 148–51, 165
Community Reinvestment Act of 1977, 48, 85, 135, 191; local laws pursuant to, 98–100
Comprehensive Housing Affordability Strategy (CHAS), 66; in St. Paul, 66, 136; in Los Angeles, 166
Conversion restrictions, on subsidized housing, 90–91, 96–98, 181–82 (Table 7.2)

239

Subject Index

Council of State Community Affairs Agencies (COSCAA), 77

De facto devolution, 35–37
Detroit, rent control in, 96
Deukmejian, George (California governor), opposition to housing, 72
Downtown development, impact on housing, 81, 87, 105–7, 112–13, 190–91
Dukakis, Michael (Massachusetts governor), housing policy, 54, 92

Economic constraints, on local policy-making, 5–14, 81, 170–71, 176–77, 193–97
Emergency Low-Income Housing Preservation Act, 97
Enterprise Foundation, 120
Expiring use restrictions, 39, 88, 96–97, 137, 181

Fair share housing, 95. *See also* Inclusionary zoning
Federal era housing policy, 19–26, 42–43; in Los Angeles, 139–41
Federal Home Loan Bank Act, 20
FHA, 21–22, 25–27, 43
FIRREA, 99
Florida: housing coalition, 65–67; land-use controls, 100
FNMA, 20–22, 26
Frank Amendment, 92

Gentrification, 80, 87, 191
Georgia Housing Coalition, 63–64, 67
Great Depression, impact on federal housing policy, 20–22

Harlem rent strike, 46–47
Hartford Housing Preservation and Replacement Ordinance, 93

Hawaii, developer exactions, 100–101
HMDA, 48, 99, 191
HOME, 199
Home Owners Loan Corporation (HOLC), 20–22
Homeless coalitions, 59, 62; advocacy of, 71–72, 110
Homelessness: in Los Angeles, 144–47; rent control and, 95, 223n.85
Homeownership, policy bias toward, 25, 43, 85
Housing Act of 1949, 23
Housing and Community Development Act of 1987, 74, 92
Housing Assistance Council, 56
Housing finance agencies (HFAs), state level, 27–28
Housing L.A., 135, 149–52, 163
Housing Now!, 75
Housing trust funds, 5, 86; in Illinois, 102–4; in San Antonio, 104; in San Diego, 70; in Seattle, 129; in Texas, 70; use of, 101–5, 181–82 (Table 7.2)
HUD: control over CDBG, 24; foreclosed homes, 71; lobbying of, 26; production levels, 118; spending levels, 4, 199; study of regulatory barriers, 101

Illinois, housing trust fund, 102–4
Illinois Statewide Housing Action Coalition: activities of, 64, 66–67, 102–4; rent control defense, 96; technical assistance provided by, 136
Inclusionary zoning, 84, 90–91, 101; in Burlington, 70; use of, 94–95, 175 (Table 7.1), 193

Johnson, President Lyndon, Great Society programs of, 115, 188

Kennedy, President John F., housing policies of, 23
Kentucky housing coalition, 68

Land-use regulations, for affordable housing, 4, 51, 86, 89, 193
Leasehold co-op, 86
Limited equity co-op, 86, 88–89
Linkage programs, 4, 81, 84, 86, 193; in Los Angeles, 159; in San Francisco, 94; use of, 90–91, 93–94, 175 (Table 7.1)
LISC, 118, 120, 133; in Los Angeles, 153, 160–61, 163
Local housing movement, 14, 36–37, 193, 196; and national movement, 73–75; electoral success of, 70; growth of, 52–56, 75–76; impact on city policies, 169–70, 176; impact on state policies, 177–80, 182–83, 187; in California, 72–73; in Los Angeles, 149, 162–66; in Maryland, 73; in Ohio, 110–12; origins of, 45–50, 75, 188; professionalization of, 52, 70–71
Local housing policy: during federal era, 26–29; progressive nature of, 80–87; use of progressive policies, 87–112; response to federal cutbacks, 38–41; spending levels, 3, 78–80, 198–99. *See also* Postfederal housing policy, Progressive housing
Los Angeles: Blue Ribbon Committee on Housing, 142, 148, 156–59, 164; CDCs in, 152–54; CHAS, 166; city council, 154–57; Community Development Department, 141–42, 157, 167; downtown development in, 143–47; economic restructuring of, 143–44, 162, 167; growth control in, 147, 155; homelessness in, 144–47, 167; housing movement in, 149, 162–66; Housing Partnership, 156, 159–60; Housing Production and Preservation Department, 157–59, 167; Legal Aid advocacy in, 147, 154, 163; linkage, 159; rent control in, 151–52; SRO housing in, 145; use of CDBG, 141; use of mortgage bonds, 141. *See also* Community Redevelopment Agency of Los Angeles, Housing L.A.

Los Angeles Times: impact on housing policy, 164; series on housing conditions, 154, 162, 164; survey of garage dwellers, 144, 162
Low-income housing advocacy coalitions (LIHACs), 37, 45–46; growth in number of, 52–53; impact on state policy, 67–69, 178–80; in California, 72–73; in Maryland, 73; organizational resources, 62–64; organizational structure, 57–59; political activities of, 63–67, 69–72; reasons for, 54–56; urban-rural tensions in, 64–66. *See also* Local housing movement
Low-income housing tax credit, 34

McKinney Homeless Act of 1987, 109, 199
Maryland housing coalition, 66, 98
Massachusetts Housing Partnership, 98
Minneapolis: Consortium of Nonprofits, 136; housing advocacy in, 58, 71–72, 109; replacement housing program, 93
Minnesota: capacity-building program, 125; Housing Finance Agency, 28; spending for housing, 198
Mortgage interest deduction, 24–25
Mortgage revenue bonds, 27–28; in Los Angeles, 141
Mount Laurel II, 94

NAHRO, 10
National Affordable Housing Act of 1990, 66, 74, 199
National Association of Home Builders (NAHB), 10, 24, 26
National Association of Real Estate Boards (NAREB), 26
National Association of Realtors (NAR), 10
National Coalition for the Homeless, 51–52, 74–75

National Congress for Community Economic Development (NCCED), 116–18,
National Housing Law Project, 74
National Low Income Housing Coalition, 10, 52, 74–75
Neighborhood movement, 45, 48–49, 115, 188, 191
New Jersey, inclusionary housing program, 95
New York, community reinvestment program, 99
New York City: housing groups in, 58–59; J-51 program, 105; preservation of SROs, 92; spending for housing, 79
Nixon, President Richard: federalism reforms of, 24, 31; housing policy of, 24–27, 37
Nonprofit housing: advantages over for-profit, 88, 116; in Los Angeles, 152–54; roles for organizations, 118–19
Nonprofit sector, 114, 192–93

Ohio, housing movement in, 110–12
One-for-one replacement, 70, 86, 90–91, 199; use of, 92–93, 175 (Table 7.1), 181–82 (Table 7.2)

Pennsylvania housing coalition, 64, 70
Philadelphia, tenant activism in, 58
Pico-Union Neighborhood Council, 143
Pittsburgh, capacity-building program, 125
Political culture, 172–73, 177, 183, 185
Postfederal housing policy, 37, 41, 43, 77, 80, 86; in Los Angeles, 157–58. *See also* Local housing policy, Progressive housing
Preservation, of affordable housing, 86; use of, 90–92, 175 (Table 7.1), 181–82 (Table 7.2)
Progressive development, 170, 189–90
Progressive housing: economic determinants of, 185–86; explanations of, 170–73, 180; in Ohio, 111–12; policy paradigm of, 45, 80–87, 199–200; social action and, 184–85; spread of, 87–110, 174, 181–83; state level, 180–83. *See also* Local housing policy, Postfederal housing policy

Reagan, President Ronald: federalism reforms of, 9–10, 29–35, 42, 75; housing budget cuts of, 1, 29–30, 34–36, 42, 50, 53–54; social spending cuts, 35, 38, 42, 50
Rent control, 4–5, 47, 86, 90–91, 101; in Los Angeles, 151–52; use of, 95–96, 175 (Table 7.1)
Residential hotels. *See* SRO housing

St. Paul: housing coalition, 135–36; replacement housing program, 93
San Antonio, housing trust fund, 104
San Francisco: CDBG program, 132; homeless advocacy, 110; housing movement in, 47–48, 50, 70, 184; linkage program, 94; preservation of SROs, 92; support for CDCs, 131–32
Seattle: CDCs in, 128–30; housing levy program in, 79–80, 129
Section 8 program, 24, 37; for SROs, 109
Section 221(d)(3) program, 23, 26, 89
Section 235 program, 23, 43
Section 236 program, 23, 27–28, 43
South Atlanta Land Trust (SALT), 88
Southern California Association of Non-Profit Housing (SCANPH), 153, 163
SRO housing, 5, 70, 87; elimination of, 106–9, 190; in Los Angeles, 145, 168; in San Diego, 108–9; use of policies to preserve, 91–92, 107 (Table 4.3), 174–75 (Table 7.1), 181 (Table 7.2)
Swap-and-turn-back proposal, 31, 33, 42

Subject Index 243

Tampa, community reinvestment program, 99
Tenant management, 86
Tenant movement, 45–47
Tennessee housing coalition, 69, 178
Texas housing coalition, 70

UDAG, 79, 92, 173
Uneven development, housing impact of, 171–72, 177, 184–86
Uniform Relocation Act, 105
Union of the Homeless, 75
Urban economic restructuring, 189; economic constraints, 7–8; housing impacts, 11, 112–13, 196–97; housing policy impacts, 185–86, 197–99; in Los Angeles, 143–44, 162. *See also* Uneven development
Urban renewal program, 23; housing impacts of, 105; opposition to, 47. *See also* Downtown development

Vermont, capacity-building program, 125

Washington, Harold (Chicago mayor), 83–84
Washington, D.C., rent control, 96
Wisconsin Housing Partnership, 134

Author Index

Abramson, Alan J., 225n.4
Albritton, Robert B., 216n.53
Alinsky, Saul D., 214n.25
Altschuler, Alan, 220n.30, 236nn. 2, 4
Andrew, Christine I., 231n.48
Apgar, William C., Jr., 237n.14
Appelbaum, Richard P., 206n.11, 213n.11, 220n.33, 221nn. 58, 59, 60, 222nn. 83, 85
Atlas, John, 213nn. 6, 10, 13

Banfield, Edward, 229n.2
Barad, Beth, 227nn. 24, 25, 26, 29, 231n.38
Barker, Michael, 208n.38, 209nn. 41, 43
Barnekov, Timothy, 202n.13, 218n.11
Bartelt, David, 221nn. 59, 60, 223n.85
Beam, David R., 210n.58
Beauregard, Robert A., 230n.15, 237n.27
Bellush, Jewell, 207n.18
Berenyi, Eileen B., 201n.5, 211n.89, 218n.7
Bergman, Edward M., 202n.13
Bingham, Richard D., 224n.102, 233n.24
Birdsell, Charlotte T., 113, 225n.122
Bluestone, Barry, 204n.35, 210n.67, 215n.29
Booms, Bernard H., 235n.34
Booth, Heather, 237n.7
Bosselman, Fred C., 231n.48
Bowman, Ann O'M., 94, 202n.14, 221nn. 49, 51
Boyle, Robin, 202n.13

Boyte, Harry, 214n.22, 226n.7, 236n.7
Bradshaw, Calvin, 222nn. 74, 75
Bratt, Rachel G., 121, 137, 205n.4, 206nn. 7, 10, 207n.25, 208n.26, 212n.100, 213n.13, 224n.104, 226nn. 16, 23, 227nn. 31, 32, 229nn. 53, 60, 61
Brizius, Jack A., 209n.53
Brooks, Mary E., 223n.87
Brophy, Paul C., 208n.38, 220n.35
Brown, H. James, 237n.14
Bruyn, Severyn T., 192, 219nn. 21, 24, 25, 26, 226n.9, 227n.26

Callies, David L., 223n.82
Caves, Roger W., 207n.20, 208n.35
Champion, Hale, 210n.62
Chavez, Stephanie, 230n.24
Checkoway, Barry, 206n.7
Christensen, Karen S., 211nn. 84, 87, 91, 95, 212n.102, 226n.9, 227n.26
Clark, Terry N., 229n.2
Clarke, Susan E., 82, 173, 204n.38, 219nn. 17, 18, 19, 232nn. 2, 8, 233n.23
Clavel, Pierre, 82, 172, 219nn. 12, 16, 20, 220nn. 28, 29, 232nn. 2, 4, 233n.14, 236n.7
Clay, Philip L., 212n.98, 222n.67
Clifford, Frank, 231n.45, 232n.56
Cloward, Richard A., 14, 126, 128, 165, 204n.42, 214n.18, 228n.46
Colyer, George, 211n.86
Cowart, Andrew T., 233n.13
Cowley, John, 213n.13

245

Danielson, Michael N., 209n.49, 220nn. 36, 37, 38
David, Stephen, 8, 201n.8, 203nn. 19, 21, 22, 32, 233n.22
Davis, John Emmaus, 195–96, 237nn. 25, 26
Davis, Mike, 145, 230nn. 19, 22, 23, 26, 27, 32, 231n.36
DeLeon, Richard E., 235n.34
Delgado, Gary, 214n.24, 215n.28
Dentler, Robert A., 214n.18
DiGaetano, Alan, 204n.41, 232nn. 3, 7
Doig, Jameson W., 209n.49, 220nn. 36, 37, 38
Dolbeare, Cushing N., 201n.1, 207n.25, 208n.26
Dolny, Michael, 221n.59
Dommel, Paul R., 207n.24, 209nn. 56, 57, 211nn. 91, 95, 229n.5
Doolittle, Fred C., 201nn. 3, 4, 210n.68
Dorsett, Lyle, 237n.19
Downs, Anthony, 208n.32
Dreier, Peter, 171, 212n.99, 213nn. 6, 10, 13, 217nn. 63, 64, 219nn. 12, 23, 221n.59, 226n.15, 229n.62, 232n.5, 238n.31
Dye, Thomas R., 235nn. 32, 36

Elazar, Daniel J., 171–72, 233nn. 16, 18, 234n.24
Elkin, Stephen L., 204n.37
Ellwood, John William, 210n.70
England, Robert E., 212n.106
Erlich, Bruce, 219n.12

Fainstein, Norman I., 188, 195, 202n.11, 213n.15, 219n.11, 236n.4, 237nn. 20, 23, 28
Fainstein, Susan S., 188, 195, 202n.11, 213n.15, 219n.11, 236n.4, 237nn. 20, 23, 28
Farber, Stephen B., 210n.75
Fava, Sylvia F., 206n.11

Feagin, Joe R., 187, 192, 213n.12, 214n.16, 221n.61, 230n.15, 232nn. 3, 10, 237n.9
Fenton, John H., 180, 235n.35
Ferlauto, Richard C., 201nn. 1, 2, 7
Finder, Alan, 220n.41
Fisher, Robert M., 206n.9, 214nn. 22, 23, 24, 25
Foard, Ashley, 205nn. 2, 3, 4
Foley, Bernard, 221n.53
Franklin, Scott B., 220n.34
Frantz, Douglas, 215n.28
Frantz, John M., 205nn. 2, 3, 4
Frieden, Bernard J., 203n.20, 223n.93
Friedland, Roger, 207n.19
Friedman, Lawrence M., 206n.8
Fulton, William, 222n.81

Gappert, Gary, 203n.33
Gelfand, Mark I., 207n.15
Gilderbloom, John I., 206n.11, 213n.11, 220n.33, 221nn. 58, 59, 60, 223nn. 83, 85
Giles, Susan L., 229nn. 55, 56, 57
Gittel, Marilyn, 14, 125–26, 165, 204n.43, 228nn. 43, 44, 45
Gladstein, Eva, 215n.36
Glickman, Norman J., 232n.10
Goddard, Antony, 224n.99
Goetz, Edward G., 204n.36, 212nn. 101, 104, 215n.31, 219nn. 12, 14, 220n.46, 221nn. 50, 51, 52, 224n.114, 225n.1, 228n.51, 230nn. 29, 30, 231nn. 34, 35, 232nn. 24, 25, 236n.5, 237n.10
Gottdeiner, Mark, 201n.8, 203n.32
Gove, Samuel K., 216n.44
Gray, Virginia, 216n.53
Green, Roy E., 224n.102
Green, Sandra, 223n.92
Greenstone, J. David, 140, 142, 163, 229nn. 3, 4, 230n.13
Greiner, Ann, 225n.123
Grimes, Kenneth, 217n.61

Author Index 247

Gunn, Christopher, 102, 192, 204n.44, 219n.22, 223n.88, 228n.48, 237n.13
Gunn, Hazel Dayton, 102, 192, 204n.44, 219n.22, 223n.88, 228n.48, 237n.13

Haas, Gilda, 229n.9, 230nn. 14, 28, 31, 237n.11
Hagstrom, Jerry, 211nn. 80, 81, 82
Hahn, Harlan, 214n.16
Halldorsen, James R., 235n.34
Hamburg, Jill, 224n.104
Harrison, Bennett, 204n.35, 210n.67, 215n.29
Hartman, Chester W., 47, 54, 205nn. 1, 4, 206nn. 7, 10, 207nn. 21, 22, 25, 208n.26, 213nn. 6, 13, 214nn. 18, 19, 215n.33, 223n.93, 224n.104, 236n.39
Harvey, David, 201n.8, 203n.34
Haught, Amy, 223n.92
Hausknecht, Murray, 207n.18
Hawkins, Brett W., 233n.24
Hays, R. Allen, 203n.25, 205nn. 1, 5, 206n.6, 207nn. 20, 23, 209n.55, 217n.75
Hendershott, Patric H., 205n.5
Herrero, Teresa R., 94, 220n.46, 221n.51
Heskin, Allan David, 213nn. 3, 9, 11, 229n.9, 230nn. 14, 28, 31, 231n.37
Hickerson, Matthew, 216n.57
Hill, Richard Child, 202n.11
Hinds, Michael Decourcey, 216n.56
Hoch, Charles, 223n.94, 224nn. 96, 98, 103
Hofferbert, Richard I., 233n.13
Hoffman, Daniel N., 201nn. 1, 2, 7
Holden, J. David, 110, 133, 140, 209n.46, 211nn. 86, 90, 224n.111, 225n.115, 226n.14, 227n.27, 229nn. 54, 1
Hopper, Kim, 224n.104
Horan, Cynthia, 204n.39

Hoskins, Anne E., 223n.92
Hughes, Mark A., 221n.55
Huttman, Elizabeth, 206n.11

Jacob, Herbert, 216n.53
Jadrijevic, Claudia, 223n.92
Johnson, Reuben B., III, 213n.8
Judd, Dennis, 195, 202n.11, 218n.11, 219n.15, 221n.53, 228n.51, 236n.41, 237nn. 19, 21, 22

Kahane, Fred, 227nn. 24, 25, 26, 29, 231n.38
Kann, Mark E., 236n.7
Kantor, Paul, 8, 201n.8, 203nn. 19, 21, 22, 32, 233n.22
Kasarda, John D., 202n.17
Katz, Jeffrey L., 215n.27
Keating, W. Dennis, 171, 217nn. 62, 64, 219n.12, 220nn. 46, 47, 227n.40, 232nn. 5, 6, 238n.31
Keefe, Frank, 208n.38, 209nn. 41, 43
Keller, Marlene, 237n.20
Kincaid, John, 233nn. 19, 21, 234n.24
Kleniewski, Nancy, 172, 219n.20, 220nn. 28, 29, 232nn. 2, 4, 233n.14
Klimkowsky, Beverly, 211n.81
Knight, Richard V., 203n.33
Kotler, Milton, 236n.2
Kotlowitz, Alex, 206n.13

Ladd, Everett Carll, 209n.50
Larson, Janet, 222n.69
Lawson, Ronald, 213nn. 3, 8, 214n.20, 221nn. 59, 60, 223n.85
Lazere, Edward B., 201n.1
Leibschutz, Sarah F., 209n.57
Leiterman, Mindy, 29, 211nn. 86, 94, 212n.97, 226n.14
Lemann, Nicholas, 206n.13
Lenz, Thomas J., 126, 128, 204n.44, 228n.47

Leonard, Paul A., 201n.1
Levine, Marc V., 218n.11
Lewis, Carol, 209n.50, 228n.51
Liebschutz, Sarah F., 209n.57
Lilley, William, III, 207n.21, 208n.33
Lineberry, Robert L., 236n.3
Liner, E. Blaine, 30, 209nn. 52, 53, 210nn. 65, 75
Lipsky, Michael J., 213n.4, 227n.33
Logan, John R., 195, 203n.31, 219n.20, 232nn. 58, 4, 237n.25
Lowi, Theodore J., 210nn. 62, 63, 66
Lukermann, Barbara, 224n.114
Lund, Michael S., 209n.50, 210nn. 58, 62, 77

McAfee, Kathy, 213n.13
McConnell, Grant, 237n.15
Mallach, Alan, 209n.49, 221nn. 54, 56, 57
Mandel, Michael, 221n.62
Marcuse, Peter, 213nn. 4, 5, 7, 214n.17
Markusen, Ann, 220n.27
Martin, Judith A., 224n.99
Masotti, Louis H., 216n.44
Matthei, Charles, 219n.25
Max, Steve, 237n.7
Mayer, Neil, 201n.2
Meehan, Edward J., 203n.24, 206nn. 9, 10, 12
Meehan, James, 192, 219nn. 21, 24, 25, 26, 226n.9, 227n.26
Merriam, Dwight H., 231n.48
Meyerson, Ann, 205n.4, 206nn. 7, 10, 207n.25, 208n.26, 213n.13, 224n.104
Middleton, D. Scott, 229nn. 55, 56, 57
Mitchell, J. Paul, 203n.24, 205nn. 1, 2, 3, 4, 5, 206n.8, 208nn. 28, 29, 30, 36
Mittle, Robert N., 29, 211nn. 86, 94, 212n.97, 226n.14
Mollenkopf, John H., 202n.13, 203n.26, 207n.20, 214n.18
Molotch, Harvey L., 195, 202n.13, 232n.4, 237nn. 18, 25

Morgan, David R., 212n.106
Morris, Peter R., 201n.6, 208nn. 38, 39, 209nn. 44, 45
Motley, Susan, 225n.6, 228n.42

Nathan, Richard P., 2, 30, 33–36, 38, 68, 201nn. 3, 4, 203nn. 27, 29, 208n.37, 209nn. 51, 54, 57, 210nn. 59, 60, 64, 68, 69, 75, 76, 78, 211nn. 79, 81, 83, 85, 88, 216n.55
Neff, Jack, 227nn. 24, 25, 26, 29, 231n.38
Nenno, Mary K., 208n.38, 211n.86, 220n.35
Netter, Edith M., 220n.44

Osborne, David, 190, 219nn. 12, 13, 225n.124, 232n.8, 236n.6
Ostrow, Irving, 229n.2

Palmer, John L., 210n.75, 225n.4
Pamuk, Ayse, 211nn. 84, 87, 91, 95, 212n.102, 226n.9, 227n.26
Papenfuss, Mary, 224n.97
Parker, Robert, 187, 192, 213n.12, 221n.61, 237n.9
Parkinson, Michael, 195, 219n.15, 221n.53, 236n.41, 237nn. 21, 22
Patterson, Samuel C., 216n.53
Pearlman, Daniel D., Esq., 222nn. 69, 70, 72
Peirce, Neal R., 41, 212n.103, 225n.6
Peterson, George E., 209n.50, 228n.51
Peterson, Paul E., 5–6, 8, 11, 140, 142, 163, 171, 195, 201nn. 16, 17, 203nn. 23, 30, 32, 204n.40, 229nn. 3, 4, 230n.13, 237n.24
Pick, Nancy, 218n.10
Pickman, James, 29, 211nn. 86, 94, 212n.97, 226n.14
Piven, Frances Fox, 14, 126, 128, 165, 204n.42, 214n.18, 228n.46

Porter, Douglas R., 220n.48, 231n.48
Portz, John, 192, 237n.12
Pye, Lucian W., 233n.15
Pynoos, Jon, 205n.1, 207n.21

Quinn, James, 230n.24

Ready, Randy L., 228n.51
Reichley, A. James, 203n.25
Rich, Daniel, 202n.13, 218n.11
Rich, Michael J., 173, 209n.56, 211n.92, 212n.106, 219n.19, 232nn. 2, 8, 233n.23, 234n.24
Ritzdorf, Marsha, 224n.102
Roberts, Benson F., 29, 211nn. 86, 94, 212n.97, 226n.14
Rom, Mark C., 202n.17
Rosenthal, Alan, 216n.53
Rosner, Kathy, 225n.118
Ross, Michael J., 216n.53
Rossi, Peter H., 214n.18
Rubinowitz, Leonard S., 209n.56

Sagalyn, Lynne B., 203n.20, 223n.93
Salamon, Lester M., 209n.50, 210nn. 58, 62, 77, 225n. 4, 5, 227n.30
Salins, Peter D., 208nn. 28, 34
Saltzstein, Alan L., 229n.2, 231n.43
Sanders, Heywood T., 202n.11, 203n.31, 204nn. 37, 38
Sassen, Saskia, 204n.35, 230nn. 15, 17, 232nn. 10, 11
Savitch, Hank V., 231n.43
Sawhill, Isabel V., 225n.4
Schafer, Robert, 205n.1, 207n.21
Schattschneider, E. E., 236n.1
Schwartz, David C., 201nn. 1, 2, 7, 210nn. 71, 72, 74, 211n.93
Schwartz, Joel, 214n.20
Semer, Milton P., 205nn. 2, 3, 4
Sharkansky, Ira, 173, 233nn. 13, 20, 234n.24, 236n.3
Sharpe, Sumner M., 224n.102

Shiffman, Ronald, 225n.6, 228n.42
Slayton, Robert A., 223n.94, 224nn. 96, 98, 103
Smith, Michael Peter, 202n.11, 221n.53, 230n.15, 232nn. 3, 10, 237n.20
Smith, Steven Rathgeb, 227n.33
Smith-Heimer, Michael, 211nn. 84, 87, 91, 95, 212n.102
Soifer, Steven D., 219n.25, 220n.30
Soja, Edward W., 230nn. 15, 16, 18, 232nn. 10, 11
Sonenshein, Raphael J., 229n.2, 231n.43
Squires, Gregory D., 202nn. 12, 15, 215n.30
Stach, Patricia Burgess, 220n.39
Stegman, Michael A., 110, 133, 140, 209n.46, 211nn. 86, 90, 224n.111, 225n.115, 226n.14, 227n.27, 229nn. 54, 1
Steinbach, Carol, 225n.6
Stewart, Jill, 229nn. 10, 12, 21, 231nn. 42, 45
Stone, Clarence N., 202n.11, 203n.31, 204nn. 37, 38
Struyk, Raymond J., 201n.2, 210n.60
Stumberg, Robert, 100 (Table 4.2), 222nn. 77, 78, 79, 80
Suchman, Diane R., 224nn. 100, 106, 107, 109, 229nn. 55, 56, 57
Swanstrom, Todd, 171, 201nn. 8, 10, 202n.13, 202nn. 18, 31, 203n.31, 208nn. 31, 32, 219n.20, 232nn. 58, 4, 9, 237nn. 10, 17

Taggert, Robert, 206n.9
Thomas, John Clayton, 231n.43
Tiebout, Charles M., 201n.10
Treadway, Jack M., 233n.12, 235nn. 31, 33, 35, 236n.36
Tuccillo, John A., 201n.2
Tucker, William, 221n.59, 223n.85
Turner, Charles, 219n.26
Turner, Robyne S., 223n.81

Van, Jon, 215n.28
van Vliet, Willem, 206n.11
Vandoren, Peter M., 221n.55
Varady, David P., 113, 225n.122
Verba, Sidney, 172, 233n.15
Vidal, Avis C., 211n.96, 226nn. 8, 10, 11, 12, 20, 22, 227n.35, 228n.41, 229n.55
Villani, Kevin E., 205n.5

Walton, John, 167, 185, 197, 232n.58, 236n.40, 238n.29
Warner, Sam Bass, Jr., 233n.19
Warren, Charles R., 203n.28, 210nn. 60, 61, 77, 211n.81
Weicher, John C., 205n.1

Weiss, Marc A., 207nn. 14, 15, 16, 223n.93
White, Kirby, 219n.25
White, Sammis B., 224n.102
Wilson, James Q., 207n.18, 229n.2
Wolkoff, Michael J., 218n.2
Wong, Kenneth, 202n.11, 212n.105
Wood, Robert C., 211n.81
Wrightson, Margaret T., 210n.57

Yates, Larry, 222n.69

Zdenek, Robert, 225n.6
Zimmerman, Julian H., 205nn. 2, 3, 4